ETHNOGRAPHIES OF ISLAM

EXPLORING MUSLIM CONTEXTS

Series Editor: Abdou Filali-Ansary

Books in the series include

*Development Models in Muslim Contexts:
Chinese, "Islamic" and Neo-Liberal Alternatives
Edited by* Robert Springborg

*The Challenge of Pluralism:
Paradigms from Muslim Contexts
Edited by* Abdou Filali-Ansary
and Sikeena Karmali Ahmed

*Ethnographies of Islam:
Ritual Performances and Everyday Practices
Edited by* Baudouin Dupret, Thomas Pierret,
Paulo G. Pinto *and* Kathryn Spellman-Poots

*Cosmopolitanisms in Muslim Contexts:
Perspectives from the Past
Edited by* Derryl N. MacLean *and*
Sikeena Karmali Ahmed

www.euppublishing.com/series/ecmc

Ethnographies of Islam

Ritual Performances and Everyday Practices

Edited by Baudouin Dupret,
Thomas Pierret, Paulo G. Pinto
and Kathryn Spellman-Poots

EDINBURGH
University Press

IN ASSOCIATION WITH

THE AGA KHAN UNIVERSITY
Institute for the Study of Muslim Civilisations

The opinions expressed in this volume are those of the authors and do not necessarily reflect those of the Aga Khan University, Institute for the Study of Muslim Civilisations.

© Editorial matter and organisation Baudouin Dupret, Thomas Pierret, Paulo G. Pinto and Kathryn Spellman-Poots, 2012
© The chapters, their several authors, 2012

Edinburgh University Press Ltd
22 George Square, Edinburgh EH8 9LF
www.euppublishing.com

Typeset in Goudy Oldstyle by
Koinonia, Manchester

A CIP record for this book is available from the British Library

ISBN 978 0 7486 4550 3 (hardback)
ISBN 978 0 7486 4551 0 (webready PDF)
ISBN 978 0 7486 5479 6 (epub)
ISBN 978 0 7486 5478 9 (Amazon ebook)

The right of the contributors to be identified as authors of this work has been asserted in accordance with the Copyright, Designs and Patents Act 1988.

Contents

Introduction   1
*Baudouin Dupret, Thomas Pierret, Paulo Pinto
and Kathryn Spellman-Poots*

PART ONE: PERFORMING RITUALS

1. Black Magic, Divination and Remedial Reproductive Agency
   in Northern Pakistan   11
   Emma Varley
2. Preparing for the Hajj in Contemporary Tunisia: Between Religious
   and Administrative Ritual   21
   Katia Boissevain
3. "There Used To Be Terrible Disbelief": Mourning and Social
   Change in Northern Syria   31
   Katharina Lange
4. Manifestations of Ashura among Young British Shi'is   40
   Kathryn Spellman-Poots
5. The Ma'ruf: An Ethnography of Ritual (South Algeria)   50
   Yazid Ben Hounet
6. The Sufi Ritual of the Darb al-Shish and the Ethnography
   of Religious Experience   62
   Paulo G. Pinto
7. Preaching for Converts: Knowledge and Power in the Sunni
   Community in Rio de Janeiro   71
   Gisele Fonseca Chagas

8. Worshipping the Martyr President: The *Darih* of Rafiq Hariri in Beirut   80
Ward Vloeberghs

9. Staging the Authority of the Ulama: The Celebration of the Mawlid in Urban Syria   93
Thomas Pierret

Part Two: Contextualising Interactions

10. The Salafi and the Others: An Ethnography of Intracommunal Relations in French Islam   105
Cédric Baylocq and Akila Drici-Bechikh

11. Describing Religious Practices among University Students: A Case Study from the University of Jordan, Amman   115
Daniele Cantini

12. Referring to Islam in Mutual Teasing: Notes on an Encounter between Two Tanzanian Revivalists   124
Sigurd D'hondt

13. Salafis as Shaykhs: Othering the Pious in Cairo   135
Aymon Kreil

14. Ethics of Care, Politics of Solidarity: Islamic Charitable Organisations in Turkey   144
Hilal Alkan-Zeybek

15. Making Shari'a Alive: Court Practice under an Ethnographic Lens   153
Susanne Dahlgren

16. Referring to Islam as a Practice: Audiences, Relevancies and Language Games within the Egyptian Parliament   162
Enrique Klaus and Baudouin Dupret

17. Contesting Public Images of 'Abd al-Halim Mahmud (1910–78): Who is an Authentic Scholar?   170
Hatsuki Aishima

Part Three: The Ethnography of History

18. Possessed of Documents: Hybrid Laws and Translated Texts in the Hadhrami Diaspora   181
Michael Gilsenan

About the Contributors   193
Index   196

Introduction

BAUDOUIN DUPRET, THOMAS PIERRET,
PAULO PINTO AND KATHRYN SPELLMAN-POOTS

In the past three decades, the social sciences in general, and anthropology in particular, have developed an ambiguous relationship with their descriptive traditions, as epistemic relativism and self-defeating critique have led scholars to reflexive deadlocks and fruitless glossing over issues. Instead of attempting to describe the social world as it unfolds when empirically observed, researchers often lose the actual object of interest and propose new narratives in its place that are devoid of the contextual and praxiological specificities of any actual situation. This holds especially true where religious phenomena are concerned. This is probably due to a theorising attitude, what Wittgenstein called the "craving for generality", that looks for big explicative schemes and neglects the situational and self-producing capacity of the social world to produce its own endogenous order. Without advocating a return to positivism, we contend that the social sciences should pay closer attention to actual social practices and adopt a more empirical and analytical attitude vis-à-vis their object of scrutiny.

We can identify at least three problems in the social sciences which justify some sort of ethnographic re-specification of our attitude vis-à-vis "the real". The first one is the tendency to seek for the nature of things instead of their workings, which often results in a "descriptive gap". The second is the quest for data which is often oblivious to the conditions of how this data is produced and thus provide the reader with sketches that somehow miss the phenomena under scrutiny. The third problem resides in the depreciation of descriptive work due to its limited capacity for explanation; although an adequate description is nothing less than a thorough analysis of a chunk of the world as it actually functions.

An important development in the social sciences over the past three decades has been the spread of the ethnographic approach beyond the boundaries of anthropology. Nowadays it is fairly common to have researchers in other academic disciplines such as sociology and political science, who use ethnography. This trend has allowed the social sciences to gradually shift their focus from the structural organisation of social systems to the role of people in producing and reproducing social processes through their everyday practices.

Let us first define precisely what we mean by "ethnography". Recently, it has become increasingly common to call any anthropological research that is based on fieldwork "ethnography". In this volume, we adopt a different approach by defining ethnography as the description and analysis of practices *from the perspective of the social context in which they were produced*. From this point of view, formal interviews are not ethnographic instruments if they are used to collect *ex post* accounts of practices that were performed in another context; their ethnographic relevance is limited to the moment of the interview itself.

Conversely, carrying out ethnography does not necessarily imply that the researcher is *present* during the interactions s/he studies. Ethnographies can be based on video recordings, as well as written documents, as long as they are not approached as mere *contents* but as *contextualised practices*. Any document is the outcome of an action that was performed for all practical purposes, that is, that had a teleological aim constraining the way in which this document was written. The practice of writing a text can therefore be retrieved from the close scrutiny of its internal organisation, its lexicon, its sequential ordering, its orientation to the context of its production, its embedment into a whole set of various documents, and its capacity to look restrospectively and prospectively at the process it is a part of.

The ethnographic approach allows a researcher to describe the complex ways in which people orient themselves to normative codes, material, corporal and social constraints, as well as the intentional strategies that inform their social practices. This is particularly important for the study of religious phenomena, for ethnography allows for a more complex and pluralistic understanding of how people attach and belong to religious communities, and how religious subjectification affects cultural and individual practices.

It is also necessary here to specify what we consider as "Islamic" practices. From the point of view of social sciences, "Islam" is neither a set of practices and beliefs precisely bounded by textual "orthodoxy", nor just any social practice carried out by people who happen to be Muslim; discourses and practices are "Islamic" when Muslims refer to them as such.

The contributions to this volume all refer to Islam as a practice; and therefore as something which must be described in action. We are more likely to gain an understanding of the meaning of religious practice through the close description of people's orientation to, and reification of, religious categories as it emerges from their actual experiences in a given social context.

INTRODUCTION

This volume does not, however, offer a methodology. Neither does it propose a reflection on methodology. Instead it proposes an exploration of the various possibilities that ethnography creates for the understanding of Islam in particular social contexts. Therefore, this volume aims to promote a pluralistic use of ethnography in research about Islam in anthropology and the other social sciences. All the contributors to the volume have used ethnography to engage with and relate to specific empirical realities. The aim is to show the strength of this approach, despite variations in terms of the object of analysis, the theoretical frameworks or the disciplinary traditions of the researcher. We argue that this attitude, what we could also call an epistemology, allows for a more precise and complex understanding of the practices and discourses that constitute social realities constructed and perceived as "Islamic" by those who live them.

Another aim of this book is to encourage ethnography in the study of Muslim practices that have seldom been approached in this way, that is, the "literate", "urban", or "upper class" aspects of Islam. The focus of ethnographers on "folk", "popular" Islam has its roots in the colonial division of academic labour between anthropology and the disciplines related to the Orientalist tradition (philology, history, philosophy). Whereas the former was characterised from the outset by a focus on social spaces that were peripheral to urban political centres (countryside, tribes, popular religiosity), the second exerted a de facto monopoly on the study of the textual tradition and, more generally, on "high" urban culture.[1] Tellingly, whereas in Europe Durkheimian sociology was chiefly concerned with the rapid social transformations entailed by industrialisation, when transposed into colonial North Africa, it turned into "Durkheimian anthropology" and devoted itself to the analysis of "traditional" forms of social organisation.[2]

This situation did not change much in the early postcolonial era. In the heyday of modernisation theories (the 1950s–1960s), the social sciences in general were very uninterested in Muslim religious practices, which were seen as mere remnants of "passing traditional society".[3] Such an intellectual context only reinforced the "marginal" bias of the anthropological tradition. At a time when most social scientists were obsessed with "secularisation", "urbanisation" and "mass literacy", major anthropological works on Islam dealt with saints and tribes (Ernest Gellner), jinn-related therapeutic rituals (Vincent Crapanzano) and Sufi brotherhoods (Michael Gilsenan).[4] Clifford Geertz proposed a more ambitious approach, showing how Muslim practices and beliefs were invested with cultural meanings and shaped cultural systems, which were expressed in specific *epitomic* places like the mosque, the bazaar or the tribunal.[5]

Some contemporary ethnographic enquiries that departed from this dominant trend were just as revealing of the "peripheralisation" of Islam in the social sciences. Indeed, although Dale Eickelman and Richard Antoun wrote the social biographies of literate men of religion, both of them chose to concentrate on figures living in the countryside. Moreover, Eickelman depicted his Moroccan religious judge as the representative of a model of religious authority that was rapidly being rendered irrelevant by modernisation.[6]

Other ethnographies led to a deeper criticism of the analytical framework used to understand Islam and Muslim societies. Through their ethnographic account of the *mevlud* recitals, a ritual performance that celebrates the birth of the Prophet Muhammad in Turkey, Richard and Nancy Tapper brought a critical reassessment of the conceptual dichotomy that dominated the analyses of Islam (orthodoxy/heterodoxy) and gender relations in Muslim societies (male dominance/female subordination). In doing so, they showed how both men's and women's recitals are integral parts of the ritual construction of the religious persona of the Prophet, as a powerful symbolic reference in Turkish religious culture.[7]

From the early 1980s on, the Iranian revolution and the rise of political Islam have considerably revived academic interest in Muslim religious practices. However, new research trends that appeared at this stage were more inspired by the Orientalist tradition and political sciences than by anthropology; the focus was on discourses, historical accounts and structures more than on the observation of practices in context. As a result, ethnographic enquiries on topics that fall beyond the scope of "traditional" anthropology have remained relatively rare except, to a certain extent, for legal practices,[8] and mosque-based communities or educational groups.[9] For instance, there are still very few similar studies on issues such as Islamic scholarship,[10] political Islam,[11] and official religious administrations.[12] Because we think that our knowledge of such topics has much to gain from ethnographic insights, we have included articles in this volume on the ulama in Egypt and Syria (Aishima, Pierret), Islamic charities in Turkey (Alkan-Zeybek), Salafis in France and Egypt (Baylocq & Drici-Bechikh), the cult that developed around the tomb of the late Lebanese prime minister Rafiq al-Hariri (Vloeberghs), and reference to Islam in the Egyptian Parliament (Klaus & Dupret).

The first part of the volume, entitled *Performing Rituals*, deals with "traditional" subjects of the anthropology of religion, namely rituals and symbols. The rituals described here include therapeutic magic in Gilgit, Pakistan (Varley), the preparation of the *Hajj* (pilgrimage to Mecca) in Tunisia (Boissevain), the transformation of mourning practices in the Syrian countryside (Lange), the evolution of Ashura rituals among British Shi'is (Spellman-Poots), a collective ritual prayer in Saharan Algeria (Ben Hounet), the Sufi ritual of *darb al-shish* (body-piercing) in Syria (Pinto), the religious socialisation of Brazilian converts to Islam in Rio de Janeiro (Fonseca Chagas), the celebration of the Prophet's birthday by the Syrian ulama (Pierret) and the devotional practices at Rafiq al-Hariri's tomb in Lebanon (Vloeberghs).

Instead of solely privileging the role of these elements of Islamic religiosity in the construction of group solidarity or the reproduction of normative guidelines of the religious system, the ethnographic approaches in the articles of this section reveal how rituals and symbols function as performative and communicative arenas in which the religious agents construct and negotiate their belonging to a particular Muslim community. In this sense, Islamic rituals and symbols will be scrutinised in each context not only for what they *mean* but also for what they *produce* in terms of creating, shaping and affirming religious subjectivities, cultural expectations, power relations and patterns of authority and community.

Ethnography allows for a better understanding of how ritual and symbolic idioms are constituted and used to connect meanings and norms to the selves of the agents. Empirical data produced through participant observation provides the basis of analytical models that take into account the tense relationship between Islam as a normative construct in textual or oral discourses and the multiple discursive, practical and experiential dimensions that it receives once it is mobilised in the religious practices of Muslim communities. Therefore, this part of the volume deals with the effects of the ethnographic approach on the conceptualisation and analysis of Islam as a shared cultural idiom in specific social contexts.

The second part of the volume, *Contextualising Interactions*, is concerned with interactions that are not religious rituals, but that nevertheless orient themselves and make reference to Islam: inter-community relations within French Islam (Baylocq & Drici-Bechikh), daily religiosity on a Jordanian university campus (Cantini), informal conversations between young Muslim revivalists in Tanzania (D'hondt), perceptions of Salafi Muslims in Egypt (Kreil), relationships between Turkish Islamic charity volunteers and their beneficiaries (Alkan-Zeybek), the handling of a divorce-case in a Yemeni court (Dahlgren), reference to Islam in Egyptian parliamentary debates (Klaus & Dupret) and controversies over the public image of the late Shaykh al-Azhar 'Abd al-Halim Mahmud (Aishima).

Social actions are irreducibly events or actions in a social order where words are parts of "language-games". Instead of looking for "big concepts", which are often constructed as "floating entities" independent of any instantiation or context of use, we suggest in this part of the volume that it would be better to ask how the members of any social group conduct their activities and eventually give it a label (for example "Islamic"). In the case of Islamic law, for instance, this means to focus on how *people*, in their many settings, orient themselves to something they call "Islamic law" and how *they* refer legal issues to the Islamic-law model. Such an attitude suggests that we focus on the methods people use locally to produce the truth and intelligibility that allow them to cooperate and interact in a more or less ordered way.

There is a missing "what" in much research on religion, in that social scientists tend to describe various social influences on the growth and development of institutions while taking for granted the many practicalities that constitute ordinary action and reasoning. There is a real descriptive failing, which only permits researchers to advance worldviews that are alternative to those of the actors or to remain insensitive to practice as it is understood by daily practitioners. We speak of a descriptive gap. In order to bridge this gap and to fill the missing "what", we must re-orient ourselves to the content of ordinary practices and the place that references to religion can occupy within it. This would allow paying close attention to the technicalities of the many settings in which this action or referring takes place, its situated character, and the specific modes of reasoning which are attached to social practices.

The book ends with a special section, *The ethnography of history*, which aims to point to other possible uses of the ethnographic approach, in this case in a dialogue with history. Michael Gilsenan's chapter presents an ethnography of the Hadhrami diaspora in South-east Asia through the claims that their members pose to history. Documents, genealogies, historical references and nostalgic remembrance appear in Gilsenan's ethnography as cultural devices that connect the Hadhramis in South-east Asia to the imagined pasts and homelands that allow them to live their diasporic identities in local contexts.

The overall ambition of this book is to highlight the various uses and conceptions of ethnography that can be mobilised for a deeper understanding of Islamic practices, discourses and forms of subjectivity. The articles here show how researchers, coming from various areas of the social sciences, were able to produce detailed descriptions that could convey the complexity and dynamics of the social phenomena defined as Islamic by the agents that live and experience them. We hope that these examples provide support for further debate on the impact of ethnography on the ways in which Islam is portrayed and understood in the various social sciences.

This volume is the result of the workshop *Ethnographies of Islam*, co-convened by the editors from 4 to 7 November 2009 at the Aga Khan University, Institute for the Study of Muslim Civilisations in London (AKU-ISMC). The editors want to thank the Aga Khan University, Institute for the Study of Muslim Civilisations for hosting and co-sponsoring the event, as well as the Wenner-Gren Foundation for the generous grant that made the workshop and the book possible.

NOTES

1. Charles Lindhom, "The New Middle Eastern Ethnography", *Man*, vol. 1, no. 4, November 1995, p. 806.
2. See Jean-Noël Ferrié, *La religion de la vie quotidienne chez les Marocains musulmans: rites, règles et routine*, Paris: Karthala, 2005.
3. Daniel Lerner, *The Passing of Traditional Society: Modernizing the Middle East*, Glencoe, IL: Free Press, 1958.
4. Ernest Gellner, *Saints of the Atlas*, London: Weidenfeld & Nicolson, 1969; Crapanzano, Vincent, *The Hamadsha; A Study in Moroccan Ethnopsychiatry*, Berkeley: University of California Press, 1973; Michael Gilsenan, *Saints and Sufi in Modern Egypt: An Essay in the Sociology of Religion*, Oxford: Clarendon Press, 1973; *Recognizing Islam: Religion and Society in the Modern Middle East*, London: Croom Helm, 1982. While Gilsenan initially (1973) subscribed to the modernist idea that Sufi brotherhoods were declining "popular", "traditional" social structures, in his later writings (1982) he recognised the continuing presence of Sufi religiosity in the Middle East and underlined its connections with the literate religious elite. He also highlighted the successful adaptation of certain Sufi brotherhoods to social change.
5. Clifford Geertz, *The Religion of Java*, Chicago: University of Chicago Press, 1960; *Islam Observed; Religious Development in Morocco and Indonesia*, Chicago: University of Chicago Press, 1968; *Local Knowledge: Further Essays in Interpretative Anthropology*, New York: Basic Books, 1983.
6. Dale Eickelman, *Knowledge and Power in Morocco*, Princeton: Princeton University Press, 1985; Richard Antoun, *Muslim Preacher in the Modern World. A Jordanian Case Study* Princeton: Princeton University Press, 1989.
7. Nancy Tapper and Richard Tapper, "The Birth of the Prophet: Ritual and Gender in Turkish Islam", *Man*, vol. 22, no. 1, March 1987, pp. 69–92.
8. Lawrence Rosen, *The Justice of Islam: Comparative Perspectives on Islamic Law and Society*, New York: Oxford University Press, 1999; Baudouin Dupret, *Le jugement en action: ethnométhodologie du droit, de la morale et de la justice en Égypte*, Geneva: Droz, 2006; Hussein Ali Agrama, "Ethics, Authority, Tradition: Towards an Anthropology of the Fatwa", *American Ethnologist*, vol. 37, no. 4, November 2010, pp. 2–18; Susanne Dahlgren, *Contesting Realities: The Public Sphere and Morality in Southern Yemen*, Syracuse, NY: Syracuse University Press, 2010.
9. See for instance: Saba Mahmood, *Politics of Piety: The Islamic Revival and the Feminist Subject*, Princeton: Princeton University Press, 2005; Alexander Horstmann, "The Inculturation of a Transnational Islamic Missionary Movement: Tablighi Jamaat al-Dawa and Muslim Society in Southern Thailand", *Sojourn: Journal of Social Issues in Southeast Asia*, vol. 22, no. 1, April 2007, pp. 107–30; Victoria Lee, "The Mosque and Black Islam: Towards an Ethnographic Study of Islam in the Inner City", *Ethnography*, vol. 11, no. 1, January 2010, pp. 145–63.
10. Michael Fischer, *Iran: From Religious Dispute to Revolution*, Cambridge, MA: Harvard University Press, 1980; Brinkley Messick, *The Calligraphic State: Textual Domination and History in a Muslim Society*, Berkeley: University of California Press, 1996; Kai Kresse, *Philosophising in Mombasa: Knowledge, Islam and Intellectual Practice on the Swahili Coast*, Edinburgh: Edinburgh University Press, 2007.

11. Cihan Tugal, "The Appeal of Islamic Politics: Ritual and Dialogue in a Poor District of Turkey", *Sociological Quarterly*, vol. 47, no. 2, April 2006, pp. 245–73; Jenny White, *Islamist Mobilization in Turkey: A Study in Vernacular Politics*, Seattle: University of Washington Press, 2002.
12. Richard Antoun, "Fundamentalism, Bureaucratization and the State's Co-optation of Religion: A Jordanian Case Study", *International Journal of Middle East Studies*, vol. 38, no. 3, August 2006, pp. 369–93.

PART ONE

Performing Rituals

Chapter 1

Black Magic, Divination and Remedial Reproductive Agency in Northern Pakistan

Emma Varley

I seek refuge with (Allah), the Lord of the daybreak,
From the evil of what He has created,
From the evil of intense darkness, when it comes,
And from the evil of those who practice witchcraft
    when they blow in the knots,
And from the evil of the envier when he envies.[1]

Anthropologists are increasingly and critically attentive to the symbolic, ideological and political dimensions of women's observance and ritual practice of Islam throughout Muslim contexts.[2] However, few researchers focus on the eclectic modalities inherent to Muslim women's formal engagements with occult practices in Pakistan, notwithstanding growing research on sorcery in the South Asian Muslim diaspora.[3] In particular, the available literature demonstrates a lack of attention to the impacts of sorcery on women's sense of physical wellbeing, or to the cosmological mechanisms women employ to protect themselves from harm. In response, I draw on ethnographic fieldwork (2004–5) in Gilgit Town, the multi-sectarian capital of Gilgit-Baltistan, to explore Sunni women's creative and agentive efforts to resolve the ailments associated with relational discord and "black magic".

Using my experiences with women-centred divination as an analytical platform, I examine the social, symbolic and moral economies underlying northern Pakistani women's perception that sorcery underlies, or contributes to, many reproductive health crises. By illuminating women-centred divination as a corrective ritual, I explicate the interlinkages between sorcery, conflictive gendered sociality, and Gilgiti and Islamic cosmologies.

Afflictive Sorcery and Modes of Recourse

While my doctoral research analysed the impacts of Shia[4]–Sunni conflict for Gilgiti Sunni women's health service access and, thereafter, their maternal health outcomes, I attend here to my participants' insistence that many of their reproductive ailments resulted from sorcery unleashed against them by other women. With women's public confrontation of their rivals or enemies (*dushman*)[5] actively discouraged, sorcery was thought to permit covert redress of emotional, socio-economic and material imbalances. Pointing to co-wives (*habaynee*), mothers- and sisters-in-law (*šaš; saroni*) as their primary antagonists and the source for magically precipitated harms, Gilgiti Sunni women proactively engaged with Islamic clerics, diviners and even sorcery to offset, redress or "bounce back" afflictive cosmological forces. Because of widespread economic uncertainty and the spatial frictions of extended family households, women competed over the financial and emotional resources provided by adult male relatives. Because Gilgiti women's social and familial status is inextricably dependent on marriage and childbearing, and with their bodies already over-determined by the religio-cultural concept of honour (*izzat*), their fertility provided the most frequent target for symbolic vengeance.

As occult phenomena, *as'sihr* (Islamic sorcery) and *kala jadu* (black magic) are often treated as analytical equivalences within the wider Islamic and anthropological literature.[6] As ontological categories, however, Islamic sorcery and black magic in Gilgit are marked by conceptual, discursive and practical differences. For example, kala jadu draws on and bridges a more extensive arsenal of materials, rituals and local beliefs than as'sihr, which is bound to Qur'anic and prophetic sources. Kala jadu, for instance, was said to originate in Bangladesh and involve the use of a bricolage of Sanskritic Hindi, Persian and Urdu *mantr* (incantations, spells), bodily matter (blood, hair, nails) and herbs such as turmeric. Bodily substances might be placed in food, drinks or on clothing to permeate and unsettle women's bodily processes or temperament. Jadu is also proposed to work through the strategic placement of items in spaces otherwise forbidden to human interference, such as graves (*qabar*). In mechanistic terms, kala jadu refracts and re-uses many of the same devices employed by Islamic protective and therapeutic measures. For example, jadu frequently involves spoken spells and amulets whereby women or *jadugar* (magicians) re-order and invert Qur'anic *ayat* (verses), thereby negating the healing benefits ordinarily associated with certain phrases. Bodily substances were also said to be placed in food, drinks or on clothing to permeate and unsettle women's bodily processes or temperament. At a primary level, participants stated that sorcery's effects included uterine "weakness", menstrual irregularities, dizziness, insomnia, unexplained emotional instability, and infant distress, foetal abnormalities and

Black Magic, Divination and Remedial Reproductive Agency

death. Both as'sihr and kala jadu focus primarily on issues of sociality, relationality and well-being. Sexual dysfunction, infertility and the birth of daughters were described as being foremost among sorcery's most harmful consequences. Participants characterised each of these outcomes, which were considered preconditions for divorce (*talaq*), as a type of social death.

When enmities became public and lines of social allegiance were openly drawn, it was strategically important for victims to take the moral high-road by conspicuously resorting to mainstream Islamic prescriptive therapies. Women strove to spiritually safeguard their fertility or existing pregnancies by pre-emptively disabling afflictive sorcery through ritual modes of piety. Formal defensive remedies and counter-measures predominantly drew on Islamic knowledge (*adab*, *ilm*), prayers (*namaz*) and amulets (*tawiz*). However, women were sometimes quietly advised to nullify current complaints and repel future attacks through the same systems employed by their antagonists, regardless of the spiritual repercussions arising from kala jadu's "immoral", "un-Islamic" measures.

Diagnosing and remedying the harms associated with enmity and sorcery involved a vast series of inter-related practices. In Gilgit's religious bookstores, a wide variety of Sunni Islamic texts and pamphlets detailed prayers, counter-spells and amulet-based prescriptions offsetting as'sihr and kala jadu. In addition to Sunni clergy, a number of female diviners (*daiyahl*) worked to diagnose sorcery and make protective tawiz. Clients either praised diviners' abilities or derided their strangeness. Many professed to being frightened by the divination experience. Working from their family homes, diviners took fees that were roughly equivalent to those charged by clerics for defensive or remedial tawiz. Women diviners from Gilgit's Ismaili, Shia and Sunni communities communicated with Islamic *jinn*[7] and fairies (*parri*), who, broadly speaking, are representative of Gilgiti traditional beliefs. These beings were enlisted to locate and materialise the hidden objects of sorcery. Recovered tawiz often evidenced the use of symbols, formulaic sets of numbers or Arabic letters. Some were written in Urdu and used victims' names or contained crudely-drawn, "idolatrous" human images (*naqshé*).[8] Women were advised to destroy amulets by fire or throw them into clean water to dispel their power.

Because the harms born of interpersonal discord and sorcery are central to women's own understandings of their health, I provide a case study of Gilgiti women's solicitation of diagnostic and defensive mechanisms from women diviners. With my own ailments serving as a methodological segue, I attended numerous sessions wherein diviners communicated with jinn to retrieve the hidden objects causing harm to their clients. As the wife of a Sunni Gilgiti and the mother and stepmother of seven children, the extent of my access to and participation with Sunni women's private worlds and practices was highly unusual.

Mediating Harm

In mid-July 2005, after I had endured prolonged reproductive health complaints that were unresolved by physicians in Canada and also Gilgit, my husband, Wadood, invited the local *qari* (cleric) to our home to discuss the potential for Islamic recourse. Because of the lack of a solution for my problems, my in-laws suggested that the underlying aetiology of my "illnesses" was supernatural in origin. Protracted friction with my husband's first wife suggested a likely source for afflictive sorcery, so women urged me to seek assistance or risk facing the possibility of more unwieldy and socially problematic ailments, such as infertility.

The qari arrived at dusk to sit in our garden and have tea with Wadood. As one of the only men entitled to hear the intimacies of women's reproductive health, the qari was quietly appraised by Wadood as to the nature, symptoms and duration of my health concerns. The qari advised that, in light of Wadood's ex-wife's hatred for me, and with her having once asked him to produce a tawiz to cause our divorce, I should solicit a diviner to locate and remove the objects of jadu she might have procured against me. With jadu typically anchored to objects, divination would allow for the materialisation and subsequent destruction of those items through which afflictive jadu was thought to exert harm. He advised Wadood that a woman renowned for her divination abilities lived not far to the south of Gilgit Town. She would, he said, be able to assist me by covertly halting the corrosive effects of sorcery. Secrecy was essential. Knowledge of our efforts to extricate the vehicles of jadu would inevitably lead my antagonist to replace the original objects. After arranging to meet us the next morning to make the trip south, the qari returned to the mosque for prayers.

The next day began hot and still. During the drive, the qari articulated the scope of afflictive magic intended to destabilise happy marriages vis-à-vis the erosion of wives' reproductive well-being and fertility. After an hour had passed, he instructed Wadood to slow the car at a point along the Karakoram Highway. Peering up through the dense foliage lining the road, he remarked that we had arrived. With a woman friend from Gilgit accompanying us to act as my interpreter, we walked up a steep hillside, along a roughly cobbled stone path through thickets of trees and prickly flowering bushes. Minutes later we arrived at a small, multi-level, whitewashed stone house. The house was in poor condition; roughly hewn wooden beams, haphazardly daubed with paint, comprised the ceiling of four dark interior rooms. Homespun carpets lay across uneven dirt floors. Striding out to meet us from one of the rooms was the diviner, a woman no more than thirty-five years of age, wearing a cream coloured *shalwar kameez* and a white cotton veil. She firmly shook my hand, and gestured for Wadood and the qari to be led into an adjoining guest room, perched precariously on the edge of the steep hillside, facing Nanga Parbat's glacier-capped peak. I was taken to a much smaller, darker room at the back of the house in which sat four women, who were accompanied by several young children and toddlers. After shaking each of their hands in greeting, I sat against one of the walls of the room.

The diviner, greeted by each of the women as *pfiffi* (auntie), entered the room after me and walked directly to a cupboard inset on one of the azure blue walls. She opened the cupboard, keeping her hands out of sight while she shifted objects around inside for several minutes. She then took four incense sticks, lit them one by one, and placed them in between wooden beams at each of the room's four corners. She returned to the cupboard, from which she took several pens, and then seated herself against the wall beside me. Her manner was quiet and withdrawn. She kept her eyes focused on the ground in front of her as she leaned back and rested her head against the wall.

At this point, a large-eyed, older woman rose and moved over to kneel on the ground immediately in front of the diviner. The other women ceased talking and turned to watch the diviner, who took a pad of paper from the floor beside her and began fanning herself with it. She held a small bottle of perfume to her nose, rolling the applicator ball back and forth with her thumb and inhaling deeply. She glanced occasionally at the far, upper corners of the room where, the qari had forewarned me, two jinn sisters sat to converse with her. For nearly five minutes, the diviner continued smelling the perfume, yawning deeply and fanning her face with the papers. She then began to hiccup, catching her breath violently. The whites of her eyes became prominent, and her forehead tilted sharply ahead. Her arms and shoulders began to shake. The woman kneeling in front of her moved over to catch and hold the diviner's quavering hands. This woman, who took on the role of the diviner's assistant and interpreter while she was in a trance, then gestured for one of the waiting women to come and sit in front of the diviner.

The shaking and hiccupping then slowed somewhat and the diviner, sitting with slouched shoulders, dropped the pad of paper from her now listless hands. As the client sat cross-legged in front of her, the diviner raised her right hand limply in greeting. The assistant instructed the client, "*Salaam tey*" ("Say hello"). The young woman, obviously unsettled, hesitatingly shook the diviner's outstretched hand. With her hiccupping subsiding, the diviner looked alternately, unblinking, at the client and then at the upper corner of the room, her lips moving silently. The assistant began speaking to the jinn through the diviner. The jinn were informed that the client's mother-in-law and sister-in-law in the Punjab were mistreating her, and that her husband's business, a small retail shop, was not succeeding. "What is affecting them?" queried the assistant. The diviner reached out for the client's left hand, which the assistant forcibly brought forward with the client's palm facing upwards. The diviner grasped the client's wrist using her right hand, and with her left index finger touched the open palm lightly. The assistant asked again, "What has caused this?" The diviner responded in a gravelly voice, "Jadu". Her diagnosis was repeated excitedly by the assistant and the client.

In a monotone voice, the diviner described how afflictive tawiz had been placed in the client's husband's shop and several other places. She noted these were now going to be "opened and removed". As the assistant continued to ask questions of the jinn, prompted by the client, the diviner reached down and picked up the pad of paper and, placing it across her right knee, turned to a blank page. Using a fountain pen, she wrote line after line in spidery blue Urdu script, her penmanship shifting between tightly controlled and looping and deformed. With no small amount of alarm, my friend observed that the diviner – amidst lines of illegible "nonsense" – was also able to produce "complicated Persian and Urdu words". After writing ten lines of script on one sheet of paper, she tore the page from the pad and folded it in half, and then tore again to create two, then three, then four increasingly smaller, triangular pieces of folded paper. On the outer corners of each triangular tawiz she drew small symbols and, one by one, dropped them into the client's hands with instructions about where each was to be used. "Who has done this against them?" asked the assistant. The diviner, with small beads of sweat forming on her upper lip, merely shook her head. "She doesn't give out names", the assistant interpreted.

The diviner then took out a fresh piece of paper and wrote three lines of script on it before placing the pad of paper under the client's right knee. Using her right hand, which still clutched the perfume, the diviner pushed down hard on the client's knee. In her left hand, the diviner firmly held the pad of paper down on the ground underneath the client's knee. Without moving her hands and arms, the diviner began to shake and hiccup violently once again for almost a minute, after which time the diviner pulled the pad of paper out from under the client's knee and, left behind on the carpet, barely visible in the dim light, were three small folded and worn pieces of paper. The diviner picked them up with pinched fingertips and dropped them into the client's lap, saying, "Take these and throw them into the river, into clean water. These are the tawiz that have been made against you." She asked for Rs 247 (CDN $5), her and the jinn's fee for their services. After being paid, she whispered a few words of instruction to the client, inaudible to anyone else, before the client got up and returned to her original place against the wall.

The assistant gestured it was my turn. Prompted by the assistant, my friend described my situation. "Emma has had problems since marrying her *baroč* [husband] ... she has had problems becoming pregnant and having healthy babies."

The assistant interrupted to ask, "How many children does she have with him?"

"*Duoh chuneh pučei* [two small sons]. She also lost a pregnancy, and had a son who died."

"Yes, these are problems ... some women have such problems", the assistant said sympathetically.

"Emma wants to know why these problems are happening to her. She has no medical answers and no doctor can help her."

The diviner took my right hand palm-side up and placed her index finger on my pulse. Looking inquisitively at my hand, she whispered "Jadu ... someone has placed three tawiz against you in your path, around your home ... I can open these after three days on *Juma* [Friday]." At the same time, she began writing lines of blue Urdu script on a blank piece of paper, folding and tearing the paper so that, ultimately, she produced nine tawiz. Two, she said, were to be worn by me – one on a string around my neck and the other on a string around my waist, with the amulet to rest "on the *bachidani* [womb]". The remaining seven tawiz were to be put in milk, left for the ink to dissolve, and then drunk by me each night for the next week. As she completed the last of the tawiz, I was asked if I had any more questions. I said, "Yes ... my husband's ex-wife is disturbing me and my family, and we want her to stop. Why is she doing this?" My friend intervened to add that Wadood's first wife had been throwing rocks at our home, following me, and trying to contact me by telephone. Confusion arose between the diviner's assistant and my friend concerning whether Wadood had divorced his first wife or not. "*Talaq thoon?*" ("Is the divorce done?") the assistant asked of the diviner, who answered so softly we strained to listen, "Yes, he divorced her."

I then asked the diviner if we would have any more children, and the diviner began to produce yet another tawiz, marking its outer folded edges with symbols. She whispered to the assistant, who nodded and confirmed, "Yes, there will be more children." The tawiz was passed to me with the instruction, "Place it in the ground in the *gullee* [lane] where the first wife lives, in her path." The diviner then leaned over towards the assistant, mumbling quietly. The assistant turned to me, saying, "You need to come back after three days, because the jadu is *sacht* [hard] and pfiffi has to cut *chillah* for you."[9] In order to complete the chillah process, I was to return with five kinds of fruit, almond oil, and three packets of cooked meat prepared with a quarter-kilogram of *desi ghee* (clarified butter), turmeric, black pepper and dried garlic. The diviner then produced yet another tawiz, intended for the entire family to imbibe after its ink was dissolved into water. One final tawiz was given to be worn by the "*sabse chota baccha*" ("youngest child"). Speaking to my friend, the diviner asked for her and the jinn's fees; Rs 347 for chillah, and Rs 247 for the tawiz. I was later informed by the qari that the jinn kept most of the fees and left only Rs 20 from each session for the diviner.

She then sat back and looked with large eyes, the whites showing prominently, toward the room's back corner; her lips moving as if in conversation, and beads of sweat forming again on her upper lip. The assistant moved quickly to sit before the diviner, who started shaking, her head rocking and hiccupping violently. The assistant's hand then shot forward to catch the diviner's head as it suddenly fell forward. Once the trance subsided, the diviner sat back, wan and exhausted, against the wall. I tried clarifying what I needed to bring on Juma, but the assistant reprimanded me, saying, "You can't ask questions once it's over – you can only ask her such questions while it lasts!"

With our return interrupted by several days of violence and army curfews in Gilgit Town, Wadood, the qari, a woman cousin and I were only able to journey back to the diviner a week later. The food I had been instructed to bring was taken to her by one of the diviner's relatives, in order for her to blow a *dhum* (prayer) onto each of the items, which I was told to consume over the subsequent five days. As one of the last clients of the day, I was taken immediately to sit in front of the diviner, who had already begun preparing written tawiz for me in blue ink. I was pushed to sit cross-legged with my right knee closest to the diviner, who placed the pad of paper underneath my right knee. Her right hand, which clutched the fountain pen and perfume bottle, pushed down hard on my knee; her arm began shaking slightly and she started hiccupping, her eyes fixed on mine. Suddenly she pulled the pad of paper out from underneath my leg. I tried to move, but the assistant and diviner both pushed my knee back down towards the ground, the diviner saying "*Sabr tey*" ("Patience"). A minute passed and then the diviner, with outstretched fingers, reached underneath my knee and plucked out a small rusted padlock. She dropped it into a blank piece of paper laid on the floor beside her, and folded the paper up quickly around the lock. In a low voice, she instructed me to "Break the lock and throw the pieces in clean water ... in the river perhaps." The room was abuzz with the other clients' comments as they crowded around to see the padlock, which Wadood's cousin quickly slipped into her purse. During the commotion, the diviner exited the trance while hiccupping loudly, her head swaying and the assistant ready to catch her as she slumped forward.

From where she sat beside me, the cousin looked aghast, saying in a shaky voice, "*Trcheké* [look]! It's to make your mind, your heart and your body *bandh* [closed, locked]! Do you understand? Do you know what this means? She's tried to lock your hearts against one another!" And, to the women around us, "Why would someone want to do something like this to her? She's innocent and not from this place ... she didn't do anything to anybody!" In conversation afterwards, the qari clarified that the "locking" of objects, or the tying of knots in string or hair, was among the most commonly-used vehicles of afflictive sorcery. In this way, the padlock simultaneously represented the potential for, and operated as an explanatory mechanism for, marital dysfunction, breached spiritual boundaries and, given the particulars of my case, impaired fertility and bodily functioning. In ways that confirmed my in-laws' belief in remedial divination, and restored my faith in the fixity of positive spiritual boundaries surrounding and underpinning my health, the safe arrival of my fifth child ten months later symbolised the success of the diviner's cosmological mediation and her interruption of intended harm.

Conclusion

As this ethnographic case study demonstrates, besides indexing women's vulnerability to unseen forces, sorcery's somatic effects vocalised and called attention to unresolved interpersonal discord. At a primary level, by ascribing their physical symptoms to sorcery, women achieved far-reaching commentary on their insecurities and enmities. Even when biomedical explanations could be applied to their health complaints, allopathic diagnoses ultimately reduced women's opportunity to express disatisfaction with their life's circumstances, comment on social discord, or enact agency. By relation, the ill effects ascribed to sorcery offered women powerfully evocative, yet also indirect means by which to address the real-world harms they experienced in the course of married and family life. Divination also enabled women to account for and mediate misfortune, trauma and injustice. Equally importantly, divination confirmed women's perceptions of ill intent and the existence of afflictive sorcery. Women used diviners to disrupt and disempower afflictive sorcery and offset the manifold uncertainties and vulnerabilities associated with gendered sociality and domestic settings. In this way, spirit diviners permitted women the agentive opportunity to render visible, and neutralise, otherwise invisible and inaccessible, malevolent realms, sociality and practices. By harnessing sorcery's offensive properties, divination permitted women a forceful and far-reaching sense of personal agency, ironic insofar as it initially arose from a perceived lack of agency. And with women's autonomy undermined by the systemic inequities accompanying married life in extended family households, as well as by the increasingly restrictive influence of Islamist conservatism on Gilgiti women's social mobility, education and financial autonomy, women-centred divination operated as instantiations of power.[10] Ultimately, divination functioned as a crucial opportunity for Gilgiti women to simultaneously assign blame for inflicted harms and heal the vulnerable, permeable, corporeal and spiritual self.

Notes

1. Qur'an 113.5. [*The Holy Qur'an*, trans. Muhammed Marmaduke Pickthall, New Delhi: Kitab Bhavan, 1996].
2. Janice Boddy, *Wombs and Alien Spirits: Women, Men, and the Zar Cult in Northern Sudan*, Madison: University of Wisconsin Press, 1989; Eleanor Abdella Duomato, *Getting God's Ear: Women, Islam, and Healing in Saudi Arabia and the Gulf*, New York: Columbia University Press, 2000; Saba Mahmood, *Politics of Piety: The Islamic Revival and the Feminist Subject*, Princeton, NJ: Princeton University Press, 2005.
3. David Pinault, *Notes from the Fortune-telling Parrot: Islam and the Struggle for Religious Pluralism in Pakistan*, London: Equinox Publishing, 2008; Pnina Werbner, *Pilgrims of Love: The Anthropology of a Global Sufi Cult*, Bloomington: Hurst Publishers and Indiana University Press, 2003; Alyson Callan, "'What Else Do We Bengalis Do?' Sorcery, Overseas Migration, and the New Inequalities in Sylhet, Bangladesh", *The Journal of the Royal Anthropological Institute*, vol. 13, 2007, pp. 331–43.
4. Although for the sake of terminological consistency across chapters the editors of this volume have chosen to use the term "Shi'i" instead of "Shia", Twelver "Shi'i" in Gilgit-Baltistan are uniformly referred to as being "Shia". In the interest of ethnographic accuracy, I therefore prefer to use the term "Shia".
5. Foreign language terms employed within this chapter are predominantly drawn from the Shina language. Some terms also draw from Urdu.
6. Syed Noumanul Haq, "Occult Sciences and Medicine", in Michael Cook (ed.), *The New Cambridge History of Islam*, Cambridge: Cambridge University Press, 2010, p. 640.
7. By contrast to humans (*inn*), who are made of earth, Islamic doctrine holds that *jinn* are formed from fire and can be considered "dual dimensional, with the ability to live and operate in both manifest and invisible domains"; see Amira El-Zein, *Islam, Arabs, and the Intelligent World of the Jinn*, Syracuse: Syracuse University Press, 2009, p. 1.
8. Shina language variant of *naqsh/naqoosh* (Urdu).
9. *Chillah* involves spiritual retreat, prayer, fasting and meditation, whereby individuals or their proxies are able to disrupt, reverse and/or end afflictive cosmological or sorcery-related harm.
10. Galena Lindquist, *Conjuring Hope: Healing and Magic in Contemporary Russia*, London: Berghahn Books, 2007, p. 18.

Chapter 2

Preparing for the Hajj in Contemporary Tunisia: Between Religious and Administrative Ritual

Katia Boissevain

In Tunisia, as in other Muslim-majority nations and communities, the pilgrimage to Mecca involves a number of national and family rituals, before and after the actual event. In this article, although I shall be writing about the Hajj, I intend to limit description and discussion to a ritual sequence, referred to in Tunisia as the *qar'a*, a term meaning "draw", a selective procedure of pilgrims which is carefully managed by the State.[1] This ritual context becomes the locus of negotiation between an individual and a collective religious manifestation and the State's religious and administrative duties.[2]

The Hajj requires the mobilisation of huge resources, and the process of preparing the pilgrims involves important management skills. Drawing on my ethnographic material, I suggest that the Hajj is both a religious ritual and an administrative ritual and I will show how the administrative dimension is intertwined with religious issues and emotional dimensions. The ethnographic method and the comparison of practices past and present based on a single ritual sequence gives us insight into the evolving relations between the State and citizens (who in the Tunisian case are 99 per cent Muslim), and the discourses they generate.

Method

Studying the only pilgrimage which is exclusively accessible to Muslims, without being Muslim myself, entails a particular methodological positioning. This research has the singularity of observing something other than its central object. The aim is to show that the material preparation for this ritual represents an important aspect of the pilgrimage which informs the observer on the social workings of a society. Indeed, from the pilgrims' selection process through to their return to Tunisian soil, a State official is always present, along with national flags, portraits of the (then) president Zine el Abidine Ali and cameras of national TV stations, ready to capture and broadcast scenes of rejoicing and emotion, which are no doubt a factor in raising the hopes of would-be pilgrims.[3]

There have been recent anthropological accounts "from within", such as Abdellah Hammoudi's excellent account,[4] but the aim differs in that the author is simultaneously on a research project and on a personal quest. Further back, the nineteenth century gave incognito travellers such as Burckhardt (1814), Sir Richard Burton (1853) and Snouck Hurgronje (1885)[5] the opportunity to enter Mecca and partake in the rituals of the Great Pilgrimage. However, not only have entrance controls to Mecca drastically changed over the last century and a half, but I am also interested in the whole process of the endeavour rather than only what occurs "on site". Therefore, apart from formal interviews and informal conversations with actors who have effectively accomplished the pilgrimage themselves, I have also paid special attention to different stages of the "pre-" and "post-" ritual, such as administrative and religious preparation, departure ceremony in domestic settings, airport departures, telephone contact during the stay in Saudi Arabia, the place religious TV channels take up during that time, return celebrations among families and friends, occasional visits to local saints on return and, of course, post-pilgrimage narratives. All these involve different instances of institutions, practices and beliefs, and it is through combining methods of participant observation and interviews that I am able to envisage the Hajj preparation as a wide social and cultural arena in contemporary Tunisia.

The Qar'a: Administrative Luck as a Gateway to Mecca

The annual pilgrimage is now familiar to television audiences worldwide. The biggest annual human gathering on the planet and the largest global pilgrimage, the Hajj seems set to continue growing. The Hajj organisation committee in Saudi Arabia, which is part of the Ministry of Hajj and Waqfs, recorded a 15 per cent increase in the number of potential pilgrims for 2010. The total number of Hajj season visitors in 2009 was 3.3 million, as compared with 3.1 million in 2008.

Overwhelmed by the growing success of the pilgrimage, Saudi Arabia decided to impose a quota on the number of pilgrims for the Hajj in 1987. Rumours have been circulating in Tunisia and elsewhere that the 'Umra (the lesser pilgrimage which can be undertaken at any time of year) might also be subjected to similar rules in future, at least during the most popular months.[6]

The current Hajj quota system allows each Muslim country to send one pilgrim per 1,000 inhabitants, giving Tunisia a total allocation of 10,000 pilgrims per year. In 2008, some 50,000[7] Tunisians applied for the Hajj, which means an acceptance rate of only one in five candidates, of whom 49 per cent were women. Forty thousand candidates and their families were left disappointed and frustrated by not being able to fulfil their religious duty. In order to manage or cater for the 10,000 successful candidates, the Tunisian State mobilised sixty-six religious guides and a sixty-person medical service, staffed by twenty-one specialist doctors and thirty-nine paramedical personnel. Prior to the draw, 46,496 candidates underwent medical examinations, 1,403 of whom proved to be unfit to undertake the pilgrimage. In 2009, the Tunisian government cancelled the Hajj for public health reasons: the country had not received the vaccines against the H1N1 flu early enough to ensure the pilgrims' security. It was considered safer to cancel the Hajj altogether.[8]

Each year the Tunisian State is responsible for designating future pilgrims. Like any highly selective procedure, the draw, organised in each municipality (Arabic: *mu'tamdiyya*, French: *délégation*), inevitably attracts criticism. Though the official line and protocol would suggest otherwise, fate and the "luck of the draw" are not the only factors at work. It has to be said that this "luck under control" seems to be generally accepted in the sense that certain tacit rules counterbalance pure chance and reintroduce a dose of rationality in a process that would otherwise be perceived as being too random, maybe too close to a mere game. Street discourse claims that it is not possible to be refused access to Hajj more than seven times. Such a series of refusals would be interpreted as if Allah himself was not favourable to the Hajj and could throw the believer into terrible grief. Another unwritten rule is that candidates over eighty years of age usually have priority. However, those who take care of pilgrims on the journey from Tunis to Mecca, the *mutawwaffun*,[9] as well as doctors, firmly discourage the senior generation from launching themselves into the tremendously tiring endeavour of the Hajj. If one has already been on the Great Pilgrimage, it is unlikely that one's name will be drawn a second time.

Furthermore, it is often said that knowing "somebody" in the local administration may increase one's chances of being selected for the Hajj. In the local Arabic, having such informal relations in a place of bureaucratic importance is referred to as having *ktaf*, literally "having shoulders", those of others, who are ready and willing to support you. Given all these factors, it seems true to say - broadly speaking - that for a fair number of pilgrimage-candidates several criteria have to be satisfied for their name to figure on the list. A candidate should not be too young (one can always try again), nor too old (one might not be able to cope with the testing conditions), and one should not be ill. I found that those who had been to Mecca many times (either for the 'Umra or the Hajj) had not gone through formal government channels. They had opted for the private travel company that is allotted a set number of places for pilgrims (within the national quota) and sells them at a much higher rate.

The Selection of Pilgrims: An Ocean of Paperwork

A few months before the date of the Hajj, the Minister of Religious Affairs announces in a press release that it is possible for the public to register for Hajj at a local *délégation* during a given time period. For the 2010 Hajj, the month-long registration period started on 28 April.

The pilgrimage selection process is arduous and heavily bureaucratic. Despite knowing that most candidates are not selected, the hopeful pilgrim places his/her name on the official list. Once the pre-registration has been recorded by the administration, the candidate is required to go through a full medical examination, which also involves tests for infectious diseases and compulsory vaccinations, including meningitis and, from 2010, avian flu. Should the aspiring pilgrim's application be unsuccessful, these formalities are required again for subsequent applications. All this has a financial cost, and for most would-be women pilgrims, the undertaking also involves a gradual "moral preparation", such as increased praying or fasting, and a visible change in self-presentation towards greater modesty. This heavy investment is the reason for the very strong disappointment and sadness felt by the unlucky majority who have to try again the following year.

I will now describe the experience of Hajja S. as an example of a pilgrim's trajectory. Hajja S. is a very pious woman. At the time of our last meeting, she had been a widow for twenty-four years. Her son was thirty-five and still single, a status that worried her; her adopted daughter, then eighteen, had had a rather chaotic schooling. She explained to me that on the death of her husband she had decided to adopt the veil and to devote herself entirely to God and her children. As a single mother and sole breadwinner in the household, she had always worked. She devoted her free time to reading the holy texts and prayer and drew obvious satisfaction from her religious practice.

When I interviewed her, S. had undertaken three 'Umras. She performed her first 'Umra in 1987, two years after her husband's death. The second was in 1992, the third in 2000. Her trip on the 'Umra was as part of a group, as the office for which she worked organised regular group pilgrimages for women, accompanied by male chaperones. In 2005, the third time she had registered for the Hajj draw, her name came up for the Great Pilgrimage. S. explained to me that she would go to Mecca every year if she could, so great was the call, so intense was the pull of the Holy Places. As she did not have any close male relatives apart from her brother and her son, it is the latter who signed the paperwork allowing her to travel to Saudi Arabia. With her women friends, she often talks of their pilgrimages: they are times of great happiness, punctuated with moments of great stress. Freed of the constraints of domestic life for two or three weeks, during the Hajj, the women recharge their batteries through prayer, relaxation and jovial socialising, and spend happy times helping each other prepare home-cooked food with products brought discreetly from Tunisia.[10]

After her first 'Umra, S. had a dream one summer night which fed her desire to undertake the Great Pilgrimage. In this dream, she saw the Al-Ahram Mosque in Mecca, dark carpets and a flight of stairs which seemed to call her upwards. There, she found herself in the presence of a man "dressed like the Ka'aba". She explained to me that in the Book of the Prophets (*Kitab al-Anbiya*), the Ka'aba is described as being "like a prophet". She was not able, however, to explain exactly what was meant by this. Filled with the intensity of faith of the entire umma, this man called her without uttering a single word. On waking, she understood that she had to register on a list for the Hajj-draw and prepare herself for the pilgrimage. Twice, in 1992 and 2000, she was one of the disappointed majority.[11] On the third try, she was finally among the lucky few. At the local *délégation* office, S. learned that she had been accepted when the results were announced without any religious decorum. She strongly regretted this, stating that she had preferred the religious atmosphere she had encountered previously, when accompanying friends. Apart from a ritual formula "*itqabal Allah*" (which means "May God accept your prayer"), the municipal official gave her the name of the mosque where she was required to go to prepare for the pilgrimage, and that was all. She began to prepare herself properly for the Great Pilgrimage by attending the state-organised meetings and classes set up to train future pilgrims. These meetings took place in the local mosque, and the imam explained the different stages of the Hajj and their religious significance. Finally, S. prepared the *bsissa*[12] to distribute to family, friends and acquaintances, some of them quite distant – her son's colleagues and the parents of her daughter's friends – to formally announce her pilgrimage.

Potential pilgrims thus go through a whole series of steps: medical preparation, administrative paperwork, religious and moral preparation, as well as a physical process, when fasting is increased or a change in clothing is adopted.

The Draw and Religious Emotion

Until recent years, the drawing of names was a ceremony. This event would be attended by all potential pilgrims and their families, who would dress in their best clothing, women with their heads covered and men in their best *jbaiyyb* (long tunics decorated with intricate embroidery). There would be recitation of the Qur'an by the men present, and sometimes a *Sulemya* group of musicians and singers would chant a religious repertoire, underscored by the deep rhythmic beat of the *bendir*.[13] Incense was burnt during the solemn moment of the actual draw, which led to a dramatic climax as names were pulled out from the box, one by one. The atmosphere was described as extremely solemn and joyous, with the women going into strident *zaghrita* (ululations), and the men echoing them with deep exclamations of "*Allah-hu-Akbar*" ("God is great"), as the names were read out aloud by the official in the presence of imams from the neighbourhood mosques. There was *jaw*, a term generally used to refer to a positive atmosphere. To satisfy Allah, dress would be both modest (no '*awra*[14] part of the body would be revealed) and pleasing to the senses (dresses, *jbaiyyb*, and large pieces of white cloth still used by some women to cover their heads and bodies in the street – *sifsariyyaat* – were of the best materials, cotton and silk) and subtle and pleasant scents such as musk or jasmine or other perfumes were worn.

Avoiding the Formal Draw: Legal Solutions, Illegal Stratagems

I would like to recall another one of my informant's comments on getting around the rules: "You have to understand that in this case the illegal is not immoral."

With adequate funds, it is possible to avoid the official pilgrimage scheme. Until the late 1990s, it was possible to travel to Mecca for the Hajj as part of a travel agency package. In light of accusations of inadequate accommodation and travel arrangements in 1998, the Tunisian State granted a monopoly on organising Hajj travel to a single private company, Montazah Gammarth (renamed Société de services nationaux et des résidences (SSNR)), owned by members of the then president's wife's family.[15] The aim was to sideline the unscrupulous travel agencies who, until then, had shared the small but lucrative private market. In 2010, Montazah Gammarth clients paid around 7,000 Tunisian dinars (around 3,500 euros at the 2010 exchange rate), to go on the Hajj. This was roughly double the State rate.

People with limited funds, who have been unlucky in the draw but who desperately wish to accomplish this religious duty, may use "illegal means" to ensure a place. They argue that the house of God is the house of all Muslims. Thus, despite the authorities' opposition, certain individuals persist in dealing with illegal "service providers" offering low-quality accommodation and transport. Shady bus companies run services to Saudi Arabia leaving from the large coastal centres of Monastir and Sousse. Pilgrims travelling in this way are not part of the official quota and cannot hope to obtain a visa for the Hajj, delivered solely by the Saudi Arabian Embassy in a pilgrim's home country through official channels. The trick is to travel to Saudi Arabia to undertake an 'Umra during the period leading up to the Hajj and then to remain in the country illegally until the time of the Hajj, during the month of *Dhul Hijja*. Certain pilgrims undertake the whole journey by road, crossing Libya, Egypt and Saudi Arabia. It takes around three months and participants return home extremely proud of their achievement. At the very least, this shows how believers' financial conditions have an impact on the way they execute their religious obligation.

Another way of ensuring one's presence on the Hajj is to travel to Saudi Arabia by plane for the 'Umra one or two months before the period of the Great Pilgrimage and then stay on. A small number of Tunisian pilgrims manage to perform their Hajj using this stratagem. However, the Saudi Hajj and 'Umra Office stresses that this dodge is increasingly frowned upon and exploiters of this loophole are penalised. It is during the Ramadan 'Umra that a significant number of pilgrims intentionally miss their planes home to undertake the Hajj, despite their lack of visa (and special passport). To cope with this phenomenon, the Saudi authorities have adopted new precautionary procedures. These measures include intensive inspections and check-points in the Mecca and Jeddah areas and a major media offensive to ensure the cooperation of local citizens and residents.

The most evident retaliatory measure is that offenders can now be subject to prison sentences and fines running up to 100,000 Saudi riyals, in addition to expulsion from Saudi Arabia with a formal prohibition banning the offender from returning to the Wahhabi Kingdom within a given number of years. A further measure places the blame squarely on the national community: the number of offenders is subtracted from the number of visas – and of places – available for the following year.

Cooperation between nation-states, between Saudi Arabia and the sender-countries, has become essential in the organisation of the pilgrimage: each country sends specially trained guides, or *mutawwaffun*, to look after groups. They are responsible for their material and spiritual guidance. Such guides were already at work in the nineteenth century, providing spiritual guidance and ensuring the pilgrimage's success in material terms. It could be argued that through the *mutawwafun*, the groups remain cantoned off from each other, reducing exchange with others. Sylvia Chiffoleau even underlines certain similarities with other organised travel groups, notably package tours, in the sense that national ties are constantly reaffirmed.[16] In this extraordinary event, the believer is faced with a constant oscillation between the dissolution of the individual, alone before God, into the immensity of the Muslim umma assembled and the reaffirmation of national ties. For many pilgrims today, especially the poorest, for whom this may be the first trip abroad, the sheer scale of the process, the number of languages spoken and the difficulty of communicating with other Muslims is a real challenge and is said to be almost frightening. In this case, staying with one's national flock is described as comforting.

Here again, we see how individual religious practice is tightly framed by social condition and the way public policy deals with religion.

Conclusion

I would like to emphasise the fact that the angle chosen here for studying the phenomenon of the Hajj is a marginal one with heuristic interest. Instead of participating in the trip myself and observing the ritual from within, with its different phases, rhythms, spaces, infrastructures and levels of spiritual engagements of the pilgrims, I decided, for obvious material reasons and sociological interest, to focus on the preparation of this ritual in the city of Tunis. In a larger study I have observed the economic issues of the Great Pilgrimage on a domestic/family level.[17] In a complementary study, I wish to analyse the discourses and practices at work during the course of religious preparatory teachings in the mosques of the capital with a comparison to those in nearby villages. For this present article, I decided to unpack the administrative ritual of the "draw". By doing this, I was able to show how the State is involved in the organisation and the control of the Hajj, as yet another example of its involvement in all religious matters (for example, imams are trained, selected and paid by the State). Studies of the Hajj tend to insist on the personal and religious aspect, rather than the pragmatic social and political event, which it also is. At one level, I have shown that it is a family occasion, as family members are involved in the preparations, and people usually travel with close relations though they apply individually (married couples, mothers and sons, brothers and sisters, or close friends). At another level, this chapter shows that the Hajj is a national event, solidly supervised by the State at every stage.

The ethnographic approach to the draw as an administrative ritual has enabled me to understand how different imagined communities, such as the umma, the nation, the region and the family, constitute different arenas of construction and expression of the self. In these different arenas, the pilgrim as a believer, a citizen, an Arab, a mother or father, may activate different – and sometimes contradictory – moralities and rationalities. For example, I have shown how the "chance" of the draw is counterbalanced by administrative rules, while the moral and religious preparation may go hand in hand with the implementation of illegal stratagems in order to reach one's goal.

Notes

1. On relations between state and religion in Tunisia, see Mustapha Al-Ahnaf, "Tunisie: un débat sur les rapports état/religion", *Monde Arabe-Maghreb-Machrek*, no. 126, 1989, pp. 93–108; Jean-Philippe Bras, "L'islam administré en Tunisie", in Mohamed Kerrou (ed.), *Public et privé en Islam. Espaces, autorités et libertés*, Paris: Maisonneuve & Larose, 2002, p. 227–46; Frank Fregosi, "Les rapports entre l'islam et l'État en Algérie et en Tunisie: de leur revalorisation à leur contestation", *Annuaire de l'Afrique du Nord 1995*, vol. 34, 1997, pp. 103–23; Mohamed Tozy, "Islam et État au Maghreb", *Monde Arabe-Maghreb-Machrek*, no. 126, 1989, pp. 25–46.

2. In this chapter I present data from fieldwork in Tunisia, undertaken in 2008, funded by the Idemec (Institut d'ethnologie méditerranéenne et européenne comparée), CNRS.
3. The 2011 Hajj will, no doubt, be staged differently, as Ben Ali's portraits have disappeared since mid-January 2010. It will be interesting to observe where the symbolic changes will occur.
4. Abdellah Hammoudi, *Une saison à la Mecque, récit de pèlerinage*, Paris: Le Seuil, 2005.
5. John Lewis Burckhardt, *Travels in Syria and the Holy Land*, London: African Association, 1822; Richard F. Burton, *Personal Narrative of a Pilgrimage to Al Medinah and Meccah* New York: Dover Publications, 1964 [1855]; George Henry Bousquet, and Joseph Schacht, *Oeuvres choisies de C. Snouck Hurgronje*, Leiden: E. J. Brill, 1957.
6. There is greater affluence during the month of Ramadan and during the period of *Mawlid al-Nabi*, the Prophet Muhammad's birthday.
7. According to the Minister of Religious Affairs, the exact number of pilgrimage candidates for 2008 was 51,741. Nine thousand candidates were accepted, of whom 6,400 were selected by draw and 1,740 were invited by workers residing in Saudi Arabia. The remainder (960 pilgrims) travelled with Montazah Gammarth, a travel company subsequently renamed Société de services nationaux et des résidences (SSNR).
8. This is the official version. Béchir Turki, in his recent book (*Ben Ali le ripou*, Paris: http://samibenabdallah.rsfblog.org/archive/2011/01/31/ben-ali-le-ripoux-ouvrage-en-pdf.html, 2011), claims that the flu was only a pretext to hide the conflict between Tunisia and Saudi Arabia over the fact that the company which centralises the flow of pilgrims in Tunisia (the sole agent) had not paid its bills to Saudi Arabia for 2007 and 2008. According to this author, many of the would-be pilgrims of 2009 have not yet been reimbursed.
9. For a colourful description of these guides who were already present 100 years ago, see David Long, *The Hajj Today: A Survey of the Contemporary Mekkah Pilgrimage*, Albany: State University of New York Press, 1979, p. 28.
10. It is forbidden to bring unauthorised food products into Saudi Arabia. However, many pilgrims break this rule because food is considered to be expensive in the Holy Places, in particular during the Hajj and Ramadan. As is true for other pilgrimage-related issues, the points of view expressed by the pilgrims vary considerably according to salary. Wealthier pilgrims who had travelled with a travel agency assured me that food was not expensive in Saudi Arabia and that it was possible to eat cheaply, in street restaurants and even in quality restaurants.
11. The local term is "*rûfzu*" which derives from the French word "refusé", in the sense that they have been "refused".
12. Highly calorific paste, made from a ground cereal mix of wheat, barley, peanuts, carob, sugar and olive oil, often eaten at important liminal events in the lifecycle.
13. Large percussion instrument consisting of a circular wooden frame and sheep skin.
14. '*Awra*, in religious contexts, refers to parts of the body which cannot be shown in public (that is, in front of people of the opposite sex with whom one has no family ties). '*Awra* for women (in some contexts) is the whole body except for the face, hands and feet.

15. As this book goes to press, only a few months after Ben Ali's departure on 14 January 2011, this company still has the monopoly on travel for the Hajj or 'Umra.
16. Sylvia Chiffoleau, "Le pèlerinage à La Mecque à l'époque coloniale: matrice d'une opinion publique musulmane?", in Sylvia Chiffoleau and Anna Madoeuf (eds), *Les pèlerinages au Maghreb et au Moyen-Orient. Espaces publics, espaces du public*, Damas: Ifpo, 2005, pp. 131–63.
17. In press is an article on the economic involvement of families in financing the Hajj and the gendered and cross-generational dimension it presents: Katia Boissevain, "Préparatifs d'un pèlerinage à La Mecque: organisation étatique et transactions domestiques en Tunisie", in Dionigi Albera and Melissa Blanchard (eds), *Pellegrini del Nuovo Millennio: Aspetti Economici e Politici delle Mobilita' Religiose*, Messina, Mesogea and Paris: Karthala, 2011.

CHAPTER 3

"There Used To Be Terrible Disbelief":
Mourning and Social Change in Northern Syria

Katharina Lange

This chapter addresses changing burial and mourning practices in villages of northern Syria. Locally, these transformations are articulated mainly in terms of changing understandings of religious prescriptions. However, analysing religious discourse is not sufficient to comprehend the changes – changing social relations and economics must be taken into consideration as well. Through a close ethnographic description of actions, practices and discourse related to mourning and burial, this article shows how "Islamic" frameworks are invoked to make sense of changing social practice, and how, in turn, concepts of mourning labelled as Islamic are enacted in everyday life. It will also demonstrate how emergent normative concepts understood as "Islamic" are not simply appropriated, but are very much contested in actual practice – even though they may not be challenged discursively.

Adopting an ethnographic approach is essential for the description and discussion of these issues. The observation of social practice (while not excluding local discourse) is a precondition for understanding the emergence and application of "Islamic" normativities in everyday contexts. Furthermore, describing change over time necessitates a longer-term acquaintance with, and, ideally, research presence in, the field, which represents a classical element of ethnographic methodology. Fieldwork in Syria was conducted between October 2002 and January 2004 in the framework of research on local (tribal) histories. This period was preceded, and followed, by a number of visits, most recently in April 2011.[1]

The villagers in this region are mostly Sunni Muslims who identify with different Arab *'asha'ir* (tribal groups) – tribal affiliation, expressed in the idiom of common descent, being one of the important local categories of social order.

People in other parts of Syria refer to this population as *Shawaya*. Originally designating small livestock herders, this term has pejorative connotations, indicating backwardness, primitiveness and a low social status in wider Syrian society.

Large-scale transformations have taken place here since the 1970s. Seasonally mobile livestock raising has almost ceased, while agriculture has been expanding since the 1950s. Labour migration abroad and to the Syrian metropolis is now an indispensable source of income. These changes have been accelerated by the construction of the Euphrates Dam at Tabqa in 1973. When today's Lake Asad submerged villages and fields, the population moved or was resettled in state farms or villages higher on the river bank, in the steppe or in the so-called "Arab belt" in the Syrian Jazira,[2] resulting in the geographical dispersal of relatives over hundreds of kilometres.[3]

Ethnography

On the last evening of August 2003, I was sitting in the courtyard of a house in the village of Rasm Hammud.[4] I was there to offer my condolences to the family of Abu Salama, the forty-six-year-old, respected director of the village school who had died unexpectedly after a motorbike accident a week before. On this evening, the week-long mourning reception (*'azza*) in Abu Salama's house was to be concluded by a *mulid*. The mulid, a religious celebration including the melodious and rhythmic reading, or chanting, of Qur'an and hadith, was taking place in a tent that had been erected beside the courtyard where I was sitting among a large crowd of women and girls. The shaykh who was leading the mulid and his "group" (*firqa*) had come from a larger village on the request of the deceased's family. As is customary, the mulid was attended by hundreds of male mourners. The equally numerous female mourners were sitting apart, in the courtyard and rooms of Abu Salama's house. With many of the women, I was listening to the rhythmic chanting of the men from afar.

About ten or fifteen minutes after the mulid had started, loud crying was suddenly heard from another corner of the courtyard. The women sitting around me interrupted their quiet conversations to ask each other about the source of the crying. My friend Khadija asked me to leave our place and look for who was weeping so noisily. It turned out to be Najwa, the unmarried daughter of the deceased who was about twenty years old. She was sitting in the embrace of an older aunt, surrounded by two other aunts and about twenty girls and young women, most of whom were crying as well. As we approached, another aunt came and admonished her to stop weeping so loudly and calm herself. However, Najwa shouted her protest and continued to weep.

On the following morning, Najwa's behaviour was discussed by a group of women who had gathered in my hosts' house. Khadija, the twenty-five-year-old girl who had witnessed the scene with me, argued that it was "normal" and acceptable for a girl in Najwa's situation to mourn and that expressing her grief would allow her to "calm down". Her mother asserted the opposite: exaggerated grieving, she said, was not "necessary" because the decision about life and death was God's and it was inappropriate to protest against his will through overly expressive mourning. To stress her point, she admitted that she herself had been guilty of "exaggerated" mourning twenty years ago when one of her children had died but she had since realised that this was wrong. Religiously acceptable mourning should look different: "When one mourns a dead person, one should sit still, and at the most cry quietly without making any noise. If we cry, we should wipe the tear off our face as soon as it has reached the cheek", Khadija's sister Maryam explained to me.

I later realised that both the commotion caused by Najwa's weeping and the following morning's debate reflected contesting normativities about expressing grief that pointed to emergent fault lines at the very heart of village life, as burials and mourning receptions are among the most central social moments in Rasm Hammud. Attending the burial, or at least the 'azza for a deceased, is considered a binding social obligation even for distant relatives and acquaintances. These occasions highlight the contradiction between the equality of death which does not differentiate – everyone will die, and be the object of divine grace – and the social hierarchy of the village which is visibly (re)produced in the celebrations of death.

When a member of the community dies, the burial is held on the same day, if possible. The closest relatives bid farewell to the deceased, whose body is washed and dressed in the shroud by a villager of the same sex known to be faithful and ritually and spiritually pure. This takes places either in the deceased's own house or, increasingly, in the village mosque, constructed in the first years of the twenty-first century. The body is then taken to the cemetery by a procession of relatives, neighbours and other mourners who have been notified immediately on occurrence of the death. The cemetery is located on a hill about a kilometre outside the village, and is also used by the neighbouring village. The body is interred while the imam recites the appropriate religious formulae. After the mourners return to the village, the 'azza begins at the deceased's house.

The mourning receptions I witnessed lasted between three and seven days, although villagers explained to me that it was "better" not to extend the 'azza beyond three days, because "exaggerated" mourning would mean questioning God's will. The higher the deceased's (or their families') social status, the more guests come and the longer the 'azza lasts. More care is also taken to observe the proprieties of hospitality and dignified behaviour. On these intensely social occasions, memories and grief are expressed, guests are hosted, and news and gossip are exchanged. Hundreds of relatives, neighbours and acquaintances may gather to pay their respects to the bereaved family. Even relatives who work abroad or those who have settled in the new villages of the "Arab belt" up to 600 kilometres away come for a day or two to join the mourners and offer their condolences.

Guests come every day from morning to night; many of them visit more than once, some attend every day. Many guests are hosted for one or more nights and they have to eat, wash, sleep, and so on.

Sharing and giving food, the essence of hospitality, is a central element of remembering and honouring the dead. When it is distributed on the occasion of a death, the food is given "for the spirit of the deceased" (*'ala ruh al mayyit*). The "classical" dishes served at the 'azza are *therid* (cooked sheep meat on top of a heap of bread drenched in broth) and *derikh* (pieces of meat roasted in a pot over the fire). It is felt that only these dishes carry the appropriate social "weight" for this occasion; they can only be cooked by older women, because the younger generation lacks the skills and experience to prepare them. However, I have also been served *lahm bi-'ajin* (a meat pie bought ready-made in the nearest market town) at an 'azza, even though it is generally considered too "light" for the occasion.

Food at the 'azza may convey spiritual qualities. During the mulid, sweets, soft drinks or salt are frequently placed in front of the shaykh. It is believed that the shaykh's "reading on" the food confers *baraka* (blessing power) on these foodstuffs which are then distributed among the guests. The blessing consumed with them will protect the mourners from material evils such as illnesses or scorpion stings.

The heavy load of hospitality is shared by the village community. Helping to cover the cost and effort of hosting an 'azza is expected of relatives and neighbours and is considered a commendable act for more distant acquaintances. Until a few years ago, it was customary to contribute in kind to the expenses of an 'azza by giving a sheep for slaughter, a sack of wheat, sugar or rice. This has changed. With the decline in raising livestock, donating a sheep has become the exception, while giving a bag of rice is now considered "cheap". Today, closer relatives and neighbours are expected to give money to help cover the costs of food, drink, soap and other expenses such as the money which is given to the shaykh and his firqa for the mulid. This donation, carefully recorded in writing so it can be reciprocated at the appropriate time, is considered an obligation (*farad*) on all relatives, rather than an entirely voluntary contribution. Not to contribute anything would be shameful; it would also mean placing oneself outside the social circle of loyalty and mutual help which functions as an insurance in times of need.

Besides material help, relatives and neighbours give their work and time. Girls share in baking bread, cooking or washing, men and boys help by serving the guests, and many village households host visitors who have come from longer distances, often for several days.

Gendered mourning

Male visitors are received in a tent (*bayt al-'azza*) which is erected close to the deceased's home for the duration of the mourning reception. In the past, this used to be a black goat hair tent of the kind commonly used during the winter and spring migrations. As many families used to own such tents, erecting the bayt al-'azza was not difficult, and did not involve any extra expense. With the decline of mobile herding, these privately owned tents are now replaced by a construction of sackcloth which is draped over metal rods, similar to models used in the Syrian cities. This has been jointly bought by the descent group to which most villagers belong, with each family contributing to the cost. On the last day of the 'azza, the mulid is held and attended only by men. Depending on the views of the shaykh leading the ceremony, it may consist of Qur'an and hadith reading only, or a more elaborate *dhikr* involving rhythmic chanting and drums.

Female guests are received in the house and courtyard of the family. At Abu Salama's 'azza (as at others I attended), the female mourners grouped together roughly according to generation. Many of the young women and girls entered a separate room to read segments of the Qur'an from thin booklets that are kept at the village mosque, and were distributed among the guests. The aim was to complete reading the whole Qur'an during the 'azza. Only the younger generation could contribute to this endeavour, since they had acquired at least basic reading skills at school, while most older women are not able to read and write. In this room, the atmosphere was quiet and controlled, no chatting took place, and the young women took care to veil their hair properly.

Older women gathered in one room or in a corner of the courtyard. From time to time, one or more of them broke into loud wailing laments (*na'wat*). Na'wat give expression to grief over a loved one's death through images of loss, separation and distance through short sentences, often rhymed, which may be traditional or made up on the spot. Although na'wat are criticised by many as a sign of backwardness, or even *haram* (forbidden), I saw lamenting at every 'azza I attended.

Women and especially young, unmarried girls are supposed to remain modest and quiet at occasions where a wider public, notably men, is present. At the 'azza, however, the usual norms for gendered behaviour may be subverted for short periods of time. As Najwa's example shows, loud weeping and lamenting may momentarily put women and even younger girls at the centre of attention.

Conversations at each 'azza I witnessed were usually conducted in low voices, and mourners took care to behave decorously. In contrast to other social occasions, girls and young women did not put on make-up and wore muted colours. The mood was sombre, but not necessarily tearful as burial receptions also offer a chance to meet with long-missed relatives and friends, to exchange the latest news and gossip. However, the mood changed quickly to one of sadness whenever a mourner expressed her sorrow through na'wat. Recited in a raised voice with a wailing, plaintive tone, these laments sound very much like loud weeping. Every time I witnessed a woman breaking into na'wat, her crying quickly moved the other mourners to tears as well. The women saying na'wat are not always close relatives of the deceased, and the mourners do not necessarily (or exclusively) mourn the deceased for whom the 'azza is being held. Because an 'azza reminds the mourners of their own losses, one may hear a mother mourning a dead child, or a wife grieving for a husband who has passed away some time before. Since the lamented individuals are not named, the knowledge of who is crying for whom arises from the knowledge of social relations in the community; it can also be inferred from the wording of the lament.

During the lamenting, I was not able to discern any words (let alone remember them for my notes, which I always took after, never during, an 'azza) and therefore asked female interlocutors to recount some na'wat for me later. Younger women and girls usually knew at least a few, but the "experts" in this kind of mourning were older women. Responding to my request, some recited na'wat in small, private sessions where no men or strangers were present – never in the "authentic" wailing style, but dictated word for word. Sometimes, however, my interlocutors hesitated to repeat these extremely emotionally evocative sayings to me because they did not feel comfortable doing so even in the sober atmosphere of an ordinary conversation.

Women's expressions of grief are currently under pressure to become less visible and audible. Besides the criticism of female voices raised in mourning, other bodily practices (tearing one's clothes and hair, scratching or blackening one's face) are condemned. Yet one of the most recent, and most noticeable, changes is the disappearance of women from the cemetery. When Abu Salama was buried, his body was laid to rest by male and female mourners. Only three days later, his cousin Abu Ali who had died from a heart attack during Abu Salama's 'azza, was interred only by men. The female relatives who had wanted to join the funeral procession for Abu Ali had been held back by the men.

This significant difference was inspired by admonitions from Shaykh Abdallah, a young imam from another village who had attended Abu Salama's 'azza. In the men's tent, Shaykh Abdallah, who had studied at Al-Azhar University, had voiced his disapproval of women's mourning behaviour which, he said, was not only "inappropriate", but violated religious prescriptions.

In other villages of the region, females have also gradually abstained from joining funeral processions over the past decade. When I visited in 2008–9, only on the early mornings of Eid al-Adha and Eid al-Fitr did female villagers still go to the cemetery to remember and mourn the dead. In many villages of the region, even outside the socially and ritually formalised occasions of burials, women do not visit the graves any more. Umm Hasan, a sixty-five-year-old widow whose husband died in 1999, lives in the village of Al-Beida, about 20 kilometres north-east of Rasm Hammud. When I first got to know her in February 2001, she used to start each day at sunrise by visiting her husband's grave, reciting the *fatiha* (opening sura of the Qur'an), talking with the deceased and keeping him up to date on family and village affairs. When I visited her in 2006, Umm Hasan had ceased to do this because "people said that it was wrong". Unwilling to resist village social pressure, she now recites the *fatiha* for Abu Hasan at home.

The condemnation of the "indignity" of female mourning has been supplemented and, it sometimes seems to me, almost replaced by another argument. During a field visit I made in spring 2007, Umm Muhammad of Rasm Hammud explained to me: "As the dead lie in their graves, they see those who visit the graves – but they perceive them without any clothes on. So they will necessarily look at the female *'awra* [nakedness; see Chapter 2, note 14, in this volume] if women visit the graves." This would blemish the spiritual record not only of the mourners whose *'awra* would be plainly visible to all the dead that are buried in the cemetery, it would also weigh against the dead themselves on judgement day. Visiting the graves has thus been turned from a "commendable act" into its opposite.

Analysis and Comments

The changes described above – shortening the duration of the *'azza*, suppressing emphatic mourning, and so on – can be summarised as a process of rationalisation. The villagers themselves subscribe to a discourse of progress and enlightenment to explain these changes and, in doing so, simultaneously take up transnational Islamisation as well as Syrian state-sponsored modernisation paradigms.

Similar to other Muslim societies,[5] expressive mourning in the Syrian Euphrates valley is placed in a framework of cultural hierarchies. It is portrayed as a sign of "backwardness" and lack of culture which supposedly characterises the villagers of this region, in contrast to the more refined urban population in the Syrian metropolis. Many villagers say that they are now more "aware" than in earlier times, thanks to increased formal schooling in the countryside – a central feature of Ba'thist modernisation policies. This education, they say, has enabled them to read (religious) texts. Furthermore, TV and radio shows have contributed to a better understanding of religious prescriptions. Others also point to the importance of an increasingly better-educated religious elite. In addition, labour migrants returning from Saudi Arabia and other Arab countries bring back new ideas on properly "Islamic" lifestyles with a notable emphasis on gender segregation.

"Inappropriate" forms of grieving and mourning are discursively firmly placed in the past. "There used to be terrible disbelief (*kufr*) before", Umm Muhammad summed up her account of traditional mourning practices. There are indeed a number of Prophet's traditions that advise against expressive or emphatic mourning, although none of my interlocutors (male or female) were able to quote any of them.

However, looking at the wider picture, it becomes clear that the transformations described above are not (exclusively) motivated by religious considerations, but point equally to changes in infrastructure, social relations and economic circumstances. Social relations between villagers are increasingly characterised by geographical dispersal (and social estrangement) of family members, economic scarcity and conflicts over money. As geographical and social divisions separating the villagers become more prominent, and many villagers actually live elsewhere, it becomes practically and financially increasingly difficult to organise a long 'azza. Many households are not equipped to host guests well. Furthermore, for unskilled labourers in a precarious labour market, each missed daily wage is sorely noticed so that time taken off work to fulfil social obligations is kept as short as possible.

The significance of the described changes for gender relations is evident. Emphatic mourning and lamenting have been discussed in terms of women's empowerment versus subordination to a patriarchal order with regard to Muslim as well as non-Muslim societies. Especially ethnographies of Shi'i communities have emphasised the empowering aspects of expressive female mourning. In contrast, Abu-Lughod sees female mourning among the Awlad Ali as "an important means by which women publicly enact their own moral, and ultimately social, inferiority" to men, and Goluboff reaches a similar conclusion for Mountain Jewish communities in Azerbaijan.[6]

On the Syrian Euphrates female mourning is also associated with "backwardness" and "indignity". Yet despite the general, vocal agreement with "Islamic" prescriptions curbing more expressive ways of mourning, the ethnographic observation of social practice shows that "progressive" ways have not replaced the more "backward" ones. Notwithstanding the affirmations that mourning receptions should be cut short, an 'azza for a very distinguished man may still last two weeks or even more. Equally, I have witnessed older women and younger girls express their grief by tearing their clothes, scratching their faces and weeping and lamenting loudly.

It may be only a question of time until these practices do disappear. But perhaps their persistence in the face of such strong opposition can also be read as an indication that the rational grieving supposedly prescribed by "proper Islam" is not felt to be adequate for dealing with the strong emotions caused by death and loss. Umm Hasan expressed this in her own way when we spoke of her deceased husband, whose passing she still mourns. She admitted that in principle she agreed with critiques of expressive mourning as *haram* by people "who knew better than her". Yet after a short pause, she said: "But how can you dance *dabke* without a *zummara*?"⁷ – How can you grieve without expressing it?

Notes

1. Research was funded by the German Research Association.
2. This refers to a chain of villages in the Kurdish areas of the Syrian Jazira. Founded in the 1970s, it resettled Arab villagers from the Lake Asad area, simultaneously breaking up the Kurdish areas of settlement in north-eastern Syria; see Jordi Tejel, *Syria's Kurds: History, Politics and Society*, London: Routledge, 2009, pp. 61–2.
3. See Annika Rabo, *Change on the Euphrates: Villagers, Townsmen and Employees in Northeast Syria*, Stockholm: Akademitryck, Minab/Gotab, 1986; Günter Meyer, *Ländliche Lebens und Wirtschaftsformen Syriens im Wandel*, Erlangen: Selbstverlag der Fränkischen Geographischen Gesellschaft 1984; Sulayman Khalaf, *Family, Village and the Political Party: Articulation of Social Change in Contemporary Rural Syria*, unpublished PhD thesis, University of California, Los Angeles, 1981; Myriam Ababsa, *Raqqa: territoires et pratiques sociales d'une ville syrienne*, Beirut: IFPO, 2009; also Gennaro Ghirardelli, "Annäherung an ein versunkenes Dorf. Raumvorstellungen und soziale Organisation in Habuba Kabira / Syrien", *Acta Praehistorica et Archaeologica*, vol. 24, 1992, pp. 205–19.
4. Names of villages and individuals have been changed.
5. For the Egyptian case, see Nadia Abu-Zahra, "The comparative study of Muslim societies and Islamic rituals", in Nadia Abu-Zahra, *The Pure and Powerful. Studies in Contemporary Muslim Society*, 2nd edn, Reading: Ithaca Press, 1999, pp. 35–83.
6. Lila Abu-Lughod, "Islam and the Gendered Discourses of Death", *International Journal of Middle Eastern Studies*, vol. 25, no. 2, May 1993, p. 203; Sascha L Goluboff, "Patriarchy through lamentation in Azerbaijan", *American Ethnologist*, vol. 35, no. 1, February 2008, pp. 81–94.
7. *Dabke* is a popular line dance, and *zummara* is a wind instrument similar to a simple oboe, played primarily at weddings.

Chapter 4

Manifestations of Ashura Among Young British Shi'is

Kathryn Spellman-Poots

This chapter demonstrates how the ethnographic research method provides a vantage point to describe the ways in which embedded conceptions and practices of the Shi'i faith are actively being questioned and reoriented by young Shi'is in British society.[1] Concentrating particularly on the prototypical Shi'i tradition, *Ashura*, this chapter describes some ways that young Shi'is are reworking religious practices through public performances and embodied experiences in British society. Looking specifically at the annual Ashura procession through Hyde Park and the Imam Hussein Blood Donation Campaign demonstrates how these performative spaces are used by the younger generations to negotiate, challenge and communicate the various, and sometimes conflicting, customs of the Ashura ritual among their parents' generation, as well as the normative and legal views of the custom in mainstream British society. This chapter aims to show how an ethnographic study of religious events, as they are in action, allows a researcher to take a closer look at the ways in which young Shi'is are simultaneously engaged in internal conflicts and struggles while actively trying to develop a wider British Shi'i identity.

British Shi'is make up approximately 15 per cent of the estimated two million Muslims living in Britain, and come from a range of educational, socio-economic, generational and ethno-national backgrounds including South Asian, East African, Iranian, Iraqi, Afghani, Indian, Lebanese, Bahraini, Saudi Arabian and Kuwaiti. Although Shi'is hold much in common with Sunnis, including an adherence to the sacred sources of Islam, many of their overlapping laws and ritual practices have evolved separately. Shi'is, for example, place great significance on the historical Battle of Karbala in 680, where Hussein, along with seventy-two of his family and supporters, was killed by the troops of the second Umayyad caliph, Yezid. Although the veneration of the Battle of Karbala varies in relation to the sundry backgrounds of British Shi'is, the tragic events, particularly the martyrdom of Hussein, have continued to play a central role in ritual practices, symbolism and identity construction in the UK. Despite internal differences of ritual practice and interpretations of meaning, Ashura is often associated with public processions and the performance of *latmiya*, also known as *zanjeer zani, ma'tam, qaama-e zani*, and *tatbir* which is a ritualised self-flagellation of one's body in grief. Stereotypically, shirtless men and boys dressed in black trousers parade through the streets, chanting and beating their chests with a whip of chains and blades, called a *zanjeer*; whilst women line the streets and observe the men flagellate or cut their foreheads until blood streams from their bodies. In addition to expressing regret and solidarity with Hussein's suffering, the lamentations are believed to bring a divine reward, or *ajr*, which can be utilised on judgement day.

Shi'i supreme religious leaders or *marja'*, who are deemed to be the most learned juridical authority figures for Shi'is around the globe, have varied rulings on how Ashura rituals should be performed. Although the marja' are mainly based in holy cities in Iran and Iraq, the most prominent have international headquarters and representatives in London, as well as interactive websites, for Shi'is to refer to for answers on jurisprudential rulings for religious matters. While several prominent marja', such as Grand Ayatollah Sayyid Ali al-Husseini al-Sistani, Grand Ayatollah Ali Husseini Khamenei and the late Grand Ayatollah Muhammad Hussein Fadl-Allah have discouraged or banned self-harm both on religious grounds and for creating a backward and negative image of Shi'i Muslims, others, such as Ayatollah Muhammad al-Shirazi, defend the practice and find it at the essence of Shi'i faith.

Although self-flagellation is not practised by the vast majority of British Shi'is, it has become a topic of heated debate among young Shi'is in Britain. This is partly due to the critical coverage that bloodletting rituals have received among segments of the Sunni population, as well as the British mainstream press. Several high-profile court cases have stirred public interest on the interface of self-flagellation in relation to British law. The best known case happened in 2008 at Manchester Crown Court, when Syed Mustafe Zaidi, aged forty-four, was convicted of child cruelty for encouraging his two sons, aged thirteen and fifteen, to self-flagellate until their backs bled during an Ashura ceremony at an Islamic centre in Manchester. Zaidi was given a twenty-six-week jail sentence for child cruelty. Violent pictures of bloody backs and foreheads, which were largely taken in Pakistan, featured in the British media, and generated controversial public discussions on the harmful effects of certain Muslim customs. Although the practice was being evaluated by Shi'is and non-Shi'is in relation to British law, human rights discourses and the normative codes in British society, it was equally important for Shi'is, young and old, to critically evaluate the legitimacy of performing the ritual from "within" the Shi'i tradition. My field research on Muharram commemorations provides a first-hand account of how Shi'is, mainly in their late teens to thirties, orientate themselves to these varying conceptions of Ashura practices; and how commemoration events have become active spaces to contest, negotiate and promote different ritual performances and meanings of Ashura in Britain.

Since the mid-1990s I have been attending Shi'i religious events as part of my ethnographic research on Iranian Shi'i religious networks and practices in London. In recent years I have carried out research with a wider range of Shi'i communities in both London and Manchester; meeting with networks of men and women, across generations, that actively associate themselves with religious centres and a wider Shi'i community. The meetings have taken place in mosques and religious centres, as well as restaurants, university common rooms, homes and at religious events, such as the Ashura procession in Central London and the Imam Hussein Blood Donation Campaign.

Ashura Procession in Central London

The annual Ashura procession in Hyde Park was first organised by a prominent family of Iraqi descent and the predominately Iranian Islamic Universal Association, also known as the Holland Park *Majma'*. Starting at Marble Arch and finishing at the Holland Park Majma', hundreds, and in more recent years, thousands of Shi'is march three miles through the park and streets to honour the martyrdom of Imam Hussein. The organisers, in line with the rulings of the most prominent *marji'i*, do not condone the practice of self-harm during the public procession. The first time I attended the Ashura march in 1997, several hundred participants, mainly from Iranian and Iraqi backgrounds, walked through the park and streets holding banners written in Arabic and Persian, beating their chests and chanting in grief to the rhythm of horns, crash cymbals and drums. Notable local Shi'i leaders in black turbans led the procession, followed by the rest of the men, with and without shirts. The procession was tailed by women donned in black chadors, and children of all ages wearing green headbands bearing Hussein's name. The London Metropolitan Police assisted the march while onlookers viewed the spectacle in relative bewilderment.

Unlike the majority of marches that are organised in Hyde Park, which aim to make an outward-facing public statement, the Ashura procession was first and foremost an inward-looking communal religious experience that emulated customary practices from "back home". Ethnographic enquiry provided me with the nuanced observational tools needed to understand the importance for pious Shi'i to organise and participate in a religious procession through the streets of

London. What was significant was the actual form of the procession itself, as it was integral to the ritual performance of commemorating Ashura and in turn an explicit part of religious life for the participants.

Over the years the procession has become larger, younger, more diverse and less insular. The 2010 Ashura procession, for example, brought together approximately 4,000–5,000 Shi'is who live in London or were bussed in from locations around the UK. Throughout the afternoon, people talked about how the procession provided a rare opportunity to bring together Shi'is from different socio-economic, ethno-national and regional backgrounds. Similar to past processions, it was punctuated with men playing instruments and a leader chanting emotive lamentation elegies in Arabic and Persian through megaphones about the suffering and injustice of Imam Hussein and his entourage. The English language, however, was also widely spoken and heard. Men, women and children intermittently invoked the name of Hussein in unison as they lightly hit their chests. Sporadically, small groups of men and boys clustered around the orators and struck their chests with greater fervour to the rhythm of the drums, cymbals and the chants. Some women responded to these efforts by taking notice of the men and chanting louder. Similar to ethnographic accounts of Ashura processions around the world, there is a carnivalesque atmosphere where the conventional social rules and conduct between sexes are softened by the intensity of the day. The elegies to Hussein are interwoven with participants socialising with each other, talking on mobile phones, and taking videos of the procession to be uploaded, as many noted, to Facebook and other networking sites. Stations of people along the route distributed water, dates and soup, catering for those breaking *Faaqeh*, a customary fast on Ashura that ends after *asr*, or mid-afternoon prayer.

Reflecting wider patterns of Shi'i organisations and activities in British society, the Ashura procession has also become more inclusive, structured and institutionalised. Greater coordination and communication existed between the individual participants, the sundry Shi'i organisations, the Metropolitan Police, the on-lookers, and the growing presence of Western and non-Western press. The organisers designated official stewards – who were mainly young males and females – to assist the police and the organisers in monitoring the order and flow of the procession. I spoke to several stewards, dressed in fluorescent yellow jackets labelled with the Persian word *entzamat* (steward), not only about their duty to ensure crowd control and general safety, but also to make sure that participants do not get carried away while performing latmiya.

Groups of youth used the procession as a platform to promote a range of social, religious or political messages. Taking advantage of the large numbers of attendees and onlookers, as well as the Shi'i and non-Shi'i press, they also advertised lecture programmes and activities hosted by their student clubs. I spoke to young men and women as they were distributing English-language pamphlets with both historical and modern interpretations of Hussein's martyrdom. They talked a lot about the need to publicise the universal lessons of the Battle of Karbala to the wider British public. Many complained that Ashura is epitomised in the UK by physical beating, crying and grief, and portrayed by the media as a violent and barbaric ritual. I heard many jokes about the cultural gulf between the stereotypical enactments of Ashura commemorations in relation to the "reserved" and "emotionally introverted" British society. As one interlocutor joked: "'*Tatbir*' – is *so* – 'un-British'". This led to more serious conversations about how Muharram commemorations should move away from being merely ritualistic. A group of young men in their twenties spoke critically of men who mourned Hussein by self-flagellating, or women by crying hysterically, arguing that they are caught up in a hollow ritual devoid of the central purpose of the remembrance of the tragedy: namely to awaken the heart and mind to the injustices in the world today. Many young attendees stressed that the commemoration of Ashura should be both inward- and outward-facing: a time for both self-reflection and personal purification and a time to renew one's allegiance to Hussein's stance against root evil and societal injustices.

The fundamental role of women during the tragic events in Karbala was also emphasised by the attendees. Many spoke in particular about the bravery of Zaynab (Hussein's sister) during the Battle of Karbala and the brave public lectures she gave against the injustices of Yazid and his followers in Damascus. One participant noted: "Remembering Zaynab helps me to reconnect to my faith; her bravery and sacrifice inspire me to become a better person." Young girls stressed how they were outspoken, like Zaynab, and not merely passive observers at Muharram events. In addition to self-reflection, they described their involvement in organising Muharram events: producing and distributing English-language educational material and canvassing for different political and social causes.

As I walked through the procession, talking to old and new contacts, I observed a contested field of ways to commemorate the martyrs of Karbala. The Ahl al-Bayt Society, for example, drawing from the episode at Karbala when Yazid's army prevented Hussein's camp from taking water from the Euphrates, spearheaded their human rights campaign to end water poverty in the developing world. They passed out information and carried placards, stating: "To end water poverty is to continue Hussein's revolution". For others the tragedy of Karbala was used as a metaphor for political injustices in Gaza, Iraq and Afghanistan. A number of young men wore black and white chequered scarves as a symbol of solidarity with the Palestinian cause and resistance to the Israeli occupation. Several males and females spoke out against the US/Western foreign policy as well as the anti-Shi'i propaganda of the Wahhabis. Others, however, were critical of the politicisation of the tragedy of Karbala, and argued that the march was hijacked by political protestors. A man in his twenties, from an Iraqi background, noted: "I'm disappointed with the march. What we need is to make people understand the real story behind Hussein's death and sacrifice. The Iranian centres wanted the march to support the Gaza protest, which, don't get me wrong, I support, but this is not the occasion for it. Ashura should be a day devoted to *feeling* Hussein's suffering. Nothing more." He defended bloodletting during Muharram ceremonies as an essential part of the Shi'i faith and said he was leaving to attend the *majlis* (singular of *majales*) at the Hossainiyat al-Rasul al-A'zam in Cricklewood.

Others, however, who were critical of both the politicisation of Ashura and the bloodletting ritual, put forward Imam Hussein as a universal model for peace, love and kindness, and compared him to Jesus, Gandhi and other prominent figures of peace. The procession was dotted with a wide range of placards with slogans such as: "I have learned from Hussein how to be oppressed yet victorious – *Mahatma Ghandi*", "Imam Hussein – Freedom was his message", "Hands off Gaza", "End the siege on Iraq", and "Hussein's sacrifice is not limited to one country, or nation, but to all mankind".

Throughout the day, several young participants expressed mixed feelings about taking part in the procession. They spoke positively about the neutrality of the procession and how it brought together thousands of British Shi'is but were uneasy with the form of the procession, which was described as "dated" or only making sense in Iraq, Iran and other Shi'i locales. They criticised those who attended the event to socialise, and spoke negatively about flyers and advertisements that did not relate to the Battle of Karbala, including those offering Shi'i marriage and advice services, *halal* restaurant ads and takeaway menus, and pamphlets on a range of charities such as *Niyabat* or hiring a person to perform a *Ziyarat* or visits to the Holy Shrines in Iran, Iraq and Syria. They conceded that it was acceptable to pass out information on blood drives in London and around the UK, and Muharram guides that included the addresses of the various majlis or mourning ceremonies held around London.

"Which Majlis Are You Going To?"

As the procession neared its destination, conversations turned to where they were attending majlis. The manner in which majales are carried out in various London centres – such as the Islamic Universal Association in Holland Park, the Al-Khoie Foundation in north-west London, the World Federation of Khoja Shi'i Ithna-Ashari Muslim Communities in Stanmore, the Islamic Centre of England in Maida Vale, Dar-e Islam and the Hossainiyat al-Rasul al-A'zam centre, both in Cricklewood – largely depends on the ethno-national customs and languages of the older generation as well as the jurisprudential rulings and politics of the marja', financially supported and backed by each centre. Many stressed how they have grown tired of only "observing" and not being able to relate to the older generations' language and interpretations of Ashura. Whereas Shi'is from the older generations have attached themselves to religious leaders and centres based on longstanding religious practices, as well as the regional and political situations in their homelands, the younger generations have been organising youth clubs and media outlets, where they explore the various marja' rulings on different practices, and decide for themselves which serves them best. They highlighted the development of English-language majales, and drew critical comparisons between the skill and effectiveness of young orators, such as Sayed Hussein Qazwini, Sayed Mahdi Modressi and Sayed Ammar Nakshawani, who provided emotionally and/or intellectually charged narrations and modern interpretations of the tragic scenes at Karbala. Speaking passionately in English, these dynamic leaders relate the sacrifice and struggle of Imam Hussein to the challenges that young Shi'is face living in Western secular societies.

Several noted that they planned to visit various Shi'i centres including those that condone bloodletting and said they were open and even receptive to different religious rulings and cultural variations of the bloody practice. Others, adamantly against latmiya, promoted different avenues of commemoration, which encourage individual sacrifice, as well as being charitable to British society. This reflects a wider trend among young Shi'is who use the month of Muharram as a time of self-purification and atonement, a time to give charity and carry out good deeds.

The Imam Hussein Blood Donation Campaign

The day after the Ashura procession, I went to a church hall in north-west London to donate blood for the Imam Hussein Blood Donation Campaign. Donating blood, which is viewed by some Shi'i as a more "Islamic" and/or "modern" way of shedding blood in the memory of Imam Hussein, has become more widely practised by Shi'i populations around the world.[2] One of the organisers (who I knew from past research) introduced me as a sociologist interested in Shi'ism to a group of girls in their twenties, from Iraqi, East African and Lebanese backgrounds. As we filled out the medical questionnaire, required by the British National Blood Service, we giggled and joked about the explicit questions, such as: "Have you ever received payment for sex or drugs?" As we waited for the nurse to call our names, the girls, all wearing hijab, explained to me that the British National Blood Service was not equipped to have completely separate rooms for men and women. Although they said they felt uncomfortable in the presence of Shi'i men, the good deed of donating blood was a special circumstance which softened codes of behaviour. The donors and nurses were friendly towards each other; the nurses were enthusiastic and impressed by the campaign, and several donors asked to take photos with the nurses.

The young organisers then explained to me the background of the Imam Hussein Blood donation campaign, and how they encouraged British Muslims to donate blood to benefit others and honour the memory of Imam Hussein. The campaign was first organised in 1997 by a group of university students and young professionals who set up a registered charity called the Islamic Unity Society (IUS), which operates mainly in London, Manchester and Leeds. Its official aim is "to empower young people by promoting social and cultural cohesion within a multi-cultural Britain based on Islamic principles" and to "bring together Shi'i Muslims of all ethnic backgrounds, in order to meet and learn from one another". They legitimised the activity by contacting the offices of the central marja' via their internet sites, and displaying their responses of support on their website. The organisers promoted the blood drives at various Shi'i centres, internet sites and Muharram activities, such as the Hyde Park procession.

I mentioned a conversation I had with a few students at the procession who said that donating blood was a "bourgeois" practice, and not a replacement for the traditional methods of remembering the trials of Imam Hussein. Proud of their physical strength and determination, they had also made machoistic jokes about men who donate blood. This led to a lively debate about self-flagellation among the donors. Several, trying to be diplomatic, stressed how latmiya plays an integral cultural role for some Shi'is, particularly those from Pakistani backgrounds. Although IUS does not condemn bloodletting, arguing that individuals may practise as they wish in a free and open society, several donors vehemently denounced self-flagellation as a "backward" and "violent" cultural practice, particularly for young children. Several donors said they supported the rulings of the late Ayatollah Muhammad Hussein Fadlallah who issued a fatwa prohibiting self-injury. Instead of conveying a violent image of Islam, they argued that Ashura should be an occasion commemorated by all Muslims to solidify the unity of Muslims. Similar to conversations at the Hyde Park procession, they stressed that the ritual practices of their parents' generations were anachronistic, and meaningless in British society. According to Fatima, a university student in London and an Islamic Unity member, "Giving blood on Ashura has provided a positive and active way, equally for men and women, to commemorate Hussein and the Battle of Karbala." Several noted the importance of building a strong unified platform in order to spread positive messages about the values embedded in the struggles at Karbala, particularly since the bad press received after the 2008 court case. As Marwan, aged thirty, noted: "I believe we should focus on the core message of Imam Hussein, the agreed principles and widely practised commemorations, and the work Shi'is have done to benefit the British community at large through the commemoration." After donating, the 300 odd participants, with an approximately equal number of men and women, were given a black tee-shirt with red writing stating: "I gave blood for Imam Hussein".

Concluding Remarks

An ethnographic look at the discourses and experiential dimensions that underpin the Imam Hussein Blood Donation Campaign and the annual Ashura procession allows a researcher to capture the internal social and political dynamics that are being played out by the younger Shi'i generations in the UK. By "objectifying"[3] and evaluating their parents' religious traditions and practices, young Shi'is are gaining the confidence to question and transcend the ethno-national characteristics and gender roles of the older generations, while in turn building a personal and united Shi'i group identity. Along similar lines to Pnina Werbner's ethnographic study of Sunni processions in Manchester, the evolution of the Ashura procession in Hyde Park and the development of the blood donation campaign also indicate a shift in the terms in which British Muslims present and represent themselves to each other and the wider British public.[4] Observing phenomena first-hand allowed me to gain an intimate insight into the internal disagreements on the meaning and enactment of Ashura commemorations, which are actively contested and manifested during these public performances and events.

In addition, this ethnography showed how ritual performances are also being scrutinised and legitimised through the process of "individualisation",[5] whereby religious traditions, such as Ashura commemorations, become sources of inspiration, with an aim of bettering oneself, and in turn, one's position in wider British society. In presenting these manifestations of Ashura commemorations, and the underlying micro-politics of British Shi'i communities, we could also see how different interpretations of the supreme leaders' *marji'i* in Iran and Iraq and the views of young British-born lay leaders are sifted through and used to legitimise new meanings and embodied realities of Ashura rituals in the UK. These religious discourses and practices, which are reshaped and tested as they are publicly performed, are "translocal" as they are being simultaneously informed and configured by a multitude of sources of authority and contested meanings, across a number of physical and mediated spaces.[6] As young Shi'is are navigating through the various viewpoints of leaders, the conflicting customs among their parents' generation, the legal cases and the media portrayals in the British mainstream, they are actively trying to make sense of their religion in relation to their lives in Britain. An ethnographic study of the experiential dimensions of Ashura ritual practices, whether in terms of renewing past practices or legitimising new ones, has allowed me to observe how young British Shi'is are critically engaging with the power relations they operate within in British society.

Notes

1. This chapter focuses on people who adhere to the largest subdivision of the Shi'i, known as the Ithna'Ashariyya or Twelvers. Unlike other branches of the Shi'i with different lines of succession, the Twelvers believe that there were twelve successive imams from among the male descendents of the Prophet Muhammad. It is believed that the twelfth imam disappeared in 874, and will return at the end of the temporal world, as the messiah, or *mahdi*, and usher in a rule of justice and peace on earth.
2. In Lebanon, for example, the *Hezbollah* organises blood donations during Ashura in both Beirut and Nabatiyya.
3. See Dale Eickeman, "The Study of Islam in Local Contexts", *Contribution to Asian Studies*, vol. 17, Canadian Association for South Asian Studies, 1982, pp. 1–16.
4. Pnina Werbner, *Imagined Diasporas among Manchester Muslims*, Oxford: James Currey Publishers and Santa Fe: New School of American Research, 2002.
5. Olivier Roy, *Globalized Islam: The Search for a New Ummah*, New York: Hurst & Co., 2004.
6. Peter Mandaville, *Transnational Muslim Politics*, London: Taylor and Francis 2001.

Chapter 5

The Ma'ruf: An Ethnography of Ritual (South Algeria)

Yazid Ben Hounet

This chapter focuses on a ritual I frequently observed during my fieldwork in Algeria (the western part of the Saharan Atlas): the *ma'ruf*.[1] This Arabic word is commonly translated as "well known", and is used in the Saharan Atlas, as in other Arabic-speaking societies, to refer to a thing or a person "well known" – that is, "famous", "distinguished". However, it is also used locally in order to define a ritual often performed by the inhabitants of the western part of the Saharan Atlas, and to some extent, of many rural regions in North Africa. The ma'ruf, as I observed it,[2] is a type of collective prayer and a Qur'anic exhortation (*amr bi-l-ma'ruf*: commanding right) which takes place after a shared moment like a meal or one of the feasts (*wa'dat, mawsim*) that frequently occur in the Saharan Atlas.[3] It is composed of one or several *sura* (*t*) (verse(s) of the Qur'an), some invocations (*du'a*) and thanks to God and to the "host". The latter can be the person who invites the assembly for the meal or a saint in the case of a *wa'da* (*mawsim*). The ma'ruf also involves all the participants of the shared moment and not only the persons who usually pray. It can be done in different places. Finally, it is a ritual for men (women do not attend).

This ritual was formerly practised more among nomads than among settled peoples.[4] It was conducted by the *tulba* (students) who were formerly hired by the nomads to teach their children. It used to be practised at the end of lessons, after a meal offered by the nomads to the tulba. One of the aims of the ma'ruf is to transmit knowledge of the Qur'an, and it can therefore be viewed as a type or method of Qur'anic education.

Ma'ruf has changed over time amongst nomads and settled peoples, as it is no longer necessarily led by a *talab* (religious student). It is, however, practised much more amongst the *mrabtin* (descendants of saints) and *shurfa'* (descen-

The Ma'ruf: An Ethnography of Ritual

dants of Prophet Muhammad through his daughter Fatima) than amongst "lay" people – indeed, the frequent practices of this ritual seem to be a way of highlighting the religious status and prestige of these descendants.

In this chapter, I will try to offer some answers to the following questions: what are the meanings of the ma'ruf ritual? What does the analysis of this ritual suggest concerning "Islamic" practices? In order to do so, I take an ethnographical approach which articulates the study of practices and the *emic* (endogenous) significations of these practices. Instead of describing the ritual in a general fashion, I will focus on a precise episode of this ritual, within its own context, in order to understand how people act, interact and build their own singular ritual.[5] The example under study was filmed by me in June 2008 within a tent located 50 kilometres north of Ain Sefra. The ma'ruf took place after a meal offered by a semi-nomadic shepherd (see note 4). The filmed sequence lasts four minutes. It includes the entire ritual along with some seconds before and after. Through an ethnographical approach, I also aim to shed light on some aspects of this ritual, introducing, when necessary, data about cultural values and the social organisation of this region of North Africa. Furthermore, if people are involved in a routine practice and if ma'ruf could be analysed as such, this ritual cannot occur without a minimum of shared understanding that has to be implicitly negotiated during the ritual. The ethnographic method can underline these implicit negotiations that are always in context.

Describing the Ma'ruf: Actions and Significations

Liminas[6]

The film sequence starts some minutes after the end of the meal, in the tent where male guests are hosted. The domestic (family) tent is reserved for women and is located around 30 metres from the male tent. Ahmed, the semi-nomadic shepherd who has hosted the assembly, enters the tent. Someone says "ma'ruf!" Ahmed then asks people if they are satisfied (*"rakum m'amrin?"*, literally: "are you full?"). While asking this question, he quickly raises and joins his hands, and lets them fall soon after. In doing so, he suggests to people that they proceed to the ma'ruf if they are satisfied. During this action, people are talking amongst themselves. Only one or two guests respond to him and to the assembly with "ma'ruf!" Ahmed asks if people want more tea. A few more guests respond: "ma'ruf!" The ritual can now begin. During this sequence we observe how the moment of the ma'ruf ritual is decided. Ahmed cannot directly tell the assembly to proceed to the ma'ruf. He does not even pronounce the word. He only suggests, through his body language, for people to do so. He has to wait until a sufficient number of guests ask for the ma'ruf. He then raises and joins his hands for a longer time

Figure 5.1 Ahmed asking the *kbar* to lead the ma'ruf. (Film frame: Y. Ben Hounet)

(see Figure 5.1) and orientates himself toward the *kbar* (elders); without saying a word, he thus asks them to commence the ritual.

This act of asking the kbar to lead the ma'ruf appears to be the norm, since it has not been a subject of discussion. Moreover, the fact that it is not discussed suggests that it is a duty to allow the elder to lead the ritual. In fact, some informants told me that travellers, kbar, and particularly *hujaaj* (pilgrims) are the first people who must say the ma'ruf. Indeed, it is said that they are the first choice to lead because they are closer to death and thus to God. They still live thanks to God. More precisely, their lives are in the hands of God. They thus have more *baraka* (blessings) than other people. This ideal view of who should recite the ma'ruf suggests a hierarchical relationship that exists locally. It is also a way to remind people of, and sometimes to impose, this hierarchical relationship between elders and younger people. The traveller here also refers to the *wali* (saint), *darwish* (mystic) or *talab* (religious student) who formerly used to travel in North African and Muslim majority countries. Thus the leading of the ritual points toward the hierarchical relationship that places elders and religious people in a position of superiority and authority. The hierarchical relationship is, in my view and following Louis Dumont's approach,[7] different to a power relationship because it exists through a shared ideology and not through coercion, through the use or the possibility of using force. Declaiming the ma'ruf is thus a kind of gratification and acknowledgement of authority.

The Ma'ruf: An Ethnography of Ritual

The kbar must now decide who amongst them will lead the ma'ruf ritual. Hajj Brahim (Ahmed's father) does not want to lead the ma'ruf because he is the father of the host and thus does not really feel like a guest. His neighbour, out of respect for him, does not want to lead either. Hajj Brahim's neighbour thus suggests that Hajj Muhammad, a third person, should lead it (see Figure 5.2). The negotiations between Hajj Brahim and his neighbour last a few seconds and the latter suggests three times that Hajj Muhammad lead the ma'ruf, and the third time he points at him. The negotiations are now closed.[8] Hajj Muhammad, without answering Hajj Brahim and his neighbour, begins the ma'ruf.

Here again, the impact of body language is evident. The negotiations are closed and Hajj Muhammad starts the ma'ruf only after he has been pointed to by Hajj Brahim's neighbour. In order to define the ritual, David Parkin uses the concept of "formulaic spatiality".[9] This concept emphasises the importance of movement, spatial orientation and body language in the process of creating meaning during ritual activity. We can add that even during the preliminaries, gesture, body language, spatial orientation and movements are important and contribute to preparation for the ritual, or that this preparation is included within the ritual itself. The importance of gesture or body language before the proper ritual can also be analysed as a way to enter into the sacred moment of the ritual since it separates profane language (before the ritual) and sacred language (the recitation of Qur'anic verse).

Figure 5.2 Negotiations between Hajj Brahim (with glasses) and his neighbour. The latter points at Hajj Muhammad (extreme left). (Film frame: Y. Ben Hounet)

The State of Communitas

The ritual itself only actually begins with the recitation of Hajj Muhammad (see Figure 5.3). He immediately starts with the recitation of a Qur'anic verse. His posture and bearing – that is, joining hands and the intonation of his voice – indicate that the ma'ruf has just begun. After the first words of the verse are recited, everybody stops talking and joins their own hands.

Figure 5.3 Hajj Muhammad leading the ma'ruf. (Film frame: Y. Ben Hounet)

The ma'ruf ritual has a restrictive and formal aspect. All those present are involved (not only those who ordinarily pray). People do not talk or move during this ritual. They do not form lines and do not face Mecca, as during the *salat* prayer. They are, more or less, oriented towards the middle of the tent. Here, the spatial configuration refers directly to the group. Hajj Muhammad can be viewed in this situation as a kind of imam. He chooses – without asking people – the verse and the *du'a* he wants to recite. He chooses to start with the last verse of the sura of The Cow (*al-Baqara*):

> Allah does not impose upon any soul a duty but to the extent of its ability; for it is (the benefit of) what it has earned and upon it (the evil of) what it has wrought: Our Lord! do not punish us if we forget or make a mistake; Our Lord! do not lay on us a burden as Thou didst lay on those before us, Our Lord do not impose upon us that which we have not the strength to bear; and pardon us and grant us protection and have mercy on us, Thou art our Patron, so help us against the unbelieving people.[10]

During the recitation of this verse, the group is very quiet (see Figure 5.4). Most people whisper the verse, or part of it, and most of the participants concentrate. The collective recitation implies a common knowledge of Qur'anic verse but it is also a way for participants to learn it.

The verse's recitation is distinct from the one of du'a, invocations and thanks. Indeed, during this second sequence, people are more responsive. They put their

Figure 5.4 Concentration during the recitation of the Qur'anic verse. (Film frame: Y. Ben Hounet)

hands in front of their faces and respond to the invocations and thanks offered by Hajj Muhammad with *amin* (Amen) (see Figure 5.5). Below is a transcription of the invocations:

Hajj Muhammad (HM): May God give this gathering benefits!
People (P): Amin!
HM: May God give to the host all that is permitted!
P: Amin!
HM: May God put their generosity in the balance of good actions!
P: Amin!
HM: May God protect us and preserve us from evil!
P: Amin!
HM: May God lead us in the good path (direction)!
P: Amin!

HM: May God cure the sick people!
P: Amin!
HM: May God offer us mercy at our death!
P: Amin!
HM: May God bless all he gives us!
P: Amin!
HM: May God pray for Muhammad (the Prophet) and his family!
P: Amin!

Figure 5.5 Sequence of *du'a*, invocations and thanks. (Film frame: Y. Ben Hounet)

The amin here consecrates the invocations. They signify the acceptance of invocations offered by Hajj Muhammad. This sequence can be analysed as a moment of exchange between Hajj Muhammad and the participants. Through gestures and intonation, some or all of the participants can approve, deny or contest what has been said as well as the authority of the person who leads the ritual. During this sequence, some are more responsive than others but all respond with "amin" since on this occasion, the invocations are not a matter of controversy. Some, like Hajj Muhammad's neighbour (see Figure 5.5, extreme left), do not seem particularly involved in this ritual. They join their hands but do not raise them, respond "amin" with a low voice, and are not very responsive. The frequency of this ritual and by extension its banality can partly explain this fact. Rituals can also be part of routine practice, and thus are not necessarily suffused with deep meaning. However, people must participate in this ritual

The Ma'ruf: An Ethnography of Ritual

Figure 5.6 The ma'ruf ends. (Film frame: Y. Ben Hounet)

even if they are bored with it. This suggests the normative dimension of the ritual and the kind of opposition/contestation to this norm.

Following the sequence of invocations (du'a), some thanks are offered to the host. This only lasts for a few seconds. These thanks also signify that the ritual is ending. Finally, Hajj Muhammad ends with a common sentence: "peace on the Prophet and his family". Participants recite the sentence with him and raise their hands to their face and kiss them (see Figure 5.6). This last, collective and really visible gesture signifies that the ritual is now finished.

Immediately after this last action, Ahmad acknowledges the participants in the ritual. Ma'ruf is indeed a ritual activity and its meaning is to recognise the hospitality that has been provided as it usually finishes with an extension of thanks to the person or family who hosts the shared moment (collective meal or feast). As mentioned before, ma'ruf cannot be carried out by the host but only by the guests. *Sharaf* (greatness/honour) is sometimes defined as the capacity to offer hospitality, to give (food) and guide the gift along its path (to host guests and be hospitable). The hospitality and the meal offered thus have great symbolic and political impact locally and more generally in Arab and North African societies. This is also the case in Algeria, particularly in the rural areas. Thus, ma'ruf closes and consecrates the collective moment, the hospitality given. It thereby confers some importance to the host.

Ahmad's acknowledgments signify that people can (from that moment) leave the tent. They are now free to move. Even if he does not (and cannot) lead the ritual, Ahmad's role is important. He begins and ends the ritual. He uses gestures to control the opening of the ritual. By speaking at the end, he also permits participants to complete the ritual and to leave the space. Even if the host cannot actually lead the ritual, he can nonetheless control it. Ahmed therefore decides to initiate the ritual himself and to let people leave because he knows how the procedure ought to be and that ma'ruf should be completed in order to end the collective meal.

Comments on the Ma'ruf

Through this description, we observe how the ritual is built, and how people behave in order to construct the manner in which the ritual should be conducted. The analysis of one ritual in its context allows us to understand how some aspects are negotiated, but also how others are not.

The analysis of negotiated aspects (like the timing of the ritual, the exact person who leads it, the exchange of voice intonations during the sequence of invocations – du'a, and so on) are really important since these help us to understand the way people organise this single ritual in its context, the value they ascribe to each sequence and how they negotiate roles during the ritual. We also see the importance of gesture as a tool for communicating and negotiating the way the ritual should be carried out and its importance. Here, David Parkin's approach to ritual is relevant:

> My argument is that, however much participants in a ritual may dispute and debate the significance, meaning, and propriety of ritual behaviour, using words to great effect in doing so, they can only demonstrate the saliency, success, and effectiveness of what they have to say through performative practice, and issues of spatial orientation and position are the only means at their disposal, being fundamentally constituted of the ritual itself.[11]

It was also observed that other elements of the ritual were not negotiated: such as the fact that an elder must lead the ritual, the organisation of the ritual sequences (beginning with a verse of the Qur'an and following this with invocations or du'a). This shows that a common understanding is shared by most or all of the participants. Thus, the ritual is not constructed solely through explicit actions and interactions, but also through implicit ones: in other words through shared culture and norms. The norms are composed of actions that are not, or should not, be negotiated. They are not a matter for discussion. We could thus add that culture, values and norms are implicitly inscribed within the context. In other words, simple description (with our own categories) of facts and interactions cannot itself lead us to understand the whole meaning of this ritual.

We must add the *emic* or *cultural* significations (not singular and retrospective ones) that people give to their actions, and particularly implicit ones, and thus their culture and values. In this chapter I have therefore tried to add some significations that have been given to me, or that correspond to local culture, when describing aspects that are not a matter of negotiation. Without these significations, parts of the implicit aspects of the ritual cannot be understood by people who do not know the culture of this region (and values that are held as relevant). Thus, the description I have outlined includes the understanding I have of this ritual but above all, of the local culture. This is in line with, or corresponds to, the ethnographical approach as developed by the anthropological tradition.[12] Finally and in our case, normative aspects are obviously important. That is by definition one central aspect of the ritual. Ritual is indeed a repetitive and formal activity. It has a clear and predefined progress. If some aspects of the ritual can be and are negotiated, others cannot: if they could all be negotiated, the ritual itself would disappear.

Ma'ruf thus allows the group to share a common religious culture. Some verses are more appreciated than others depending on the group and the moment. The mrabtin usually recite long verses and "lay" people short ones. Ma'ruf also refers to a kind of knowledge that must be known. Qur'anic verses are not matters for discussion or analysis but just have to be memorised. However, it can also be a moment of competition. The person who recites the ma'ruf can exhibit his knowledge of the Qur'an through declaiming or reciting long and different verses. People around him can also try to declaim the verses if they know them. In fact, they often tend to do so. The attendees or participants use the ritual as an opportunity to show others the extent of their Qur'anic knowledge. That is particularly the case of the talab or the mrabtin who practise ma'ruf more often. I noticed during my observations of this ritual that ma'ruf is usually longer when declaimed by these persons, so as to signify their religious prestige. Declaiming the ma'ruf is also a kind of gratification and a sign of authority. Indeed, the person must be designated among and by the group, more precisely by the most authoritative persons, namely the elders. And, in a way, in order to determine who the leader of the group is, one has only to observe who leads the ma'ruf or who decides this. Ma'ruf is thus a space for negotiating what should be said, how the Qur'an must be learned, recited, and God (*Allah*) invoked. It is also a space for negotiations of social relationships (between participants, guests and hosts) and of the authority of the person who leads the ritual.

Conclusion: Ma'ruf and Islamic Ethnographies

What does the analysis of this ritual suggest concerning Islamic practices? This ritual shows us not only how religious norms and knowledge are shared and spread, but also how they can be negotiated. It also suggests the importance of body language in implicit negotiations. Here the ethnographical method allows us to shed light on the various forms of body language. Furthermore, an analysis of the ma'ruf helps us to know how religious knowledge and rituals are used in order to remind or impose values such as hospitality, hierarchical relationships and authority. It is useful here to remember that if reference to Islam is obvious in the case of the ma'ruf (owing to the recitation of Qur'anic verses), this ritual is not an Islamic obligation (such as salat). Therefore, it not only shows how religious ideas are inscribed in routine practice and how they infuse daily life and behaviour, but also how reference to Islam is concretely put in practice.

Notes

1. The author wishes to thank Alice Wilson, Sarah Houston and the editors who commented and corrected the initial drafts of this paper.
2. The definition of the ma'ruf ritual varies between different authors and regions. For instance, Hassan Rachik defines it with regard to Morocco as a sacrificial meal, and Emile Dermenghem with regard to Algeria as a sermon. Hassan Rachik, *Sacre et sacrifice dans le Haut Atlas Marocain*, Casablanca: Afrique-Orient, 1990; Emile Dermenghem, *Le culte des saints dans l'islam maghrébin*, Paris: Gallimard, 1954.
3. The ma'ruf and more broadly the meal can be analysed through the gift theory, in Marcel Mauss' sense. See Yazid Ben Hounet, "La tribu en pratique: le rituel de la mudawala chez les Awlad Sid Ahmad Majdub", *Alfa*, 2007, pp. 201–9.
4. Nomads (at the present time semi-nomads) were numerous in the region where I conducted my research (2004–6) and are still important today (around 22 per cent of the population of the western part of the Saharan Atlas); see Yazid Ben Hounet, *L'Algérie des tribus. Le fait tribal dans le Haut Sud-Ouest contemporain*, Paris: L'Harmattan, 2009.
5. This approach is, in a way, inspired by praxeological analysis as developed by Baudouin Dupret and Nicolas De Lavergne, "Pratiques de véridiction. Inculcation, contrôle et discipline dans une école coranique de Haute-Egypte", *Revue d'anthropologie des connaissances*, no. 2, 2008, pp. 311–43.
6. Liminas (which includes the idea of transition and separation) and *communitas* (the experience of the community) are the two main aspects of the ritual process as analysed by Victor W. Turner, *The Ritual Process. Structure and Anti-structure*, London: Routledge and Kegan Paul, 1969.
7. Louis Dumont, *Homo Hierarchicus. Le système des castes et ses implications*, Paris: Gallimard, 1966.
8. I will also present here the case of a meal I attended with a *mrabtin*, a man of religious lineage. It was a meal in honour of a member of this lineage who now lives 300 kilometres away from the locality of his lineage. At the end of the meal, and as

he was the guest, the elder, the most authoritative person of the lineage, suggested that he lead the ma'ruf. He was embarrassed. Out of respect, he refused and asked the elder to lead it. The latter did not want to as he really wished to honour the guest, considering him a *habib* or dear friend. Finally, the elder asked a talab who was present, to lead the ma'ruf. He wanted to signify that the guest was equal to him (the elder).

9. David Parkin, "Ritual as Spatial Direction and Bodily Division", in Daniel de Coppet (ed.), *Understanding Rituals*, London and New York: Routledge, 1992, pp. 11–25.
10. Qur'an 2.286. [The Holy Koran, trans. Muhammad Habib Shakir, London: Kegan Paul, 1986].
11. Parkin, "Ritual as Spatial Direction", p. 22.
12. Since Edward B. Tylor's book *Anahuac or Mexico and the Mexicans, Ancient and Modern* (London: Longman, 1861), widely regarded as one of the first classics of anthropological studies, this is the standard approach shared by most anthropologists. Paul Bohannan, in his "Preface" to Edward B. Tylor, *Research into the Early History of Mankind and the Development of Civilizations*, Chicago: University of Chicago Press, 1964, p. viii, wrote of Tylor and his book *Anahuac*: "He wanted to know not merely how Mexican life looked to a merely well-to-do English Quaker like himself, but also how it looked to Mexican Indians". Louis Dumont has particularly discussed the importance of this approach in his book *Homo Hierarchicus*.

CHAPTER 6

The Sufi Ritual of the Darb al-shish and the Ethnography of Religious Experience

PAULO G. PINTO

Anthropologists have already recognised the central role of religious experience in both the construction of symbolic meanings and values, and their ritual inscription as part of the subjectivity and corporality of the faithful.[1] However, there is still very little ethnographic understanding of the processes that make experience such a powerful tool for the constitution of social subjects. In order to address the possibilities and challenges created by an ethnographic approach to experience, I will focus the analysis on the processes of construction and communication of religious experiences in the Sufi ritual of the *darb al-shish*. The ethnographic data analysed here comes from several periods of fieldwork research among the Sufi communities in Aleppo and its surrounding countryside in northern Syria.[2]

During my research, the ritual manipulation of the body appeared as a major experiential arena for the constitution of religious subjectivities of the members of Sufi communities in northern Syria. In order to understand how the religious self of members of Sufi *zawiyas* (lodges) was informed by Sufi traditions, I started to look for processes of internalisation and the embodiment of religious principles. As a result, some informants began to mention the ritual of the darb al-shish. According to them, it was pointless to explain the issues in which I was interested through discourses, for only when I saw the darb al-shish would I fully understand them.

DESCRIPTION: THE DARB AL-SHISH RITUAL AND ITS RELIGIOUS CONTEXT

While it exists in several ritual traditions within Sufism, the darb al-shish is seen as mainly connected to the *tariqa* (Sufi order/path) Rifa'iyya, which links advancement along the mystical path with the capacity of its members to perform various sorts of *karamat* (miraculous deeds) in ritual contexts. These karamat include a vast range of extraordinary deeds, such as eating glass or burning charcoal, walking or standing on fire, licking red-hot iron skewers, handling poisonous snakes, taming wild animals, stabbing oneself with knives or iron pins attached to round handles (*rahmaniyat*) and perforating various parts of the body with iron skewers (darb al-shish) or swords (*darb al-sayf*).

The darb al-shish remains a central ritual practice among Sufi communities linked to the Rifa'iyya, as well as other Sufi traditions, such as the Qadiriyya, in Syria. The darb al-shish is defined by the Rifa'i shaykhs as a "proof of faith" (*dalil al-iman*), meaning that it is material evidence of the religious quality of the faithful self (*nafs*). It is important to note that the darb al-shish is not seen by Sufis as a form of mortification or denial of the body. On the contrary, it demonstrates the control achieved by the disciple over his nafs through the expansion of the capacities of his body.

Usually the darb al-shish is not performed by the shaykhs themselves, but rather by their disciples, as it is used both as an ordeal that the latter have to endure in order to advance through each stage of the Sufi path and simultaneously as a miraculous deed that publicly confirms the reality of the mystical states (*ahwal*, sing. *hal*) claimed to be achieved by the disciples. The miraculous character of the darb al-shish is understood by Sufis who perform it as a result of the action of *baraka* over the disciple's body. While all *baraka* is seen as ultimately flowing from God, Sufi shaykhs are unanimous in saying that they are necessary intermediaries in this process, which can only happen with their consent. Therefore, according to the doctrinal rules that regulate the darb al-shish, the disciple must volunteer and obtain permission from his shaykh in order to legitimately perform it.

The darb al-shish is widely known to be part of the religious life of many Sufi communities throughout Syria. However, it is also the centre of an ongoing religious debate about the legitimacy and authenticity of the Islamic credentials of certain Sufi rituals. This debate mobilises Sufis and non-Sufis on both sides of the divide between those who accept the Islamic character of bodily and miraculous Sufi rituals, such as the darb al-shish, and those who deny it.[3]

During my fieldwork among the Sufi communities in Syria I was able to witness performances of the darb al-shish in Aleppo and throughout the Kurd Dagh, which happened mainly in zawiyas linked to the Rifa'iyya, located in both urban and rural environments. In all these zawiyas, the instruments used in the ritual performance of the darb al-shish, such as skewers or iron pins with round handles and swords, were hung on the walls as visible symbols of the miraculous deeds that the members of these Sufi communities could perform. The ritual gathering (*hadra*) was seen by the members of these communities as the appropriated arena for the performance of the darb al-shish, as these were the occasions when the disciples of the shaykh were publicly tested in order to prove their mystical powers or to ascend to a higher stage of the Sufi path.[4]

While the darb al-shish constitutes the more elaborate form of the ordeal, it has several degrees of difficulty itself, depending on the area of the body that is pierced and the diameter of the piercing instrument.[5] The darb al-shish comprises the following acts in order of growing difficulty: the perforation of the cheeks, tongue, neck, shoulders and belly. The darb al-shish of the abdomen also has degrees of difficulty that increase with the risk of damaging vital organs, beginning with the "easy" lateral parts of the belly to the "difficult" parts around the navel. Similarly, in each part of the body there is a gradation of difficulty that begins with thin needle-like skewers and increases until reaching skewers that have a diameter of half an inch. Finally, the most difficult of all is the sword.

The articulation of the various meanings and experiences attached to the darb al-shish is well exemplified by a performance that I saw in March 2000 in the Rifa'i zawiya of Shaykh Mahmud in 'Afrin, a Kurdish town north of Aleppo. There were around eighty people in the zawiya and the crowd of participants overflowed into the courtyard, where latecomers pressed to see the action through the door of the zawiya. At a certain point of the dhikr, the rhythm of the music became frenetic, with the loud singing of *"la ilaha il Allah"* (there is no god but God) and a rapid and violent beating of drums. At this part of the ritual the shaykh's disciples could volunteer to perform an ordeal with his consent. Usually the disciples volunteered in a hierarchical order, with the ones at a lower rank performing the ordeal before those more advanced in the Sufi path.

The first performances involved the use of rahmaniyat to pierce the cheeks or to stab the chest or belly. When the more advanced disciples volunteered, the instrument changed to an iron skewer (*shish*). Then, a disciple (*murid*) went to Shaykh Mahmud and kissed his hand asking his permission to endure an ordeal in order to prove his faith in God. The shaykh consented to the request by placing his hand over the head of the disciple. Then the disciple went to the centre of the room and invoked the names of Muhammad, Ali, Abd al-Qader Jeilani and Ahmed al-Rifa'i, and recited the opening verse of the Qur'an, the *fatiha*, and the *shahada* (Muslim profession of faith). At this point the shaykh pointed to one shish hanging on the wall, revealing which ordeal the disciple would endure. The disciple lifted his shirt. Then a disciple from a higher rank in the mystical path (*jawish*) took the shish,[6] and pushed it into the *murid*'s abdomen with a rapid sharp movement, piercing through his body with the shish, which came out of his back without shedding any blood.

This was a very dramatic point in the ritual, as loud singing and the frenetic rhythm of the drums created an emotionally charged ambience that complemented the astonishment and concern of those in the audience who attentively watched the act, usually the non-initiated or disciples in the early stages of their mystical initiation. On the other hand, disciples with higher degrees of initiation regarded the performance of the darb al-shish in a very nonchalant matter-of-fact way, as they were also able to perform it themselves.

Cries of "*Allah*" (God), "*Allah-u-Akbar*" (God Almighty) and "*Ya Latif*" (Oh Gentle One) came from the audience while the man walked among the participants with the skewer pierced through his body. Everyone could visually examine the absence of bleeding from the wounds that, according to the religious tradition of this Sufi community, confirmed the miraculous nature of his deed. Those who wanted could even touch the material proof of the miracle that was taking place in the body of that disciple, and many, including myself, did so. After all those present in the room had the chance to closely examine or touch the concrete evidence of the mystical qualities of the disciple, at a sign from the shaykh the *jawish* removed the shish from the abdomen of the disciple, who then returned to his place.

During the rest of the ritual there were other less spectacular, albeit very intense and dramatic, bodily expressions of the experiential achievement of mystical states by the participants, who would violently rock their bodies back and forth or side to side, jump, fall on their knees, faint, cry, laugh or shout the names of God. Some of these religious experiences, particularly those from disciples who were initiated in the esoteric path of Sufism, were communicated according to models of mystical states set by the Sufi tradition.

However, the ordeal was not completed with just the simple performance of the act, as the esoteric (*batini*) nature of the act had to be established beyond any doubt. In the codification of the Sufi tradition that circulates in the Rifa'i zawiyas in northern Syria, extraordinary acts, such as the darb al-shish, can have two sources: God's baraka, through the mediation of the Prophet, the saints and the Sufi shaykhs, which would validate the act as a karama and demonstrate that the disciple is on the right path; or *jinns*, which would make the performance an act of magic (*sihr*) and show that the disciple did not have the mystical qualities that he claimed. In order to determine the causal source of the act, as well as the true character of the disciple, each zawiya developed its own system for identifying the precise signs that reveal the divine or the magical nature of the phenomenon.

In Shaykh Mahmud's zawiya in 'Afrin the absence of bleeding from the wounds is the first sign of a karama, as opposed to a magical act.[7] All participants carefully scrutinised the wounds left by the darb al-shish in order to see if there was any bleeding, in which case the whole performance would be declared by the shaykh as a magical act caused by jinn possession. Other signs of a karama include the closing of the wound within a two-week period and a reddish tonality to the scar occurring within another week. If the disciple fulfils these conditions he is granted success in the ordeal and either elevated to a higher stage or confirmed in his present stage of the mystical path. However, if he fails in any of them, this is seen as evidence of the weakness of his faith in God, which makes him vulnerable to the action of jinns and as a consequence, he can be downgraded in the hierarchy of the disciples, or even expelled from the zawiya.

The performance of extraordinary deeds, such as the darb al-shish, produces in the disciple a dramatically condensed experience of the Sufi path. In each performance he has to mobilise the appropriate cognitive framework and body techniques acquired during his initiation into the mystical path in order to achieve a successful result for both himself and the rest of the Sufi community.[8] The sense of having one's own body chosen as the instrument and the stage for a divine act makes it the existential ground for the doctrinal and ritual principles of Sufism. A disciple of Shaykh Mahmud summarised this by saying:

> I felt the pressure of the skewer on my skin and, after it, the coldness of the iron passing through my body. Then, I felt alive! It was love, God's love filling my heart. I could feel God in my heart and I was sure that I was close to him.

The physical sensation of the iron passing through his body was felt by the disciple simultaneously with the fact that he was unharmed by it, giving him the immediate experience that he interpreted in terms of the Sufi concept of "love" (*hubb*), understood as an emotional and intimate relation to the divine reality. This corporeal experience allowed the embodiment of the mystical concept of "love" as emotional, sensorial and existential realities that the disciples live and feel as constituent parts of their selves. In this sense, the darb al-shish constitutes a dramatic expression of the importance of the body as the experiential ground of Sufi subjectivities.

This was expressed in the conversation that I had with the disciple who endured the ordeal. When I talked to him about the ritual performance, he said:

> [The performance] proved to me who I really am. It makes me feel my connection to God and show everybody how my self (*nafsi*) was purified and blessed by Him. This feeling accompanies me in my life and makes me behave correctly, always keeping me in the straight path.

Through his speech we can see how he considered the experience of presenting his religious self through the piercing to be a defining element in his identity as a Sufi.

Comment: The Ethnographic Experience and the Ethnography of Experience

The ethnography of mystical experiences raises first of all the issue of having access to the arenas of constitution and expression of these existential spheres of religious life that are inscribed in the very body of the agents. In the case of Sufism in Syria, this means the ritual practices and esoteric initiation in the mystical path that defines one's belonging to the Sufi communities.

The ethnographic access to secret or esoteric cultural systems is mediated by the possibility that the researcher will be affected by the experiential universe that reveals the implicit layers of meaning which are inscribed in the discourses and practices of the informants.[9] Therefore, I had to negotiate my insertion into a religious system based on the mystical mysteries that should be revealed only to the initiated and could and should not be properly discussed in open and public discursive interactions.

An important turning point in the research happened when Shaykh Mahmud allowed me to take part in the activities connected to the process of initiation (*tarbiyya*) of his disciples. By accompanying the disciples throughout long periods of fasting, reading sacred texts, meditating on religious concepts and performing physically demanding spiritual exercises, I could see how they gradually acquired a cultural idiom for the expression of the experiences induced by their engagement in the Sufi rituals and religious practices. This idiom consisted of body techniques (gestures, postures, corporeal abilities); emotional schemes; and discursive categories, which should be combined in order to effectively convey the individual experiences into the models of religious experiences as they were codified by the Sufi tradition.

Both the disciples and the shaykh classified and communicated the experiential outcome of their religious practices in terms of mystical states. These states, which included *tawba* (repentance); *mukhasaba* (self accountability); *sidq* (trustfulness/righteousness), were understood as steps of the mystical path that should lead one's self to the direct experience of the divine reality (*haqiqa*). The process of initiating the disciple worked through the induction and mobilisation of desires, feelings and body sensations, and their combination and organisation into clusters that were delimited and classified as specific mystical states by the discursive categories, symbols and ritual idioms provided by the Sufi tradition.

The categories that delimit these clusters as realms of religious experience allow their perception and communication in terms of the disciplinary regime of the Sufi tradition. As we saw in the disciple's description of his experience performing the darb al-shish, the ritual induces existential states that exist as experiences in their expression through the categories and body techniques of the Sufi tradition.

The process of mystical initiation in Shaykh Mahmud's zawiya was a combination of individualised and collective religious practices – such as fasting, praying or listening to sermons or exhortations – all of them centred on the relation between the master (*murshid*) and his disciples (*murid*, plural *muridun*). The practice of reading the Qur'an or Sufi texts was not a central element of the mystical initiation under Shaykh Mahmud, unlike with the other shaykhs who allowed me to accompany their disciples in their process of initiation. Most of the religious knowledge, which included the categories of classification and principles of evaluation of the religious experiences as mystical states, was transmitted orally through sermons, mystical prayers (*wird*, plural *awrad*) and exemplary stories about the deceased shaykhs of the zawiya or the great saints of Sufism, such as Ahmad al-Rifa'i.

This predominance of oral discourses in the pedagogical practices of the mystical initiation does not mean that the codification of the Sufi tradition transmitted by Shaykh Mahmud was autonomous from the textual tradition. On the contrary, all discourses proffered by Shaykh Mahmud were full of references to the Qur'an, the hadith, Islamic jurisprudence or Sufi texts. However, the meaning of the categories transmitted in these discourses was given not only by their cognitive decodification, but also by the experiential realms that were associated with them during the process of initiation.

While Shaykh Mahmud proffered his sermons or told exemplary stories, the disciples were required to stay in specific sitting or standing postures, which after a few hours became quite demanding on the body. After the sermon, there would be a dhikr or a collective recitation of the *wird* (mystical prayer), which would also require certain postures and uses of the body. Frequently the shaykh would tell them to remain for hours in a certain posture reciting prayers or Qur'anic passages or simply meditating on certain Sufi concepts. Through these practices and exercises the disciples acquired a cultural idiom composed of categories, body techniques and emotional dispositions through which they could communicate their existential position and relationship to the Sufi tradition as religious experiences.

Interestingly, neither the darb al-shish nor the models for its performance were taught in the process of initiation. Nevertheless, the latter was central to understanding darb al-shish as it allowed me to see the process of acquisition of body techniques and embodied dispositions which made it possible. The darb al-shish is not the mechanical reproduction of a model, but rather a performative improvisation on a theme. In this sense, it shows a complete mastery of the body techniques that constitute the idiom of religious experience, revealing to the community the *virtuosi* of mystical states and creating the embodied certainties that ground their Sufi subjectivities.

It is true that the darb al-shish is an extreme example that is only performed by a small group of Sufis affiliated to certain traditions within Sufism. However, my ethnographic engagement with this ritual allowed me to understand the processes through which the induction and communication of mystical experiences created an existential ground for religious subjectivities in the Sufi contexts analysed here.

Conclusion

Besides providing new ethnographic information, my access to the practices of initiation into the Sufi path reshaped the quality of the interactions that I had with my informants in the Sufi communities. I did not claim to have any mileage on the mystical path and, as a non-Muslim, I was not perceived by anyone as having done so. However, the fact that I was disposed to spend long periods of fasting, repeating mystical prayers, listening to sermons and exemplary stories about the Sufi saints and performing physically demanding spiritual exercises was understood as proof that I had been "affected" by Sufism and wanted to experientially live its truth.

While I indeed had a set of experiences during my ethnographic engagement with the practices of mystical initiation in Shaykh Mahmud's zawiya, they could not provide me with any insights into the existential content of my informants' experiences. Nevertheless, these experiences gave me access to the cultural idiom that they were acquiring in order to effectively express their existential positioning in relation to the specific codification of Sufism transmitted by Shaykh Mahmud. Once the disciples considered that I had something to share with them in terms of corporeal sensations, emotional dispositions and unusual states of consciousness and perception or, at least, that I could understand how these realms of existence came together, they started to talk about their religious experiences.

Instead of the discourses about religious experience, the fact that I was sharing the context of its production allowed me to engage in the discourses of experience. These discourses were less articulated and more fragmentary than the former, consisting of a combination of body postures, gestures, emotions, verbal expressions, commentaries and confidences, but they conveyed the process of acquiring different degrees of proficiency in the Sufi idiom of religious experience.

Therefore, the ethnographic engagement with the ritual of the darb al-shish allowed me to understand the processes through which religious experience works as an important tool for the constitution of social subjects in Sufi communities in Syria. Sufi mystical experiences constitute cultural idioms that condense bodily and discursive domains of existence, allowing their holders to live, affirm and/or negotiate an existential position as subjects in the world.

Notes

1. Thomas Csordas, *The Sacred Self: A Cultural Phenomenology of Charismatic Healing*, Berkeley: University of California Press, 1997; Katherine Ewing, *Arguing Sainthood: Modernity, Psychoanalysis and Islam*, Durham: Duke University Press, 1997; Robert Levy, *Tahitians: Mind and Experience in the Society Islands*, Chicago: University of Chicago Press, 1973; Gananath Obeyesekere, *Medusa's Hair: An Essay on Personal Symbols and Religious Experience*, Chicago: University of Chicago Press, 1981.
2. I undertook fieldwork among the Sufi communities of Aleppo and its surrounding region from 1999 to 2001, and in several periods of one or two months in the subsequent years. The research was funded with grants from CAPES, CNPQ and FAPERJ (Brazil).
3. Sa'id Hawwa, *Tarbiyatuna al-Ruhiyya*, Beirut: Dar al-Kutub al-'Arabiyya, 1979.
4. The stages (*maqamat*) of the mystical path in the Sufi *zawiyas* on which my fieldwork was focused did not follow a general and necessary order. They were usually not clearly defined, for there was a shared idea that each individual trajectory was unique. Therefore, while one had to demonstrate that one was progressing along the mystical path, this was evaluated according to the shaykh's personal judgement of each case.
5. While technically speaking the term darb al-shish only refers to piercing the body with skewers, in practice, Sufis use it to refer to all ritual ordeals of body piercing.
6. There are four degrees of initiation among Shaykh Mahmud's disciples in his zawiya: *murid*, *jawish*, *naqib* and *khalifa*.
7. In the Rifa'i zawiyas of the Euphrates region, it is the absence of bleeding that is considered to be a magical sign.
8. The concept of body techniques elaborated by Marcel Mauss refers to the culturally acquired techniques of using the body in order to achieve an effective symbolic or material result in specific social contexts. See Marcel Mauss, "Les Techniques du Corps", in *Sociologie et Anthropologie*, Paris: PUF, 1995 [1934], pp. 365–86.
9. Jeanne Favret-Saada, *Les mots, la mort, les sorts*, Paris: Gallimard, 1977.

Chapter 7

Preaching for Converts: Knowledge and Power in the Sunni Community in Rio de Janeiro

Gisele Fonseca Chagas

This chapter focuses on how power relations are constructed and legitimised in the various contexts in which religious knowledge is transmitted and circulated among members of the Sunni Muslim community in Rio de Janeiro, Brazil. Textual, ritual and practical religious knowledge are continuously mobilised by the local religious leaders as both disciplinary devices and instances of legitimisation of their authority. These forms of knowledge are differently appropriated and inscribed in the social practices of members of the Muslim community of Rio de Janeiro according to their ethnicity, gender and social class, thus creating distinct understandings and practices of Islam.

In order to understand the relation between power and knowledge in the Sunni community in Rio de Janeiro, I looked at the various contexts in which religious knowledge is presented as a claim to authority by those who proffer it. In this case, these consisted of the Friday sermons (*khutba*) and the sessions known locally as "religion classes" that take place in the community's mosque. I also looked at how members of the audience appropriated, interpreted and challenged the knowledge they acquired in these discursive spaces of the Muslim community.

In this chapter, I will analyse the practices of teaching, preaching and listening to religious discourses within the Sunni Muslim community of Rio de Janeiro as contexts of interaction in which identities, experiences and power relations are produced, shaped and affirmed.[1] The main organisation of the Sunni Muslim community is the Muslim Beneficent Society of Rio de Janeiro (MBSRJ) (Sociedade Beneficente Muçulmana do Rio de Janeiro), which was founded in 1951. Until the 1990s, it was oriented around transmitting the cultural heritage of Arab Muslim immigrants to their descendents. After 1997, a new imam, together with a group of members, changed its character, transforming it into an organisation to spread Islam in Rio de Janeiro through the conversion of non-Muslims, according to my interlocutors from MBSRJ.

The missionary efforts of the Muslim Beneficent Society played a central role in the religious life of the community with discursive practices aiming to transmit religious knowledge. In order to reach Brazilians without Arab Muslim origins, the leadership of the community adopted Portuguese as the linguistic context of the official discourses. Therefore, sermons started to be preached in Portuguese, with Arabic being restricted to the recitation of a few Qur'anic passages.[2]

Also, the *Salafiyya* became the main source for the codification of the Islam that began to be fostered by the leadership of the community.[3] The *Salafi* definition of Islam as a set of doctrinal and ritual principles presented in the textual tradition of Islam, as enshrined in the Qur'an and the hadith, allowed the community to incorporate non-Arab Brazilian converts despite their lack of familiarity with the cultural traditions of the Arab immigrants. Furthermore, the codification of Islam as a bounded and explicit set of normative principles that can be pedagogically transmitted to those unfamiliar with them proved to be very instrumental in the missionary aims of the Muslim Beneficent Society.

The success of this strategy was expressed by the growing number of converts in the composition of the Sunni community. While in the year 2000, non-Arab Brazilian converts constituted 50 per cent of the members of the community, in 2007 they represented 85 per cent of them.[4] Besides the converts, the community included Arab immigrants and their descendants (10 per cent) and African foreign students and immigrants (5 per cent).

According to the community leaders, there are around 5,000 Muslims in Rio de Janeiro today. However, attendance at religious rituals and activities of the Muslim Beneficent Society is usually limited to 200 people. The vast majority of those who regularly go to these activities are Brazilian converts. For each activity there is a clear gender divide: for sermons and religious rituals the majority of those attending are men, while in the pedagogical activities, such as Arabic courses and courses on Islam, women form the majority of attendees.

While non-Arab Brazilian converts constitute the majority in all activities of the Muslim Beneficent Society, all positions of power are occupied by Arabic speakers both non-Brazilian and Brazilian of Arab descent. At the time of my ethnographic study, the imam was a Sudanese educated in Libya, and the teachers of the courses were all Brazilians of Arab descent (Syrian and Lebanese). The imam did not have a formal religious education and he always emphasised to the local Muslims that his religious learning was acquired in Brazil through reading books by Muslim thinkers, such as Hasan al-Banna and Sayyid Qutb. The religious elite of the community tried to legitimise their authority by claiming that their mastery of the Arabic language gave them a "direct" access to "authentic" Islamic knowledge. However, the universalistic codification of Islam that was hegemonic within the community allowed the expression of various tensions and challenges to this ethnic marking of religious power.

In order to understand the affirmation and challenge of power relations through the display of religious knowledge, we have to look at the performative arenas where these disputes are enacted by members of the community. Therefore, I will analyse here some of the ethnographic contexts in which these processes emerge through the interactions and exchanges that structure the religious life of the Sunni community of Rio de Janeiro.

Religious Knowledge in Context: "Religion Classes" and Sermons

On Friday mornings, around eighty members of the MBSRJ would gather in the mosque's small prayer room to listen to the religious teachings of the local imam. The teachings performed by Imam Abdu on this occasion were organised into two different, albeit complementary, activities: the locally-named "religion classes" and sermons (khutba). Both activities had a strong pedagogical and oral character, being the main collective arenas of transmission and acquisition of religious knowledge in the community. Orality was valued as a means to gain knowledge in a "more objective and direct way", according to one of my interlocutors, a Brazilian female convert to Islam who did not speak Arabic. According to her, the imam's oral teachings were the best way of obtaining religious knowledge for she could not read the religious texts in their original language. This made the local imam an important cultural broker[5] between an objectified and idealised normative Islamic tradition and the social context of Muslims in Brazil.

The religion classes took place about one hour before the sermon. They were pedagogically structured using a "question-and-answer" method which made them more dynamic than the sermons, for they were interactive and allowed for direct public contact between the audience and the imam. I attended the religious classes many times during my fieldwork. In these classes, Imam Abdu used to sit in front of the pulpit, which also served as *mihrab* (the niche used to indicate the direction of prayers in mosques). Frequently, the men who used to sit close to him were lay leaders of the organisation. The women who attended these classes seldom asked the imam questions in public.[6]

The majority of the questions posed to the imam reflected the sociological constituency of the community: Brazilian converts usually tried to accommodate Islamic codes within the challenges faced in the arenas of everyday life. One day, Imam Abdu was talking about the celebration of the Prophet's birthday (*mawlid*), which in his opinion was an incorrect practice. A Brazilian convert then requested permission to speak and Imam Abdu agreed. The man told us that his birthday was approaching and that his workmates were preparing a surprise party for him that would be held at his house. They contacted his wife (non-Muslim) and asked her to keep the secret but, on the assumption that Muslims do not celebrate their birthday, she thought it would be better to warn him about the problem in order not to create any embarrassment. So the man asked the imam to enlighten him about the Islamic prohibition of birthday celebrations and how he should behave with his friends. The imam argued that the Prophet Muhammad recommended that Muslims should not celebrate their birthday, but since they were living in a non-Muslim majority society, the man had to respect the celebration that his friends had organised, provided that they in turn respected his religion and did not bring anything illicit to his home, such as alcoholic drinks. Finally, the imam said that the man should use the opportunity to talk about Islam and explain certain religious principles to his friends.

Then, an Arab Muslim man asked the imam a question in Arabic. The imam answered him quickly in Arabic, and then translated the question into Portuguese for the others. The man's question referred to the use and commerce of alcohol and its relationship with Islam. The imam, while answering the question, recited a hadith of the Prophet Muhammad and then translated it. The hadith expressed opposition to any proximity between a Muslim and alcohol, as it "harms the pocket, body and mind, especially the latter, and makes people lose their ability to act with reason and make the right decisions". There were other questions asked by members of the community in this manner in order to solicit the imam's advice, such as how they should deal with non-Muslim family and friends; what kind of food and drink restrictions they had to observe; whether Muslim men could play football and whether they could go to football games in stadia; what kind of Islamic etiquette they should practise in public; what were the recommendations for women about veiling; how to prepare oneself for prayers; and so on.

After answering all the questions posed to him during the religious classes, an activity that took about an hour, Imam Abdu would leave the pulpit for a few minutes, returning later in his brown *abaya*, a symbolic clothing which publically communicated his religious authority, and also, his Arab origin. At this time, the direct spoken interactions with the imam ceased, and the audience sat in the small prayer room in silence. Then Imam Abdu stood up in the pulpit and started to preach his sermon.

In order to prepare his sermons, Imam Abdu made use of several sources of religious knowledge, ranging from the sacred texts to theological essays by Muslim authors. He also used pages on the internet, especially those produced by the Muslim diaspora in Europe and the USA. The imam told me that in order to prepare his sermons he thought it an important step to connect the

Qur'anic verses and hadiths with the theme of the sermon, aiming to make it as coherent as possible with Salafi Islamic codes. He would first choose the theme to be preached and then look for textual passages that highlighted the topic. In his opinion, this task was a bit complicated for it demanded knowledge of the Arabic language and the sacred texts.

Therefore, by connecting stories to daily situations and to Islamic doctrinal principles in the Qur'an and hadiths, the sermons preached by Imam Abdu emphasised not only moral and ethical issues – that according to him should guide each and every step taken by Muslims in the Brazilian cultural context – but also that the believer's task was to seek religious knowledge, especially by way of activities that took place at the MBSRJ.

In the following example from a sermon delivered by Imam Abdu, we can see how he focused on moral commitment to Salafi Islamic practices as a way to construct a model of conduct for his audience. He told us a story about Muslims in China. According to the story, Chinese soldiers completed the dawn prayer (*fajr*) every day despite facing the adversity of the war they were involved in and the retaliation of their commander, who did not allow them to pray. This story was presented as an example of Chinese soldiers' good religious conduct. Imam Abdu compared the religious commitment of the Chinese soldiers with the practices of MBSRJ members, who, according to him, often disregarded fajr prayers and did not care to improve their bodily movements during the prayers.

The other story Imam Abdu included in the sermon was about an imam from a mosque in London, who acted earnestly and responsibly as a Muslim when he received extra money as change from a bus ticket by returning it to the bus driver. The driver asked him if he was the new imam from the London mosque and mentioned that he would like to learn about Islam, requesting the imam's help. The London imam then "thanked God for not having changed Islam and the Islamic teachings for any money". By citing this example, Imam Abdu reinforced the importance attached to religious knowledge, its practice and the correct way of spreading it. In his words:

> It is necessary that a person has a perfect conscience with regard to religion and the information he is spreading and that he acts in line with it. I therefore advise all brothers to take this seriously. We have the greatest product of all to be presented to mankind, a message of peace, restfulness and mutual respect. We need to deliver this message, but we should not act as a lousy vendor who does not know his product and who does not know how to pack it in order to present it to the public.

The Muslim characters in the stories cited by Imam Abdu also lived in minority and diasporic Muslim communities, something that allowed the

Brazilian Muslims to connect with their struggle to follow these Islamic norms in daily life. "If a Muslim can be correct in China and in London, why can we not be correct in Brazil?" asked Imam Abdu to his audience. Moreover, we can expand the implicit meanings of Imam Abdu's speech on Islam as "a product to be sold" by stressing that a large number of the Arab members of the community were merchants and that they were "called" through the imam's speech to help the MBSRJ's religious leaders in the work of *da'wa* (call to Islam) in the Brazilian "religious market".

One of my interlocutors, a twenty-five-year old Brazilian male convert, told me in an interview that the religion classes were very important for local Muslims because they improved their understandings of Islamic codes, and corrected various aspects of their daily lives. In his opinion, he and his fellow converts should try to live a pious life in Rio de Janeiro cutting off all "old habits", such as going out to parties or cinemas. According to him, it was easier for Brazilian converts than for Arab Muslim men to be pious in the local context, since the former were fully socialised into the local cultural codes.

However, Ghada, a fifty-year-old Palestinian woman who had emigrated from the United Arab Emirates to Brazil in 1990, did not think in the same way. One day, during an informal conversation at her house, she told me that she really liked Imam Abdu and all the "brothers and sisters" of MBSRJ, but that she rarely attended the activities such as Friday religious classes and sermons. Her reason was that religious issues were not discussed in depth because

> the majority of the members in the institution are new Brazilian Muslims. They are like children who need attention to be raised in the correct Islamic way, so they have to learn how to pray, how to fast, how to have Islamic behaviour and how to speak Arabic. That is not my case, so I go to the mosque just on Islamic celebrations or when I have time. My thirteen-year-old daughter could teach these things to them.

Some of my interlocutors who had been born Muslim criticised the "radical" changes that some converts tried to implement in their daily lives. One of them, Muhammad, a man of thirty-two, told me that some converts wanted to change everything "from one day to another", aiming to become "exemplary Muslims". According to him, the converts should try to "learn Islam step by step", being aware of the challenges posed by the local cultural context. He also said they should be more tolerant of the imperfections of others.

On the other hand, the converts tried to turn their daily lives into something more "Islamic" by using special clothing such as the *hijab* and adopting new religious vocabulary (*insha'a-llah*, *al-hamdu li-llah*) and names – just like a convert named Paulo who chose Ibrahim as his Muslim name. The converts were also critical of the behaviour of those who were born Muslim, denouncing their lack of interest in participating in the community activities. Converts often referred to the sermons delivered by Imam Abdu, particularly his practical examples and stories, to explain specific issues during their conversations and when expressing opinions about certain topics. A young Brazilian female convert, for example, told me how she forgave her mother after hearing a sermon delivered by Imam Abdu on children's duty toward their parents. She told me that the sermon was a kind of "letter" sent by God because she was angry and sad with her mother for continually disagreeing with her conversion to Islam. She told me that her mother would cook pieces of pork and put them inside a pot of black beans almost every day (making a traditional Brazilian dish called *feijoada*). She would therefore argue with her mother and refuse to eat anything. After listening to the sermon and engaging in some self-reflection, my interlocutor forgave her mother. According to her,

> I stopped arguing with my mother. Islam is comprehension, so I explained to her why I should not eat pork and why Islam was good for me. She finally understood, and now she prepares my meals without *haram* ingredients.

These disputes between Brazilian Muslim converts and Arab-born Muslims came to my attention at the beginning of my fieldwork, when I started to attend the Friday prayers. While the MBSRJ did not have a person responsible for conducting the call to prayer (*muezzin*), there were two Arab members of the community who usually performed this task. One day, both were absent. Imam Abdu therefore asked for a volunteer to conduct the call. After a while, a young Brazilian convert stood up and began the call. The man did not have a good command of Arabic, although he was a very dedicated student of the language. When he finished, Imam Abdu congratulated him for his commitment to Islam, but told him that his call could not be accepted because he had not pronounced the words correctly. The imam asked an Arab man to make the call instead. He did so, and thereafter the prayer began.

Although Arab ethnicity may not be a defining element of Muslim identity, in this local context it is connected to a sphere of religious knowledge culturally inherited by the Muslim-born Arabs and their descendants, which is alien to the converts without Arab origins. This is reflected in the symbolic disputes regarding the demonstration of religious knowledge that take place between Arab-born Muslims and Brazilian converts. These disputes emerge even in the way each group assimilates the sermon. Arabic-speakers are keen to point to the fact that they are able to make sense of the Qur'anic verses that are quoted during the sermons, unlike the converts who usually do not speak Arabic.

Conclusion

This ethnographic analysis has shown how the religion classes and sermons delivered in the Sunni community of Rio de Janeiro actually represent arenas in which religious knowledge, power relations and symbolic disputes between its members are expressed. In these arenas, the imam's position and his acceptance by Muslims in Rio de Janeiro depends on the amount of religious knowledge that he can continually and publicly mobilise. In addition, it depends on his capacity to translate abstract Salafi Muslim values into practical terms connected to the community's everyday life.

In this way, the imam constructs and legitimises his authority from his ability to instruct the members of the community on how to live in a proper "Islamic" way in Rio de Janeiro, as well as from his sensibility to the particular differences among the local Muslims (Arab and non-Arab). In this sense, for example, he taught not only how a convert should deal with his/her non-Muslim friends, family and the local culture (familiar to them), but he also advised Arab Muslims who had recently moved to Rio de Janeiro on how to behave in the local culture, for example how to deal with local dress codes and the easy access to alcohol. While the local imam mainly asserts his religious authority by demonstrating his knowledge of doctrine and practice in a public and oral way, his authority is also strengthened by being Arab and African, and for having had his entire experience as a religious leader in Brazil. These biographical elements help him establish his position as leader of the three major ethnic groups that compose the Sunni community in Rio de Janeiro.

Therefore, the efforts of the imam and the other lay leaders of the MBSRJ to inscribe this version of Islam in the Brazilian religious sphere through a pedagogical methodology of summarising the religious codes via what is 'permitted' (*halal*) and what is 'forbidden' (haram) find a relative measure of success in the local religious community, mainly among converts, who are very enthusiastic in promoting Islam as a non-ethnic religion. On the other hand, the Muslim-born members of this community mobilise their belonging to Islam as part of their ethnic and cultural Arab identity.

Therefore, this analysis points to the use of the ethnographic method as an important methodological tool for understanding the cultural complexity of what is defined as Islam in the local context of Rio de Janeiro. The ethnographic approach allows for a multilayered comprehension of the ways in which Muslims become attached to the religious community organised around the MSBRJ and transform the normative Islamic code into a dynamic social reality through the practices of everyday life.

Notes

1. I undertook fieldwork among the Sunni Muslim community of Rio de Janeiro in 2001 and again in 2004–5.
2. The sociological profile of Muslim communities in Brazil is extremely diverse. The majority of them do not have a "missionary" goal and therefore use Arabic in all ritual contexts.
3. The *Salafiyya* is a reformist Islamic movement that emerged in the nineteenth century. Its main idea is that all the religious conduct of a Muslim should be based on the canonical religious texts (Qur'an and hadiths).
4. Paulo G. Pinto, "Arab Ethnicity and Diasporic Islam: A Comparative Approach to Processes of Identity Formation and Religious Codification in the Muslim Communities in Brazil", *Comparative Studies of South Africa and the Middle East*, vol. 31, no. 2, 2011, p. 315.
5. On this concept, see Patrick Gaffney, *The Prophet's Pulpit: Islamic Preaching in Contemporary Egypt*, Berkeley: University of California Press, 1994.
6. The women also sought Imam Abdu's teachings and advice, but in a private way: they used to meet him in the MBSRJ during the week or on Saturdays, before the public religious activities that occurred in the institution. Sometimes, they did it as a group.

Chapter 8

Worshipping the Martyr President: The Darih of Rafiq Hariri in Beirut

Ward Vloeberghs

The tomb (*darih*) of Rafiq Hariri (*Rafiq al-Hariri*) is one of two elements that make up the mausoleum of the late Lebanese tycoon-turned-politician.[1] Every year, the site draws bus-loads of visitors from inside and outside Lebanon. In spite of its touristic popularity, the burial site and the practices surrounding it have received very little scholarly attention.

Throughout the descriptive analysis below I shall present the location and development of the tomb followed by the salient characteristics of the cult attached to it. I explore the darih as a shrine defined by Eickelman as "more than just a building". In fact, shrines often encompass a whole set of "rituals, symbols, and shifting social and spiritual ties that link believers to Islam and create a sacred geography".[2]

In order to highlight the characteristics of this unique urban feature, this chapter examines both the political and religious aspects of the tomb from an ethnographic perspective. By discussing artefacts and practices found or observed on-site, I demonstrate how a detailed account of the funerary complex allows us to reveal a number of ongoing dynamics that other methods might easily overlook but which, in fact, illustrate how the tomb continues to be relevant for Lebanese actors in articulating the boundaries of their constituencies and territories. Contrary to press surveys or interviews which inevitably recall events through intermediaries, the ethnographic method encourages direct observation and first-hand access to those practices that are of interest to the researcher who aims to bridge the aforementioned descriptive gap and analyse the realities of everyday life in considerable detail. This chapter engages in substance with the (re)arrangements in the physical layout of the tomb as well as shifts in the political and religious connotations attached to it.

After the assassination of ex-prime minister Rafiq Hariri, his family acted quickly to acquire a plot of land immediately next to the luxurious Muhammad al-Amin mosque. Hariri had commissioned this mosque on Beirut's most emblematic public square as a pious coronation of his impressive if not undisputed reconstruction efforts in central Beirut.[3] The positioning of the tomb itself was hardly a coincidence and both the mosque and the tomb are inextricably connected – if only because a direct passage connects the tomb to the mosque via a couple of stairs hidden between two dedicated trees.[4]

The construction of a monumental mosque on Martyrs' Square (a strategic site that occupies a prominent place in Lebanese political history) has had a strong impact on residents as well as on occasional visitors. The will (not only Hariri's) to bestow a landmark of Muslim civilisation onto the skyline of Beirut can be seen as a meaningful gesture that has not taken long to spark acts of contestation. This became especially apparent during the activities of a paralysing sit-in (*i'tisam*) staged by opponents of Hariri's coalition between December 2006 and May 2008. The campaign not only caused an institutional deadlock but, in a subtle, complex and dialectal way, also turned the surroundings of the emerging mausoleum into a locus of spatially contested power.

Site Location and Development

On Wednesday, 16 February 2005, two days after his assassination by a heavy car bomb, tens of thousands of supporters carried Hariri's coffin from his residence in Qoraytem to its final destination in central Beirut where a large white tent structure had been erected to accommodate what was to become commonly known as *ad-darih*.[5] In the case of the tomb of Rafiq Hariri, this term designates the spacious area covered by the shelter, which hosts Hariri's tomb as well as the graves of seven of his bodyguards. Although the funeral complex (see Figure 8.1) nowadays presents itself as an integrated whole, it has gone through considerable alterations since 2005.

Initially, nothing indicated that Hariri would be buried in this particular location (or in Beirut at all) and the decision to do so can be qualified as a political one.[7] However, once the ceremony at the Muhammad al-Amin mosque was over and Hariri had been laid to rest just next to it, events rapidly succeeded each other. Vast amounts of people amassed at the nascent grave-site and soon the tomb became a popular attraction and media spectacle.

During these early days, the tomb resembled a big, green, white and red pile of souvenirs left by visitors (see Figure 8.2). Flowers heaping up on an ever-widening space atop Hariri's grave were cordoned off by a large circle of planters filled with sand and candles. The shelter covering tombs and visitors soon turned into a space that people creatively fitted out with more Lebanese flags, portraits

Figure 8.1 An overview of Hariri's grave-site (under the white shelters) bordering Martyrs' Square, the Muhammad al-Amin mosque, the Maronite cathedral of St George and the Garden of Forgiveness (under development) in 2006. (Photo: W. Vloeberghs)

of Hariri, children's drawings, tributes, wreaths and copies of the *surat al-fatiha*. One also discerned candles with pictures of Mar Charbel (a Catholic monk venerated as a saint by many Lebanese Maronites) or the Virgin Mary.

In the weeks after Hariri's dramatic assassination, the concept of *"ciné-diner-darih"* appeared as a popular locution among Beirut residents, reflecting the extent to which visiting the tomb of the ex-prime minister had become an ordinary, almost leisurely activity. Spurred on by its touch of novelty, people would pay a visit to the darih just as they might have gone for a walk along the "corniche" or visited an internet café. Other practices soon emerged, as impressive numbers of common citizens took possession of the site, now easily accessible twenty-four hours a day. Parents took their children there on an excursion, and numerous recently-married couples visited. Victorious football teams insisted on having themselves photographed in front of Hariri's grave. These practices are all in line with Eickelman's concept of a shrine, since he maintains that "visits to shrines secure blessings for the household and can be used to signal changes in personal status – marriage, the birth of a child, or mourning".[8]

Figure 8.2 Hariri's tomb in April 2005 (upper) and April 2006 (lower). (Photo: W. Vloeberghs)

Gradually the site became more properly organised by Oger Liban,[9] which oversees the maintenance of the grave-site, and large printed banners with pictures, slogans and messages of commemoration, as well as propaganda material, appeared. For instance, a digital screen was installed that counted the days that had elapsed since the day of the assassination, above which in red letters stood the phrase "*al-haqiqa ... li-ajli Lubnan*" meaning: "the truth, for the sake of Lebanon".

This call for "truth" referred to the claim for an international enquiry to determine who was responsible for the murder of Hariri. The claim was expressed repeatedly in the months following February 2005 by Hariri's family, supporters and (international) allies, and it became a political mantra for the emerging 14 March movement. In this sense, the truth and the sentence *li-ajli Lubnan* was a vengeful truth, implicitly thought to be directed against what was seen as the "lies" coming from Damascus, as well as showing opposition to a chaperoning role by Syria, perceived as hostile to a sovereign Lebanon.

As crowds continued to show up, a system had to be found to organise and manage visits to the site. Surveillance personnel appeared, as did crush barriers and, later on, a CCTV system. Soon, Hariri's own grave was being rearranged. A wide elevated bed of white flowers was installed on top of it while huge pictures showing Hariri kissing his father's hand, sitting next to his mother or visiting "his" reconstructed city centre came to surround his tomb. A giant Lebanese flag was hung from the ceiling over a lozenge-shaped space subtly sealed off by a dark-red velvet-cloaked cord, the sort of barriers one encounters in palaces or museums. On the walls behind the tomb were more Lebanese flags.

To the left of Hariri's grave (when facing it) an impressive composition of identical white flower diadems was installed. Each one bears the name of one of his (grand)children and all have the same portrait of the *pater familias* at their centre. On top of these garlands stands a similar spray, this time with red flowers – presumably offered by Hariri's wife, Nazik – with the words *ila rafiq 'umri*.[10] All floral arrangements on-site were made of fresh flowers which were specially flown in from Italy until artificial ones were installed in 2011.

To the right of Hariri's tomb, a short corridor formed by transportable barriers leads to a separate chamber accommodating the graves of seven of Hariri's private bodyguards who perished with him when their motorcade was blown up. The design of Hariri's tomb and those of his bodyguards has been carefully studied to comply with religious and aesthetic guidelines as the bodies were placed on an axis defined by the Ka'aba in Mecca and the Martyrs' Statue.

Simultaneously with the rearrangement of Hariri's grave, the tombs of his security personnel were more neatly organised. In the beginning, each of them had been decorated with flowers, little Lebanese flags, pictures of the deceased, candles and a ring of flowers bearing Hariri's picture (see Figure 8.3).

Worshipping the Martyr President

Figure 8:3 The tombs of Hariri's seven bodyguards in April 2005 (upper) and April 2006 (lower). (Photo: W. Vloeberghs)

As the site continued to be developed, the bare earth of the early days was covered with a green carpet, and a more sophisticated presentation appeared. Behind the graves, the shelter was closed off by a wide banner reproducing the Lebanese flag while a large white wreath was placed in front of each tomb. All tombs mentioned the mother's first name next to the bodyguard's full name. The tombs were now each covered by a large Lebanese flag, with a flower arrangement and a framed portrait depicting the bodyguard next to Hariri installed on top of each tomb. Strings of praying (and playing) beads (*misbaha*) hung from the corners of frames containing a picture or an Islamic blessing. Finally, behind the tombs another large display of white flowers bore a religious dedication.

During the past couple of years, the layout of the site has tended overall to exhibit fewer but more strictly selected objects and images. This objective is accomplished through frequent and ongoing reorganisations of the posters and artefacts on display. The rationale behind this selection is not only to provide for a more orderly, choreographed space but also to create a setting that is in tune with the prevailing socio-political circumstances. Permanent artificial lighting and selected Qur'anic recitations create an atmosphere conducive to piety and worship. The main objective seems to be to generate an ever-perfect, almost sanitised portrait of Rafiq Hariri combining orderliness with enhanced visibility.

Furthermore, access is another way to analyse the changing disposition at the darih. While no formal admission procedure applied in the beginning, eventually guards would operate a brief but efficient control of visitors, asking them to open bags and sometimes, conducting full security scans.

Thus, while the site displayed a spontaneous and uncoordinated character in the beginning, it gradually developed into an ever-more elaborate and structured shrine – complete with life-size portraits, paraphernalia and an accompanying cult.[11]

An Emerging Cult

Several factors converge to explain how and why Rafiq Hariri acquired the status of a mythical "martyr". His considerable achievements in life – as the single most powerful Lebanese politician to have emerged since the late 1980s – and his international radiance with direct access to global leaders are only part of this explanation. Indeed, it is the brutality of his assassination combined with thoughtful planning and political manoeuvring that have resulted in the current reverence. The fact that he is nowadays systematically referred to as *ar-ra'is ash-shahid* (the martyr president) is but one example of this trend. Within less than a year, the darih had become a pilgrimage site that, just like its martyr during his lifetime, imposed itself on the local political liturgy.

While there may have been a brief period (in the first two months or so after Hariri's assassination) when visiting the darih was quite an acceptable mourning practice for individuals of virtually all political, social and religious backgrounds, this changed rapidly. Since the site was attached to anti-Syrian rhetoric, it soon became caught up in a climate of political polarisation whereby the Lebanese increasingly came under (social) pressure to take sides along the divide between the so-called "8 March" and "14 March" coalitions. A number of interventions and activities at the tomb and its immediate vicinity reflect a sustained and orchestrated endeavour to nourish the relevance of the grave-site as a political forum as well as efforts to renew and reformulate the legacy of Rafiq Hariri.

Some examples of such practices include a staged celebration of the first anniversary of the withdrawal of Syrian troops from Lebanon, flowers offered at the darih on the occasion of Hariri's sixty-third birthday, and the commemoration of "Day 1000" after the assassination.[12] Of particular interest in this respect is the installation at the darih of a showcase containing a solemn plaque celebrating the establishment of the basic framework for the Special Tribunal for Lebanon by the adoption of resolution 1757 by the UN Security Council in May 2007.

Among the most significant series of activities contributing to the establishment of Hariri's shrine as a new centre of political life was the phenomenon of an annual pilgrimage. Every year since 2005, a large commemorative gathering has been organised on 14 February and no expense has been spared to publicise the event or to attract supporters. These mass manifestations as well as their professional management have confirmed the centrality of the darih as a locus for political mobilisation.[13]

Furthermore, scenes of Lebanese and foreign dignitaries visiting Hariri's tomb have become standard political practice, almost since the installation of the darih. As a longstanding friend of the Hariri family, French President Jacques Chirac was the first foreign official to pay his respects to Rafiq al-Hariri at his burial site. Just hours after the latter's funeral, Chirac appeared at the freshly arranged grave, accompanied by his wife Bernadette, Nazik and Saad al-Hariri. Together they joined a large circle of Lebanese citizens surrounding the flowered, candle-lit tomb in a moment of silence and prayer.

National and international, political and religious dignitaries swiftly followed suit, eager to mark their visit to Beirut by a show of appreciation for the slain politician and his family. Among those who came to pay their respects at the darih were Kofi Annan (Secretary General of the UN), Condoleezza Rice (US Secretary of State), Nancy Pelosi (Speaker of the US House of Representatives), Angela Merkel (German Chancellor), Gulf leaders, high-ranking EU diplomats and many others. They were joined by numerous Lebanese politicians and religious dignitaries. Mufti Qabbani (Lebanon's most senior Sunni official) was frequently photographed at the darih while Walid Jumblatt, then a pillar of Hariri's coalition, was one of the first politicians to participate in such ritual visits. In March 2006, even Hizbullah's Sayyid Hasan Nasrallah came to the grave-site in person.[14]

Not only does the visit of a dignitary strengthen the cult of Hariri, it also confers considerable visibility and legitimacy upon the visitor(s) in question. These appearances must be seen as political statements and expressions of sympathy to the family, the person of Hariri and even to his allies who continue "his fight" – however they may (re)define it. Such visits perpetuate Hariri's ability to attract the world's elite and the ease with which he "circulates" among the famous and powerful. Finally, particularly during the first ten months following Hariri's inhumation, the public exhibitions of mourning and grief at his grave generated valuable scenes of trans-confessional tolerance and (inter-)national unity which fuelled Hariri's political heirs and allies.

Interestingly, however, the trajectory of the tomb as a symbol of national consensus was rather ephemeral; it soon became invested with sectarian meanings and competing narratives about truth and national unity, thus reflecting the semantic shifts that these terms, as well as the concept of "darih" itself, suffered during the waxing of Hariri's cult.

As I have indicated, during the early weeks, one could find Lebanese of varying age, descent and confession ritually burning candles, placing flowers and praying side by side.

Hariri's grave was initially surrounded by a permanent cordon of mourners: Christians praying and making the sign of the cross, Muslims next to them reading from tiny copies of the Qur'an.[15]

Later on, specific objects indicated the manifest will to create an atmosphere of Islamic piety: a large picture of Hariri performing the *Hajj*, prayer beads and written or spoken Qur'anic verses are all elements of the religious character of the cult and worship woven around the "martyr president". So there is a large stone Qur'an, standing on a book holder – obviously a present, as it is dedicated "to the soul of the martyr Rafiq al-Hariri". Next to it stands a shield-shaped plate (see Figure 8.4) displaying *surat ya sin*, a gift from the Union of Beiruti family associations.[16] Perhaps as indicative of the religious aspect of the cult are little black prayer books occasionally distributed at the darih,[17] or the ceremonial atmosphere of hushed conversations created by the tranquil transmissions of *tartil* (a specific way of Qur'an recitation) by Shaykh Khalil al-Husari. Tellingly, many attendants of the Friday prayer precede their entry to the Muhammad al-Amin mosque with a visit to the tomb.

The markedly religious character of the cult surrounding Rafiq al-Hariri at his tomb and, in particular, an apparent tendency to add Sunni elements to it must be understood in relation to a wider trend of increased communal polarisation that affected Lebanese society soon after Rafiq al-Hariri's assassination. This

Figure 8.4 Shield with Quranic verse, a gift from Beiruti families to "Rafiq of Beirut" (2009). (Photo: W. Vloeberghs)

eventually culminated, first, in a sit-in protest that lasted for eighteen months and then, in May 2008, in the violent takeover of Sunni parts of Beirut by Shi'i militias.[18]

The sit-in saw supporters of opposition parties (mainly Michel Aoun's FPM, Amal and Hizbullah) camping in tents, thus closing off downtown Beirut which is considered as government territory. Although the sit-in should not be seen as a direct response to the installation of the mausoleum but rather as a reaction to the situation prevailing after Hariri's assassination, the protestors' choice of location was highly symbolic and anything but accidental. It is therefore interesting to note how the ethnographic approach allows us to document exactly how one and the same place has been used as a locus for competing truths. This partisan mobilisation, the proliferation of counter-narratives and competition between various truths, including religious ones, around Hariri's funerary complex not only illustrates how relative truth can be; it is also an urban, spatial expression of ongoing political contest.

In a delicate but unmistakable manner, the layout of the grave-site both responded to this evolution and participated in it. In other words, the gradual elaboration of Hariri's funerary complex became caught up in a political struggle

Figure 8.5 A considerable area of the funerary complex has yet to be developed (2009). (Photo: W. Vloeberghs)

where the darih served as a formidable forum and an instrument of political mobilisation in a context of heightened communal polarisation in Lebanon.

The apparent tendency to emphasise Sunni identity at and from the darih as well as Hariri's entombment next to the mosque itself – while in contradiction to Wahhabi interpretations of Islam eschewing any form of shrine-based idolatry or person-related commemoration – provide a poignant illustration of the *social construction* of a communitarian symbol by (at least parts of) the Sunni community in Lebanon. In fact, the ethnographic account of commemorative practices observed at Hariri's grave-site presented so far shows an even more interesting phenomenon, namely the transition of an emerging national hero to a markedly communitarian symbol in reflection of an evolved political climate. This seems to be corroborated by the fact that, notwithstanding its numerous international visitors, the site nowadays attracts more confessionally uniform visitors than had been the case immediately after its installation.

Conclusion

Given all these improvised practices and orchestrated rituals, the darih appears as a sacred space entirely appropriated by the Hariri family as a sanctuary for its founding father. As to the future development of the site, it should be added that large parts of the space covered by the tents are currently left unused (see

Figure 8.5) – perhaps because the shelter is but temporary housing for the tomb. At the time of writing, one of Hariri's children – Fahd, his youngest son – was contributing to the design of a more permanent structure to accommodate what may sooner or later become a fully-fledged commemorative complex.

This ethnography of the tomb of Rafiq Hariri, its material culture and the practices associated with it enable us to understand this process and how the darih is much more than a space of remembrance devoted to a particular person. For those who visit his shrine and even more so for those who visit it frequently, the practices, convictions and sympathies attached to the grave-site are not only religious or political in nature. The meticulous ethnographic description of the characteristics of Hariri's tomb allows us to transcend initial appearances by providing a distinct understanding of the dynamics at play, most notably by indicating how they may cover various, mutually contradictory realities and visions.

The tomb is in perpetual evolution, neither its distinctive features nor its framing are ever stable but always shifting in relation to the actors' political needs and the subtle complexities of Lebanese multi-confessional society. Highlighting the ever-changing layout of the tomb as a succession of overlapping and unstable narratives helps to establish this and, moreover, how the tomb is being carefully monitored and adjusted in order to sustain and legitimise Hariri's legacy. Illustrating this process in detail allows us to better understand how a contemporary martyr is being worshipped and how a contemporary shrine is being strengthened through the social interactions of its commissioners and visitors.

Notes

1. The second constitutive element of the mausoleum, the Muhammad al-Amin mosque, is not considered here because the mosque does not actually belong to Rafiq Hariri but to the Directorate General of Islamic Awqaf, and because the cult of Rafiq Hariri can be best observed at his tomb. A detailed study can be found in Ward Vloeberghs, *A Building of Might and Faith: Rafiq al-Hariri and the Muhammad al-Amin Mosque. On the Political Dimensions of Religious Architecture in Contemporary Beirut*, PhD thesis, University of Louvain (UCL, Belgium), 2010.
2. Dale F. Eickelman, "Shrine", in John Esposito (ed.), *The Oxford Encyclopaedia of the Modern Islamic World*, vol. 4, New York – Oxford: Oxford University Press, 1995, pp. 69–71.
3. Nasser Shammaa, close to the Hariri family and chairman of Solidere (to whom the parcel of land technically belonged), was involved in the discussions of this overnight decision. However, the exact details of this transaction (surface area, price, conditions, and so on) remain undisclosed.
4. One of them, "planted in earth from all Lebanese provinces" on 10 April 2005, was dedicated to "national unity" at the occasion of the Beirut Marathon while the second tree was unveiled on 3 September 2005 as "a tree of peace for a man of

peace" by the youngsters of Hariri's Mustaqbal (Future) party.
5. The scholar Taha al-Wali informs us that a darih is usually understood to be "any luxurious tomb where a man of standing or high rank is buried or any notable or *'alim*". He cites Riad as-Solh's burial site as an example of a darih. See Taha al-Wali, *Al-Masjid fi-l Islam*, Beirut: Dar al-'Ilm lil-Malayin, 1988, pp. 126–7.
6. The structure consists of two parallel rectangular shelters (80 by 36 metres and 80 by 35 metres, respectively) and one smaller triangular tent covering the guards' tombs. Two hundred and fifty labourers from the Hariri family's contracting company Oger Liban had worked from 10 pm on Monday evening until 4 am on Wednesday morning to have the site ready in time. See *an-Nahar*, 16 February 2005.
7. Many expected that Hariri would be buried in his birth town of Saida, where he had commissioned a commemorative mosque for his mother and another even larger one to honour his father. In addition, the funeral became politicised when the Hariri family declared that it had refused a state funeral.
8. Eickelman, "Shrine", p. 70.
9. Oger Liban is a contracting company owned by the Hariri family.
10. This is a literary pun which translates either as "to my life companion" or "to Rafiq, my life".
11. I am grateful to Kathryn Spellman Poots and Paulo Pinto for pointing out similarities between the cult of Hariri and the practices of remembrance surrounding Princess Diana (1961–97) and Juán Perón (1895–1974) respectively. Also, I am grateful for an exchange with Konstantin Kastrissianakis.
12. See respectively *al-Liwa*, 27 April 2006 (on the withdrawal anniversary), *al-Liwa*, 2 November 2007 (on Hariri's birthday) and *al-Liwa*, 12 November 2007 (on the 1000 days of martyrdom).
13. Following the 2006 edition, the family thanked its supporters on billboards with the text "More than a million thanks, Saad al-Hariri".
14. See *al-Sharq al-Awsat*, 4 March 2006.
15. Nicholas Blanford, *Killing Mr Lebanon. The Assassination of Rafik Hariri and its Impact on the Middle East*, London: I. B. Tauris, 2006, p. 153 (discussing events on 21 February 2005).
16. It is dedicated to "Rafiq (companion) of Beirut", as if to boost his credentials as a Beirut *za'im* (communal leader) rather than a scion of Saida.
17. Entitled "Prayer for the Martyr President Rafiq Bahaa ad-Din al-Hariri", the eight-page prayer booklet contains fifty-two prayers. I thank Didier Leroy for providing me with a copy.
18. The strengthening of confessional identities intensified during the sit-in and reached a paroxysm in May 2008 when Shi'i militias took over Sunni parts of Beirut in a couple of hours. That traumatic event made way for a more inclusive discourse emphasising national unity and religious coexistence later on in 2008, as became evident at the inauguration ceremony of the Muhammad al-Amin mosque in October 2008. Tensions soared in 2010 and 2011 over the "Hariri Tribunal".

CHAPTER 9

Staging the Authority of the Ulama:
The Celebration of the Mawlid in Urban Syria

THOMAS PIERRET

The ulama are a particularly uncommon topic for ethnography. As the paragons of textual culture in classical Muslim societies, they have more often than not been studied through their writings and sermons, that is, through their discourse. This chapter focuses on other kinds of practices and more particularly on the annual celebration of Muhammad's birthday (*Mawlid*) in early twenty-first century Damascus, Syria.[1] Academic literature on the celebration of Muslim prophets and saints has been mostly concerned with popular pilgrimages which, like in Egypt, frequently involve what puritans describe as "un-Islamic" practices (mixing of sexes, dance, and even alcohol consumption and prostitution).[2] Little attention has been paid so far to the fact that the Mawlid is also celebrated in public by the self-proclaimed custodians of orthodoxy, that is, Muslim scholars.

The goal of this chapter is to show that ethnography allows us to grasp aspects of the "scholarly" *mawalid* that generally remain concealed within the discourses produced by social actors. These discourses can be categorised as either controversial or consensual. The first category is concerned with disputes over the definition of orthodoxy and orthopraxy, and consists either of controversies stirred up by Salafi opponents of the Mawlid,[3] or of normative statements on the boundaries of its correct performance, which entail the denunciation of the above-mentioned "un-Islamic" behaviours. The second category of discourses is mainly composed of speeches given during the celebration and of articles released in the media as the Mawlid approaches. They propagate an idealised conception of the latter's purpose, which revolves around the ideas of morality and identity: on the one hand, speakers and writers call their audience to imitate the exemplary behaviour of Muhammad and stress the need to abide by his Sunna; on the other hand, they present the birthday of the Messenger of God as the best occasion to reunite his followers against their enemies. The latter framing of the Mawlid fits functionalist conceptualisations of celebrations as devices aimed at cementing a community's unity through the remembrance of its founding episode. Unsurprising, from that point of view, is the fact that in Syria, the mawalid easily acquire political overtones. In the 1960s and 1970s, they sometimes turned into openly anti-Ba'thist meetings.[4] In 2006, celebrations started a few weeks after the Danish cartoon affair and US/EU non-recognition of the elected Hamas government in Palestine, which led to the flourishing of anti-Western speeches on these occasions.[5]

However, observing how mawalid are celebrated – rather than merely listening to what is said about or during them – reveals another important dimension of the celebrations of the Prophet's birthday. Indeed, this chapter will show that the ulama have given the mawlid a form that not only reflects their concern for orthopraxy, all "un-Islamic" practices being carefully avoided, but also conveys a strongly hierarchical meaning. As a result, in urban Syria, the mawlid appears as a celebration of the clergy rather than of the community as a whole.

This chapter relies on observations that were made between 2006 and 2008 in about twenty mosques in Damascus. Except for the urban focus (my fieldwork did not cover the countryside because the ulama are predominantly found in cities), and the fact that I was allowed to attend male celebrations only, there was no particular bias in the choice of these mosques. They were located in areas with different social and economic characteristics (from popular, semi-rural outskirts to exclusive housing estates), and my sample included both pro-regime and more independent places of worship.

Description

Every year in the cities of Syria, the twelfth day of the lunar month of Rabi' al-Awwal marks the beginning of the celebration of the Prophet's birthday (*al-ihtifal bi-l-mawlid al-nabawi al-sharif*). This period, which lasts for more or less six weeks, is one of the most important of the religious year, second only to Ramadan. Mawalid are organised every evening in different mosques, which for these occasions are decorated with light bulbs, banners and green pennants. These celebrations are a huge popular success with some of the largest mosques welcoming more than 5,000 people at a time.

Each celebration lasts for three or four hours starting from one of the two evening prayers. Following the prayer, the crowd progressively fills the neon-lit mosque and sits on the carpets facing the *qibla*. In the largest places of worship, which sometimes have several floors, staff members show visitors the way to the remaining available space. The main prayer hall is occupied by men only, whereas women congregate on a separate floor or side room. Like the men seated at the back of the mosque, women can sometimes watch the ceremony on television screens thanks to one or several cameras (depending on the organisers' financial means) whose images are edited live by a control room. In some wealthy neighbourhoods, images are also displayed on a giant screen outside the mosque. When everybody is seated, the staff distribute water, Arabic coffee (strong and non-sweetened), sugar-coated almonds wrapped in aluminium foil, and in some cases, plastic flags for children bearing slogans such as "He [Muhammad] lives in our hearts", "Let's revive His Sunna", or "We follow His Sunna".

In one corner of the mosque sits a group of *munshidun* (religious singers), whose chants in honour of the Prophet are amplified by a powerful sound system and are heard throughout the evening. The munshidun's appearance allows them to be identified as artists. Unlike clerics, they wear impeccable suits and ties and prefer a moustache, three-day stubble or even being clean-shaven to having a long beard, and unlike ordinary laymen, they often refrain from cutting their hair short at the back of the neck. However, their performance strictly abides by the rules of Shari'a as defined by the Damascene religious elite, who forbid any kind of dancing as well as the use of musical instruments except for percussion, in this case tambourines.

Against the *qibla*'s wall, facing the public, "VIPs" are seated on two or three rows of plastic chairs, benches, and, for the most distinguished of them, leather armchairs. The centre of the front row is reserved for the *shuyukh* ("shaykhs"), that is, the ulama. They are recognisable by their serious and hieratic attitude, their white turban or scarf and their distinctive dress, which for this special occasion is often a gilt-edged robe (*jubba*). By their sides sit junior clerics as well as lay notables, most of whom are merchants. The latter, who are commonly called *hajj* ("pilgrim"), often display outward signs of religiosity such as a short beard, sober ankle-length tunic (*dishdasha*), and white prayer cap (*taqiya*). In some cases, more prominent businessmen with a moustache and elegant suit are also present. For members of the private sector, enjoying a place of prestige in a mawlid is often a symbolic reward for donations to the mosque and its charitable activities. Consequently, the more warmly a merchant is greeted on his arrival and the closer to the ulama he is invited to sit, the greater his generosity. In some cases, auction-like fundraising sessions organised during the mawlid itself allow wealthy people to publicly display their readiness to spend money "in the path of God".[6] This way of enhancing one's reputation is particularly convenient for those businessmen who aim at being elected to the Parliament as "independent" deputies. For instance, during the 2007 electoral campaign, which coincided with the Mawlid season, some candidates toured the mosques of the capital in order to reap the symbolic benefits of their previous donations. The "diplomatic" dimension of the mawlid also concerns the men of religion themselves. Ulama who are on good terms systematically invite one another, while publicly welcoming a representative of a rival clerical faction is also a common means to initiate a détente.

The rows of chairs are occupied by two categories of people: on the one hand the hosts, including the shaykh of the mosque,[7] his senior disciples, and his notable supporters, and on the other guest clerics and other notables. In general, guests do not attend the entire celebration, which results in ceaseless comings and goings between the entrance of the mosque and its "choir". In order to reach the "choir", distinguished visitors have to walk through the crowd, sometimes through a passage delimited by cordons. On their way, they are greeted by a disciple of the organising shaykh. Once they reach the "choir", the ulama and notables who are already present stand up from their chairs to embrace or exchange handshakes with the newcomers. By greeting each other in this way, hosts and visitors display a sense of social equality, and therefore of superiority over common people, since the latter usually greet clerics by kissing their hand. Particularly old and respected shaykhs are subject to special treatment. When they are among the hosts, they do not stand up when guests arrive but rather wait for them to come and kiss their hand or forehead. Likewise, if they are among the visitors, they are immediately surrounded by respectful hosts when they reach the rows of chairs, which they sometimes do on an improvised litter, that is, an armchair borne by three or four young men. Some guests might also choose to sit among the audience out of modesty. In this case, the hosting shaykh sends one of his disciples to request them to join the notables on the rows of chairs.

Half a dozen times during the evening, religious hymns stop to make place for the ulama's speeches. As mentioned above, these speeches usually take advantage of the occasion to deal with issues of morality and Islamic unity. The first of them is given by the master of ceremonies, in general a close disciple of the shaykh of the mosque. The shaykh's address, which occurs later in the evening, is generally the most important moment of the ceremony. As a gesture of respect, major guest clerics are often also asked to speak. The celebration closes with an invocation (*du'a'*) led by a scholar chosen for his ripe old age – which is synonymous with godly blessing (*baraka*) – or for his remarkable eloquence, or for some other "diplomatic" reason.

Throughout the evening, the crowd watches the "show" and generally remains quiet and still. It does not sing along with the munshidun and is not even invited to do so. Except for the concluding prayer and invocation, the only participation that is requested from the audience – above all, to ensure its attention – is to pronounce the ritual formula "May Allah honour Him and grant Him peace" (*salla Allah-u 'alayhi wa sallam*) each time the Prophet's name is mentioned in a speech.

Spending many hours in Syrian mawalid has often led me to wonder if the audience was really content with the very formal ceremony that offers so little entertainment, let alone an atmosphere of spirituality similar to that of the Sufi *dhikr* sessions. A possible answer would be that people are not looking for "fun" but rather to abide by a religious and social obligation.[8] This is of course partly true, but many Syrians do expect some entertainment from the mawlid. In particular, a sizeable proportion of them are obviously more interested in its musical dimension than in anything else. For instance, one of my informants did not attend the mawlid in the mosque of his own shaykh because the hymns were sung by a choir of students whose voices he deemed "ordinary". Instead, he attended another mosque known for hiring "the best *munshid* in Syria". During another mawlid, hearing a foreign female spectator marvelling at the lead singer's voice, a woman seated next to her said: "Why do you think we're here?"[9] Accordingly, videos and CDs of the celebrations that are sold on pavements and in Islamic bookshops are frequently edited in order to cut out the ulama's speeches, thus leaving only religious hymns. The people's quest for real "fun" is also obvious in the rare outdoor mawalid that have been allowed by the authorities for a decade as part of a progressive relaxation of the restrictions on Sunni religious activities. Held in pedestrian areas or public gardens, such celebrations sometimes include more festive features like whirling dervishes, who are now mostly professional dancers. Outside the sacred space of the mosque, spectators behave differently: they remain seated but are frequently seen singing enthusiastically while "dancing" by moving their arms. Whereas the organisers prevent people from actually dancing by disapprovingly waving at the few spectators who stand up out of enthusiasm, they do not prevent the "seated dancers". Nevertheless, some clerics privately condemn this behaviour and assert that mawalid should remain inside the mosques in order to avoid such "excesses".

Even indoors, however, Muslim scholars do not always manage to prevent the crowd from turning the mawlid into a real "party". That is what I observed in a mosque of the humble southern Midan quarter in April 2007. As usual, the mawlid began as a tribute to the ulama and more precisely to the ninety-year-old, paralysed shaykh of the mosque. Emotions rose as soon as the venerable cleric was carried into the mosque by three robust men. People crowded around him to touch his clothes in order to get some of his baraka. Indeed, this shaykh is viewed as a saint because of the seventy years he spent providing religious education to the people of the quarter, his Sufi affiliation as well as his anti-regime credentials, since he took refuge in Lebanon in the uprising of the 1980s during which he was abducted by the Syrian secret service. Later in the evening, devotion to the scholar's persona constituted a pretext for the audience to break the protocol.

The "incident" occurred after the shaykh's senior students started a Sufi dhikr, which is not uncommon in a mawlid. According to the Shadhili tradition to which the shaykh is affiliated, the dhikr is a tightly organised collective practice where participants form concentric circles or squares and follow the rhythm set by the "master of ceremonies". In this case, however, ranks rapidly broke apart when enthusiastic young people headed towards the centre of the prayer hall and started running in circles around the shaykh's chair. Seeing that things were getting completely out of control, the organisers abruptly put an end to the dhikr. In order to calm the participants, they invited them to stand in a queue in order to kiss a relic of the Prophet contained in a small cushion (a practice known as *taqbil al-athar*, "kissing the relic"). Whereas in such circumstances the faithful generally wait for their turn in a very orderly fashion, this time, overexcited young people were literally fighting with each other to get access to the cushion. Staff then asked the audience to leave the mosque, throwing handfuls of candy into the courtyard in order to encourage the younger members to do so. After a few more attempts at fighting between young teenagers, the mosque eventually emptied.

Comments

Syrian ulama often oppose the orthopraxy of their mawalid to the "un-Islamic" practices that are observed in the religious festivals of countries like Egypt. Indeed, in the latter case, reformist attempts at "civilising" popular religious festivals have only partially succeeded,[10] whereas in Syrian cities, the "scholarly" mawlid – which is in no way a recent custom[11] – has been the only form of public Sunni religious celebration for half a century. This is partly the result of social change and the subsequent spread of modernist-reformist conceptions, which as early as the 1950s dealt a fatal blow to popular religious festivals such the "Thursday of the Shaykhs" in Homs.[12] Of course the concern of the Ba'thist regime for public order has also played a major role, since most outdoor Sunni festivals were banned from the 1960s onwards, thus leaving mosques as the only venues for such celebrations. However, as we have seen, a fundamental tension remains between two competing conceptions of the performance of the mawlid: on the one hand, the clergymen's ceremonious approach, and on the other, the audience's quest for entertainment.

Even though it is probably easier to force puritan Damascene bourgeois to sit quietly for several hours than to do the same with peasants of the Nile Delta, the modalities of the mawlid I have described in this article are not a mere expression of Syria's "sober" urban culture. In more popular neighbourhoods, in particular, these modalities remain under the permanent threat of "carnivalisation", with the result that the rules of "proper" conduct must be reasserted by the organisers. What is the cause of the Syrian ulama's strong commitment to this particular form of mawlid performance? In my view, concerns for orthopraxy are important but do not constitute a sufficient explanation.

Using Mikhael Bakhtin's conceptualisation, Samuli Schielke describes the popular Egyptian saints' festivals as "carnivals", which means that they are characterised by the temporary suspension of usual social norms, and that they know no separation between participants and spectators since they are performed by the latter themselves in a spontaneous and disorderly way. In Bakhtin's view, the subversive potential of carnivals explains the dominant classes' attempts at turning them into "spectacles", that is, celebrations where performers are clearly distinct from a passive audience.[13] Schielke, who is chiefly concerned with state policies towards the mawlid, shows that a diffusionist model – that is, the spread of modernist conceptions of order and public morality since the nineteenth century – better explain modern attempts at reforming the mawlid than Bakhtin's class analysis.[14] In my case study, however, I think that what is at stake is a certain conception of social order. What Syrian Muslim scholars are protecting by retaining the current form of mawlid – which existed centuries before the emergence of modernist ideas – is their own prestige and authority. Indeed, as it is performed in Syria, the mawlid is a theatrical device that stages an idealised social order dominated by the ulama and their notable friends, and celebrates them rather than the community as a whole.

In Bakhtinian terms, the Syrian urban mawlid constitutes an ideal type of "anti-carnival" because it is a highly ritualised spectacle. The clerics' authority is not only displayed through their monopoly on speech but, more importantly, through the "formulaic spatiality" of the celebration.[15] Interestingly, this organisation radically contradicts the egalitarian scheme of the Muslim collective prayer, where all believers pray in the same direction and, as far as possible, side by side. In contrast, during the mawlid clerics and notables sit on chairs and *face* common people, who sit on carpets. Hierarchy is thus made even more visible than in the Friday sermon, at the end of which the preacher comes back down from his pulpit in order to pray in company with his co-religionists, or in the Sufi dhikr, where the shaykh also occupies a central position but takes his place on the perimeter of a circle or square formed by his disciples. In the mawlid, moreover, the "embracing ritual" allows the audience to assess the number and quality of the shaykh's friends among the notables, that is, his social capital. He is the only one who decides who has the right to sit in pride of place, which is made very clear when distinguished visitors who choose to sit among the crowd are then publicly designated by the host as worthy of being seated with the other notables.

As noted above, the fact that the mawlid celebrates the ulama as much as it glorifies the Prophet is almost never acknowledged by local religious actors. However, a few weeks after my last stay in Syria, in the spring of 2008, I discovered a counter-example in the recently published hagiography of Shaykh 'Abd al-Karim al-Rifa'i, a Damascene scholar who died in 1973. Evoking al-Rifaʻi's commitment to the celebration of the mawlid, the text describes it in the following way:

> Those who enter the mosque on this occasion feel like they are in one of the gardens of Paradise because the ulama, these heirs of the beloved Prophet, are at the centre of the assembly. Through this crowd of Muslims, Damascus displays its joy in belonging to this religion as well as its loyalty to its ulama.[16]

This highly unusual account results from one of the many peculiarities of al-Rifaʻi's biography: whereas such texts traditionally focus on Muslim scholars' incommensurable knowledge and outstanding moral virtues, this one also pays much attention to the shaykh's social *practices*. It is probably too early to speak of a "descriptive turn" in the Islamic biography genre, but this new approach reflects deep changes in the conception of Muslim sainthood, an issue that falls outside the scope of this article.

Conclusion

In Syria, the celebration of the Mawlid is presented by its proponents as a way to invite Muslims to come back to the righteous path of the Prophet as well as an occasion for reuniting them around the founding figure of Muhammad. Ethnography, however, reveals another aspect of this celebration, that is, the fact that it is first and foremost a ritualised spectacle staging the authority of the ulama. Indeed, the spatial organisation of the ceremony and the theatrical welcome of notables, in particular merchants, make the clerics appear as the dominant element within an idealised social order. In order to maintain this hierarchical pattern, the ulama have to contain the common people's quest for enjoyment and emotion. Even though they do so in the name of orthopraxy, I have shown that what is more fundamentally at stake here is to determine who is to be celebrated during the mawlid: the clergy, or the community as a whole.

Notes

1. Depending on the context, the Arabic term *mawlid* (plural, *mawalid*) designates the Prophet's birthday itself, its actual celebration, or a celebration that follows the same modalities (see my description below) but is organised at another moment in the year, for instance on the occasion of a marriage or in honour of guests. I will use the written form "Mawlid" in the case of the former and "mawlid" in the case of the latter two.
2. J. W. McPherson, *The Moulids of Egypt (Egyptian saints-days)*, Cairo: Ptd N. M. Press, 1941; Nicolaas Biegman, *Egypt. Moulids Saints Sufis*, Den Haag: Gary Schwartz, 1990; Samuli Schielke, "On Snacks and Saints: When Discourses of Rationality

and Order Enter the Egyptian Mawlid", *Archives de sciences sociales des religions*, no. 135, pp. 117–40, *http://assr.revues.org/index3765.html* (accessed 30 March 2010).
3. See Julian Johansen, *Sufism and Islamic Reform in Egypt. The Battle for Islamic Tradition*, Oxford: Clarendon Press, 1996, pp. 70–1; Marion Holmes Katz, *The Birth of the Prophet Muhammad: Devotional Piety in Sunni Islam*, London: Routledge, 2007, pp. 169–207.
4. Sa'id Ramadan al-Buti, *Hadha Walidi* [This is my Father], Damascus: Dar al-Fikr, 1995, pp. 130–1; Sa'id Hawwa, *Hadhihi Tajribati ... wa hadhihi Shahadati* [This is my Experience ... This is my Testimony], Cairo: Dar Wahba, 1987, pp. 130–1.
5. Observations by the author.
6. Thomas Pierret and Kjetil Selvik, "Limits of Authoritarian Upgrading in Syria. Welfare Privatization, Islamic Charities and the Rise of the Zayd Movement", *International Journal of Middle East Studies*, vol. 41, no. 4, November 2009, p. 595.
7. In Syria, the shaykh of a mosque (an informal title) is the mosque's most senior *teacher*, but not necessarily its imam or Friday preacher.
8. Attending the mawlid is not a formal religious obligation like the two *Eid* prayers. However, the social importance of this event is such that many committed Syrian Muslims see it as compulsory.
9. I thank Nathalie Bontemps for this anecdote.
10. Schielke, "On Snacks and Saints", p. 135.
11. On the history of the Mawlid, see Frederick De Jong, "Mawlid", in Edmund Bosworth, Emeri van Donzel, Charles Pellat (eds), *Encyclopaedia of Islam*, 2nd edn, Leiden: Brill, 1991, vol. 6, pp. 895–7; Nico Kaptein, *Muhammad's Birthday Festival: Early History in the Central Muslim Lands and Development in the Muslim West until the 10th/16th Century*, Leiden: Brill, 1993.
12. Jean-Yves Gillon, *Anciennes fêtes de printemps à Homs* [Ancient Spring Festivals in Homs], Damas: IFPO, 1993, pp. 68–71.
13. Schielke, "On Snacks and Saints", p. 120. Schielke relies on Mikhail Bakhtin, *Rabelais and His World*, Cambridge, MA: MIT Press, 1968.
14. Schielke, "On Snacks and Saints", pp. 135–6.
15. David Parkin, "Ritual as Spatial Direction and Bodily Division", in Daniel de Coppet (ed.), *Understanding Rituals*, London: Routledge, 1992, pp. 11–25. On this concept, see Yazid Ben Hounet's contribution in this volume.
16. 'Al-Shaykh 'Abd al-Karim al-Rifa'i wa Masiratuhu al-Da'wiyya – 12 [Shaykh 'Abd al-Karim al-Rifa'i and his Course in the Islamic Call], *Sada Zayd* (website), 20 April 2008, *www.sadazaid.com/play.php?catsmktba=3165* (accessed: 30 March 2010).

Part Two

Contextualising Interactions

CHAPTER 10

The Salafi and the Others: An Ethnography of Intracommunal Relations in French Islam

Cédric Baylocq and Akila Drici-Bechikh

Salafism is a religious and/or political phenomenon that only recently emerged in Europe, at the beginning of the 1990s.[1] Etymologically, *al-salafiyya* (Salafism) designates the Companions of the Prophet, the righteous forefathers who should be imitated because they were in close contact with the perfect Muslim model (that is, the Prophet Muhammad himself). By imitating them, contemporary Salafis claim to be in search of a "pure Islam",[2] contrary to any other Muslim group (*firqa*) that does not strictly follow this path. However, we argue that even though it is important to know the doctrinal aspects of such a (non-homogeneous) movement, its comprehension, particularly in Europe, requires a focus on how this "minority within a minority" deals with its day-to-day insertion in broader local religious and social fields and how it interacts with the non-Salafi context surrounding it. For that purpose, the authors *embedded* themselves inside both Salafi and mainstream Muslim groups in order to propose an original panorama of intracommunal relationships among the different tendencies and sensibilities of French Muslims, especially between a local Salafi group on the one hand and the representative of the main mosque on the other. This chapter is divided into three parts.

In the first part, we will describe a study of a group of women who "converted" to Salafism in a suburb of Paris.[3] We will focus particularly on the representations they share concerning their co-religionists who did not follow them onto the alleged "straight path".

In the second part, we will analyse a split that occurred among Muslims in the south-western city of Bordeaux, when young Salafis left the mosque run by Tareq Oubrou, an imam and self-made scholar affiliated to the Muslim Brotherhood-oriented *Union des Organisations Islamiques de France* (UOIF).

To conclude, the third part will provide two short descriptive scenes of interaction involving Salafis and non-Salafis in order to try to further understand the attraction/repulsion between the two groups.

In our opinion, this attention to common interactions is more likely to render a faithful (as far as possible) picture of the complex threads that constitute the canvas of the pluralistic Muslim community in France. Consequently we posit ourselves regarding ethnomethodology as defined by Benson and Hugues, as we examine "the ordinary, common-sense, mundane world in which members live and do so in a way that remains faithful to the methods, procedures, practices, etc., that members themselves use in constructing and making sense of this social world".[4]

From Regular Muslima to "the Straight Path": Conceptions of the Self and of Co-religionists among Salafi Women

Religious classes are held by Salafis on a non-regular basis in the poor suburbs of Paris, where the majority of the inhabitants are North African or of North African descent. We attended one of these classes in 2007. The meeting, which was held in Fatima's 70m² apartment on the eighth floor of a typical French HLM (Habitation à Loyer Modéré/low-income housing) building constructed during the 1960s–70s, quickly reached fifteen persons.

Fatima is a forty-year-old woman. She studied Shari'a for four years in Saudi Arabia and is married to the (Salafi) imam of the local mosque. She complained about the difficulty of finding a suitable place for the classes. Consequently, she welcomed "any person who would like to strengthen their knowledge about religion" for a two-hour talk each afternoon in her own apartment., All the attendants were female and most of them were French-born. Some of our informants "did not want to get in trouble" and asked that their names and their location not be mentioned. Interestingly enough, they seemed to be more worried about how they would be regarded from outside the Muslim community than from inside. The debate on *niqab* (face veil) that arose three years later in the French public sphere would confirm their fear. Nevertheless, when we first joined the course, Fatima, the leader of the group, did not yet realise that we were there for an academic study.

In the entrance, a poster on the wall advertised products from Saudi Arabia, ranging from books written by Salafi shaykhs, to niqab, *jilbab*, gloves and a moisturising cream. The latter particularly drew the women's attention, not only due to its geographic origin, but also to its nigella-based composition (*habba sawda*), whose value is well known for having been praised by the Prophet himself. This particular religious lesson was dedicated to "the effects of *salat* on the improvement of faith". Fatima started the lesson by quoting a list of references in connection with the theme, including medieval scholar Ibn Hazm (d. 1063), a proponent of the literalist Zahiri school of fiqh.

Before starting the lesson, Fatima asked if any of the attendees had an unlimited mobile phone line in order to contact "other sisters" to allow them to benefit from the class. About ten of the attendants used this means to get in touch with acquaintances.

Fatima, dressed in a *jilbab*, began the lesson by exhorting everybody to question themselves and undergo a thorough process of self-reformation:

> Real life requires continuous strife to improve oneself, because we must be convinced that we are full of sins. We must first and foremost acknowledge that fact about ourselves in order for us to progress. And even though criticism hurts, you have to go through it because most of the time compliments are fraught with hypocrisy.

This incipit, meant to increase the audience's receptivity, is common to Salafi sermons, which begin by stressing the reality of sin in order to pave the way for the presentation of the righteous path, meaning the Salafi straight path.

During the lesson, Fatima was interrupted four times by her children whom she kept close to her throughout. These interruptions were seized as opportunities to insist on the role of women in education and the transmission of religious values. She even went as far as to say that being a good housewife does not only consist of keeping the house clean and taking care of children, but also of helping the husband out of difficult situations (professionally or otherwise) and particularly when "his faith could be weakened by the predicaments of life". She thus emphasised the religious importance of the Muslim wife on more than simply the domestic level of her common daily "duties". Contrary to the widespread belief that argues that Salafi women are totally committed and submitted to the religious authority of their husbands (which could also be true), we can see here how she engaged in a relatively feminist discourse *inside* radical Islam.

After the class, Hanan aged twenty-two, agreed to give us an account of her decision to follow this specific religious school. At the time we met, she lived in the eighteenth arrondissement of Paris. She holds a *baccalauréat* with a major in socio-medical sciences. Talking about her own religious education, she carefully said: "I worshipped as my mum said ... Ramadan ... all those little things everybody does" as a way to avoid blaming her mother but at the same time to convey the idea that the Muslim practices which were transmitted to her were insufficient. Her husband, whom she met at college, introduced her to the study of religion through bookshops initially and then via Salafi mosques.

She told us she used to be surrounded by Muslim friends whose practice of Islam was, according to her, "kept at a minimum". Moreover, she perceived the link her family had with religion as being narrow and insufficient. This link was maintained only through cultural practices and their homeland (Morocco). Her husband clearly appeared to be the key factor behind her "conversion to Salafism", as she said he was the one who encouraged her "to renew her ties with Islam". The choice of the latter expression shows that for Hanane, adhering to Salafism was akin to conversion. She then made use of an interesting comparison to account for her religiosity:

> If I may use the image of a plane, I would say that the *Ikhwan* [the Muslim Brotherhood] use only one wing. They would not take much heed of all that is forbidden; they would only pick up the brighter side of things and refrain from doing certain things in order to please other people. The Salafi, for me, invokes the image of a plane flying with the help of both its wings and which, therefore, finds balance. Some things are *halal* (licit) and others *haram* (illicit). Some things are good and others bad, whether it is in our time or in any other.

This metaphor of the plane using either one of its wings or both is interchangeable with another Salafi binary discourse on "purity" and "authenticity" versus "hypocrisy" and "innovation", and exemplary of how a dichotomy is put in relief.

Courses such as Fatima's continue to be held, and they regularly welcome new attendants. This particular Salafi group is in control of the mosque where Fatima's husband preaches. Thus, it seems to be autonomous enough not to have any relationships (or, if any, very restricted) with the so-called "Ikhwanis", who dominate French Islam administratively (through UOIF).

Same Qibla, Other Mosque: From the "Neo-Ikhwani" Mosque to the "Salafi Mosque".

As we were walking down the street on our way to the main mosque of Bordeaux (*El Huda*), nearly thirty minutes before the sermons (*khutba*) of the Friday prayer (*salat al-jum'a*), a man in his thirties, dressed in a *gandura* (robe), head covered with a typical round hat (*taqiya*), called out to us: "Are you going to the *jum'a?*" He was just leaving the Muslim library where he worked. He subsequently added, without even pausing for an answer: "Because we are going to Bègles; so you can join us if you wish, brother!" Indeed, an old Renault truck, full of other Muslim companions of his, was parked in front of the library, ready to leave; a few metres ahead, the local mosque *El Huda* was welcoming its earliest attendants for the forthcoming sermon. The local Salafis of course kept the same direction to pray (*qibla*) but had shifted towards a new mosque.

The scene described above occurred in 2008 and it bears witness to the tension between two poles of the local French "Muslim market": the central mosque administered by the *Association des Musulmans de la Gironde* (AMG),[5] a reformist branch of the *Muslim Brotherhood*, and a Salafi-oriented mosque at the urban periphery (Bègles). If the men in the Renault truck felt the need to turn to the Salafi-oriented mosque when their little library was just next door to the older and bigger mosque of the AMG, it is because they rejected the religious authority of the latter's imam, Tareq Oubrou. Under his influence, the AMG has developed strong ties outside the community with local institutions and other faith groups, including Jews, which has upset the local Salafi group and even some local mainstream Muslims.

On the other hand, Imam Tareq Oubrou reproaches the Salafis (even if not openly naming them) for the troubles and "anomie" they cause among the Muslim community and even sometimes among their own families when misusing *da'wa* (to spread the call to Islam). Indeed, in Bordeaux as in many other places, Salafis sometimes undertake *da'wa* by using the notion of *"al-firqat al-najiya"* ("saved group"). This rhetorical technique relies on the "hadith of the seventy-three sects", according to which only one out of seventy-three groups of Muslims will escape the fires of hell.

The Salafi mosque (or, more properly, prayer room) is located 15 kilometres from the inner city of Bordeaux in a suburb called Bègles. It was inaugurated in 2008 by the local mayor Noël Mamère, a prominent leader of the Green political party. Progressively, a young group of Salafis moved from the "historical" mosque to this new one. Even though this initial Salafi cell attracted other Salafi-oriented local Muslims, the congregation is far from being exclusively Salafi. Umar, the imam providing the sermon (*imam khatib*) of the mosque is in his thirties. Umar refused to have an interview with us, although we had had favourable initial contact with him right before he went "abroad for a few weeks", as he told us during the first and only short talk we had (September 2009). This could be due to the fact that we had, in the meantime, co-authored a book with Imam Tareq Oubrou. In fact, Umar used to have close relations with the two main AMG imams: Tareq Oubrou and Mahmoud Doua (see the final part of this chapter for an account of the latter). But he had broken these ties, after Imam Oubrou publicly minimised the importance of the veil for Muslim women, compared to other Muslim practices.[6]

It is notable that Umar is the first imam of sub-Saharan African origins to become the leading imam of a mosque in the whole local Muslim community. As this Salafi group is a minority within a minority, it cannot rely solely on Arab-born Muslims, but must include faithful from other origins (converts of European descent as well as youth of sub-Saharan descent). Hence, it is noticeable that there is no "Arab hegemony" among this local Salafi group, contrary to the neo-Ikhwani group which leads the older mosque. Even though there is no particular ethnic focus among this group, they are theologically committed to Saudi Arabia's Muslim scholars. As a result, while the Salafi group is not ethnically Arab-centred, it fundamentally remains so, culturally and theologically speaking. On the other hand, the heads and religious leaders of the main mosque are mostly Arab-Moroccan but claim to be culturally French and even theologically open to adapt to their cultural context when possible and necessary. Here is the interesting apparent paradox of those two groups: culture and theology are not at all defined by their respective ethnic composition.

We finally learned that Umar was excluded from preaching at the mosque of Bègles. This is not apparently due to a pressure of the attendency but we were not able to collect reliable explanations on why he was excluded. But this neo-Salafi group reacted quite quickly by opening a new prayer room, in a space measuring approximately 100 square metres, just a few hundred metres from the main mosque of Bordeaux. They named it "*L'Oasis de la science*".

A "Strained Brotherhood": Scenes of Interaction Between Salafi and Non-Salafi French Muslims

At the beginning of 2009, Samir, a twenty-nine-year-old French Muslim, asked us some questions about Shi'ism. We gave him a short account of the emergence of the Twelver Shi'i, the principles of *wilayat al-faqih*, and the status of Ali and Hussein. Our account happened to run counter to the opinion of an Algerian friend of his who was in our company and who held that the Shi'i prefer "Ali to the Prophet Muhammad", an idea commonly held among Sunni Muslims. Recently, Samir saw a copy of Imam Khomeini's *Spiritual and Political Testament* in my personal library and borrowed it in order to learn about Shi'i ideas directly from this source without any intention of sharing Shi'i views. Samir is a regular worshipper, and a *zabiba* (a mark supposedly resulting from frequent prayer) had progressively become visible on his forehead in the last five years. His commitment to Islam towards the end of his adolescence had been decisive in bringing to an end his early delinquency. But contrary to some former delinquents who directly turn to Salafism or Tabligh (an apolitical re-Islamisation movement that originated in India), Samir's religious drift did not lead him to a rupture with his multicultural background, for he has continued to maintain his taste for American rap music, Italian and Spanish culture (he has a fair level of fluency in both languages even though he does not hold academic degrees) and a large network of non-Muslim friends and acquaintances (particularly among artists and musicians). Samir has a genuine admiration for local Imam Tareq Oubrou: "His *khutba* make sense to me. It's is a *rahma* (mercy) to have him here in Bordeaux" (June 2007).

One day, as Samir was walking through the biggest mall in Bordeaux, carrying Ayatollah Khomeini's *Testament* in his hand, he came across a Salafi "brother" he had met several times before at the mosque. After the customary "*as-salam'alaykum*", the Salafi saw Khomeini's book in Samir's hand and expressed his indignation while trying to remove it from his hands (the following scene relies on Samir's account):

– *Astaghfiru'llah* ("May God forgive me"), brother, this guy is a big *shaitan*! Why do you read this?!
– Get your hand off this book! It is not mine! I have to bring it back!
– But what is the use of reading this?
– And so what!? What is it with you? Are you intending to impose a list of permissible and forbidden items on me?!

When describing the scene to us, Samir said: "Though I will not question his being in the *din* ["din" means "religion"; here it means by extension "being a good Muslim"], how can you take him seriously when he shouts at you?" Samir now imitates perfectly the markedly hustling tone of youth from the suburbs with an exaggerated slow rhythm to ridicule his contradictor: "Really, it's not good, broza'; it's not good what you're doing with respect to science [i.e. Islamic science]!" ("Franchement c'est pas bien mon frèr', c'est pas bien c'qu'tu fais au niveau de la science!"). While we were laughing at his admirable imitation, Samir concluded harshly: "Science, science ... as if one could pretend to be talking about engineering when not even holding a lower degree in mechanics and having such poor language as well."

Even though prominent local Ikhwanis, non-affiliated Muslims and local Salafis still maintained narrow ties, we noticed that these ties are maintained largely due to a charismatic man called Anas whose past illegal activities as well as his subsequent sincere repentance are known to all.

Anas is in his forties, and although he "looks like" a Salafi (long beard, *kameez* (a long shirt) and a taqiya on his head) he does not present himself as such. During our three meetings (between March and May 2010) he did not even depict himself as a member of *Ahl al-Sunna wa-l-jama'a*, even though he tries "to follow this path". He simply refuses to label himself as well as his fellow Muslims in one way or another: "Listen to me, he said; I don't want to know about all that stuff! I am just relying on God and his Prophet '*salla 'llahu'alay-hi-wa-salam!*'" ("praise and peace be on him"). For Anas, "everybody is part of the same Umma". This shows how difficult it would be to try to encapsulate a religious identity within a particular Islamic group: while looking like a Salafi or a Tablighi, Anas refuses to be labelled, thus undermining (perhaps involuntarily) the major argument used by Salafis for recruitment: their claim to being "*Al-Firqa al-Najiya*" ("the saved group").

Anas had a long career in crime (drug dealing and burglaries). He used to be very close to one of the most important godfathers of the French Mafia from southern France, assassinated in recent years during a wave of bloody reprisal. He is known among friends of North-African descent for his reputation in this environment (the nickname he gets from that period still circulates in the community, but not in front of him as far as we know). He turned to religion in jail through discussion with a convert of European descent. Thus, he particularly targets this category of the French population better than those of North-African descent as "it is their duty to be Muslim, they received the Message …" When he was released from jail, he became close to the leaders of the AMG by attending prayer and lectures on Islam in their mosques.

Anas recently reinforced his role as mediator between local Salafis and local neo-Ikhwanis after the turmoil ignited by Oubrou's statement on the veil (see note 6). Basically, the local imam relativised its importance by comparing it to other religious duties, particularly internal religious dispositions such as generosity, mercy, kindness and the like (which are all part of *al akhlaq*, the moral dimensions of Islam). While Salafis contacted a shaykh in the Middle East to ask if they "can still pray behind him [viz. Oubrou]", Anas asked Tareq Oubrou for a discussion due to the growing criticism of him by the local Salafi group. Eventually Oubrou received Anas at home for dinner a few weeks after the incident. This long discussion seems to be an important milestone in the relationship between Anas and the imam. It explains the obvious respect Anas shows when speaking about Oubrou, even though he spends part of his time with Salafi brothers. However, notwithstanding Oubrou detailing his theological views to Anas during this meeting, a more practical fact apparently attracted Anas' attention. Indeed, he focused particularly on the fact that the imam's "wife and daughter do wear *hijab*". Thus, he concluded that Oubrou is not "against" hijab, and used this to calm the Salafi beliefs about and criticism of Oubrou. We could therefore hypothesise that he used this (apparently) convincing argument to try to calm Salafi critics. Thus, his role could be deemed the most important human factor in avoiding the complete *fitna* of the local Muslim community while an urban split happened.

Moreover, Anas was also a key person when an important event occurred which could have caused a decisive rupture between local Salafis and neo-Ikhwanis. In July 2009, Imam Mahmoud Doua, who leads the prayer in Cenon (a lower to lower-middle class suburb of Bordeaux on the northern side of the Garonne river) and also teaches a course on Islamic civilisation at the University of Bordeaux, was assaulted by two Salafi youngsters. Apparently, the young Salafis refused to shake Mahmoud Doua's hand because he did not defend *niqab* during a TV programme in which he was interviewed.[7] Mahmoud Doua then quoted a hadith which states that "a scholar does not care about the gossip of an ignorant" as he was hurt by the boys' behaviour. Following this, his interlocutor violently pushed Mahmoud Doua onto the ground. Then several people standing close by separated them. Supported by AMG, Mahmoud Doua decided to lodge a complaint. The day this happened, Anas promptly visited the two youngsters in order to admonish them as "stupid" for having done such a reprehensible thing, as this was disrespectful to the imam and detrimental to the image of the community. Anas told them: "Are you visited by representatives of all kinds when they want to talk with Muslim people?! No! HE is! ... Now we are done for good everywhere because of you. It spreads on the internet and all!"

Afterwards, Anas helped negotiate a settlement between the two parties.

Conclusion

A local, ethnographic observation of the multiple trends of Islam in France shows a complex network of inter-relationships in which each group competes for religious legitimacy and authenticity as we witnessed by attending a Salafi women's course and by interviewing one of the participants. The growing distance between the local imam Tareq Oubrou (who paved his singular and independent way from within the large and multifaceted Muslim Brotherhood trend) and the local Salafi also exemplifies this fact. We also saw that some individuals went even further and physically attacked another well-known local imam they disagreed with (that is, the case of Mahmoud Doua and the issue of the niqab).

However, factors such as being a minority, urban proximity and probably a reciprocal and strenuous subconscious fear that division could cause the loss of the umma finally helped to build a *modus vivendi* between Salafis and non-Salafis (that is, neo-Ikhwanis and mainstream French Muslims in this case) that does not often exist in Muslim-majority countries.

Salafis show an increasing ability to reach youngsters, particularly those living in poor neighbourhoods. Thus, they are now in a process of elaborating alternative forms of religious socialisation through study groups of Qur'an or hadith (as we saw with the Salafi women's religious class in Paris). It is fairly clear we are witnessing "the formation of a distinct community on the public scene that is developing another identity"[8] as Marie Miran put it in the case of Wahhabism in sub-Saharan Africa.

Tension can be clearly noted between the need to maintain a social and religious life connected to "other" members of local Muslim community and that of keeping a "safe distance". And yet, local Salafis did not brand other Muslims as infidels as some ties remained between them and local neo-Ikhwanis. Nevertheless, this stability seems to be precarious and there is no evidence to suggest it will last. It remains for us to say that ethnographic enquiry allowed us to depict this precariousness and day-to-day human negotiation whereas a broad approach focusing on doctrines, religious texts or even official claims through website or videos would have (merely) depicted the surface of the social and religious "reality".

Notes

1. We would like to thank Oussama Ayara (University of Kairouan, Tunisia) for his involvement in correcting and helping translate parts of the paper and Martijn de Koning (University of Nijmegen, the Netherlands) for the critical remarks he generously provided.
2. See notably Martijn de Koning, *Zoeken naar een "zuivere" islam* [Searching for a "Pure" Islam]. *Geloofsbeleving en identiteitsvorming onder jonge Marokkaans-Nederlandse moslims*, Amsterdam: Bert Bakker, 2008 (forthcoming in English).
3. Martijn de Koning also uses the term "conversion" for Muslims who turn Salafis in "Changing Worldviews and Friendship. An Exploration of the Life Stories of Two Female Salafis in the Netherlands", in Roel Meijer (ed.), *Global Salafism. Islam's New Religious Movement*, London: Hurst & Co., 2009, p. 420.
4. Douglas Benson, and John A. Hughes, *The Perspective of Ethnomethodology*, London; New York: Longman, 1983, p. 30.
5. AMG is linked to the UOIF, which is known to be inspired by the Muslim Brotherhood. This label should be used with care, however, since it does not take into account the reform and autonomisation processes among the European "inheritors" of this movement. See Cédric Baylocq, "The autonomisation of the Muslim Brotherhood in Europe: *da'wa*, mixité and non-Muslims", in Roel Meijer and Edwin Bakker (eds), *The Muslim Brotherhood in Europe. Burdens of the Past, Challenges of the Future*, London: Hurst & Co., 2011, pp. 179–205.
6. See www.lemonde.fr/societe/article/2009/10/15/tareq-oubrou-les-musulmans-doivent-adapter-leurs-pratiques-a-la-societe-francaise_1254356_3224.html (accessed December 2009).
7. *C dans l'air*, France 5, 19 July 2009. Mahmoud Doua said that niqab does not have any kind of Islamic legitimacy but rather corresponds to a cultural practice. Nevertheless he was opposed to the ban.
8. Marie Miran, "Le wahhabisme à Abidjan, dynamisme urbain d'un islam réformiste en Côte d'Ivoire contemporaine", *Islam et sociétés au Sud du Sahara*, no. 12, 1998, p. 11.

Chapter 11

Describing Religious Practices among University Students: A Case Study from the University of Jordan, Amman

Daniele Cantini

Literature on the contemporary dimensions of Islamic movements in the Middle East has been growing steadily over the past decades. Anthropology has played its role in this process, especially in very recent years with a number of studies on piety movements, on ethical self-discipline, and on questions of identity and gender. What I believe is largely missing, however, are ethnographic accounts of how Muslims in the Middle East concretely embody and enact their religious belonging in everyday life. This is therefore the aim of this chapter, in which I will try to show how Jordanian university students represent themselves and their religiosity.

The data I present here is the result of fieldwork carried out over sixteen months between 2003 and 2005 during my PhD, mostly at the campus of the University of Jordan. I was a student myself, of Arabic, and this enabled me to spend much time with the students in their environment, to have mutual exchanges of information, and to pay close attention to their context through thorough participant observation, in which religion was just one interest among many others.

Jordan is often referred to as a "moderate" Arab country, with a pivotal role for the stability of the region; its population is quite consistent from a religious point of view, with almost 92 per cent Muslims, mostly Sunni. The educational system of the Kingdom is usually labelled as one of the best in the region, and higher education enrolment is equal to the United Kingdom, around 2.5 per cent of the total population. Like other neighbouring countries, the overall population is booming, with a consequent stress on the educational system and on access to the labour market. This is perceived as a potential threat to the stability of the country, and therefore the educational sector is given quite a prominent position within Jordanian public discourse.

Given these premises, I examined the Jordanian educational system, from within higher education, and particularly focused on students' lives and representations. I will not only try to describe their religious practices in the context in which they enact them, but also to develop some basic discourses on how students divide themselves, in order to deepen our comprehension of what it means to be a pious Muslim in a university environment; what it takes to be considered a "true" Muslim; and what are the concrete consequences of student practices. Thus, one of my aims is to show the political implications of the religious acts practised in this context, in order to highlight all the contradictions and the complexity of students' religious practices. I will begin by describing how Ramadan is lived by students, since it is one of the major religious events during the year and, as such, suitable for showing how religious practices are enacted.

Religious Practices on Campus

The ways in which people tend to live the month of Ramadan differ, of course, according to where one lives and to one's social and economic level. In Amman's crowded and popular neighbourhoods, Ramadan is indeed a total social fact, involving not only the act of fasting but the entire social life of individuals. In the more affluent and less crowded quarters, however, the holy month is spent in a more ordinary way. For example, no one wakes people up with drums at night one hour before dawn, when the fast begins; nor are there social gatherings in the streets after sunset, when the *iftar* breaks the fast and opens the very animated social life that follows at night. In these affluent areas the way of celebrating the festivity is much more in line with the Christian Christmas as it is performed today.[1]

Despite the social separation of the university campus from the city, it is possible to draw a similar distinction between the different faculties within the same university, with the interesting fact that the spatial differentiation between social groups is considerably lower than in the city. It is precisely this proximity, and the fact that it is perceived as such by many students who operate precise distinctions among the different social backgrounds of those attending certain faculties, that renders the object of this study suitable for showing contrasting ways of being religious within the same country, as well as within the same social category, such as "student" or "youth".

The campus, located on the northern edge of the city, is surrounded by walls, and its entrances are guarded by security staff. It is a pleasant, open space, with many green areas and small pathways, one of the very few spaces in town where youth can gather (almost) freely. The main gate leads to the clock tower, and to its left are the various faculties of humanities while the scientific faculties are grouped to its right. The library and the canteen are situated in the middle of the campus. Admission to the university is regulated by the marks a student obtains in the *tawjihi*, the national exam at the end of secondary school. There is a list that ranks the faculties hierarchically, from the "better" ones, in which a high grade is required for entry, to the less prestigious ones. For example, in the humanities, literature is at the top, and a student in 2003–4 required a grade of 92/100 in order to gain admission. This system was designed to be socially equitable, allowing students with better grades – regardless of their social and economic background – into the best faculties. In recent years, however, new liberalisation policies have introduced the possibility for students who do not have the required grades to pay a substantial amount of money to gain entry into the faculty they prefer. While some students of poorer origin are still present in the best faculties, the opposite is less the case since well-off students with poor grades will pay or enter private education rather than accept lower-grade faculties.

During Ramadan, class hours and academic life in general change for all faculties; days are shortened, and a couple of hours before iftar the campus is abandoned by nearly everyone. In the lower-grade faculties Ramadan is definitely an event, and life changes, even if it is just for twenty-eight days. Riad,[2] a student of education, explained that, "A lot of students leave classes to pray, and also some professors. During Ramadan, boys tend to stay more away from girls, and also the jokes are different – nobody speaks about sentimental affairs anymore." The normal chatting that takes place outside the faculties, which is usually devoted to flirting and exchanging jokes, becomes invariably devoted to the practices that one is to perform during the holy month,[3] and in general there is a certain form of competition in showing signs of religious piety.

"I love Ramadan because of the atmosphere it has; everybody behaves more properly, like it should be, and everything is better", said Yasmine, a student in her fourth year at the Faculty of Education, while other students quickly gathered around us in the courtyard, "It is a difficult month, since we have some obligations to perform, like reading the entire Qur'an and praying regularly, but all this is for the sake of God and comes easily". Another student then noted, "How very beautiful it is to perform the prayer during Ramadan", and after similar comments they recommended that I too should fast, as one stated: "If you want to understand our culture you have to understand our religion, and do as we do". I then asked what it means to fast and why it is so important; and I was told that "Fasting helps one to live like the poor people, at least for a month", "It is about learning how to control yourself, to renounce the good things in this life, like food and drinks, to gain paradise".

The situation is rather different, however, in the prestigious faculties. On the surface, the presence of Ramadan is also evident here, with the above-mentioned reduced hours and the university guards patrolling the paths of the campus – especially the areas where the less religious students are more likely to gather.[4] All eateries are closed and it is forbidden to smoke or drink anything in public. It is commonly understood that a certain degree of modesty and chastity should be deployed in all relations within the campus. Nevertheless, when I walked through the campus I was usually invited by male students to have a cigarette in a hidden place near the faculty, something that apparently was quite common among the students there who were engaging in various forms of public refusal of the imposed fasting.

Asal, a language student in her third year, once told me that she did not like Ramadan,

> because it is a period in which people want to show off their religiosity, while the true Islam should be completely different. This year I am trying to fast for the first time, I am also forcing my parents to do so even though they never did before, but I am doing it simply because I feel like doing it, and here [in the university] nobody knows about this.

This personal attitude, by which the act of fasting becomes something exotic that has to be tried in order to be added to one own experiences, is shared also by other students, such as Majd, who said that

> I'm fasting, only this year, but I really cannot live without my cigarettes, and that's why I keep smoking also while fasting. At the end, fasting is about food and beverages mostly, isn't it? I have been caught a couple of times, but I do not care.

There are of course also some religious students in these faculties and generally the two groups tend not to mingle, at least during Ramadan. As Leyla, a fourth-year student of literature, once explained me,

> I know how my companions will behave in this month, and since I believe in God I cannot accept it; also I cannot change it, so I'd rather not spend time at the university in this period and concentrate on praying and staying with the family.

"And why do you think some students behave like this?" I asked, and she replied, "They think that they'll be more cool this way, but they don't understand that they are simply offensive."

In the courtyard of the Faculty of Literature, however, segregation between boys and girls does not exist – not even during Ramadan – and mixed groups tend to gather, chatting and gossiping while waiting for the iftar to come. What is all the more interesting for this analysis, though, is the fact that those who practise Ramadan and those who do not share the same space within the campus – the Faculty of Education is less than 100 metres away from the Faculty of Literature, and in the immediate surroundings there is also the Faculty of Shari'a. They are therefore physically aware of the existence of differences, and these differences become a part of the construction of their selves, as I will show in greater detail in what follows.

Islam in Jordan is commonly understood as being quite monolithic and it is seldom questioned by anyone, including university students. Although there are exceptions to this at a personal level, the general principles of Islam remain largely unquestioned. Nevertheless, there are some differences in the understanding of how one should be Muslim, as already exemplified by Ramadan and its diverse practices. I will now further discuss the context of the university, in order to put forward a deeper understanding of what being a Muslim, in a Muslim country, entails.

One day I was having a coffee with some friends from the Faculty of Literature and I told them that I was going to the Faculty of Shari'a to conduct some interviews. The reaction was immediate, "Why do you go there? They are all backwards [*mutakhallifin*], they do not understand anything", said one of them, shortly followed by a female student who said,

> They simply impose their rules on students, regardless of their faculty; once I was chatting with a boy in the courtyard of their faculty and somebody came and started to shout at us saying that it was forbidden for a woman to speak with a boy! But of course I reacted, saying that this was nonsense and that we were inside the university, and in the end the man left.

Then another added that, "They simply state that everything is illicit (*haram*) and they're done with it".

The ways in which the students at the Faculty of Shari'a interact and socialise with each other are indeed quite different from those at the Faculty of Literature or of the best science faculties. Although the Faculty of Shari'a has an official religious character, its social and spatial dynamics are similar to many of the lower-status faculties. For example, boys and girls never mingle; they have separate stairs inside the building and they are segregated in the classrooms, with boys in the front to avoid indiscreet staring at the girls. Similarly, the lower-status faculties keep relations between boys and girls to a minimum; all girls are fully covered by the black robe (*'abaya*) which is usually associated with women of poorer social status and provincial geographical origin; interactions between the sexes are usually avoided. Consequently I had little if any interaction with girls there, and with few exceptions, the boys were also not keen to speak with a foreigner. After a lesson on the life of the Prophet, for instance, I was stopped by a boy dressed in *jalabiyya* and *taqiyya* (the Islamic headwear quite uncommon within the university campus), who approached me and started speaking about "the religion" (Islam). When I asked him why the people studying shari'a were so different from other students he told me,

> It's easy to claim to be Muslim, but this is only the case when your entire life is modelled on that of the Prophet, beginning with your dress and coming to your relations with people. When you see somebody doing something wrong for example, it's too easy to ignore that; and too many people just do that. But the religion says that we have *al-amr bi-l-ma'ruf wa al-nahi 'an al-munkar*,[5] and we simply have to abide by this obligation [*farz*].

Material Conditions of the Religious Divide

The ethnography introduced thus far has shown many different religious practices among the students, including fasting, ways of socialising and the observance of the gender divide and the prescriptions on the modesty of women. It also demonstrates how these differences are somehow consistent with the hierarchy among the faculties in the University of Jordan. What follows next will place these findings further into context by focusing on the material conditions that enable students to behave differently, in an attempt to make sense of the differences that emerged from the ethnography.

The social gatherings of students that are more common within the more privileged faculties are not to be found among the less prestigious ones, not only as a result of the different social backgrounds of the students but also because in the latter they are more likely to be seen as "haram". Here a student can be questioned or even sanctioned if he or she is doing something "wrong". I am not arguing that social control is ubiquitous, and that it somehow determines the entirety of social relations; it is nonetheless crucial to understand the importance that the context has in order to establish and sustain socialising patterns that can be described as religious.

The differences between "*shari' oroba*" (Europe Street, the courtyard immediately next to it and the nearby paths in front of the Faculty of Literature) or the "*saha al-'ilm*" (Science Square, located in the middle of the science faculties, on the opposite side of the campus to the humanities faculties) and the courtyards of the less prestigious faculties are immediately recognisable, and some students of these latter faculties, mainly males, go to the former because of the possibility of meeting girls. They are not really welcome in the groups of students at the best faculties and thus they end up in liminal spaces that are disregarded by the more privileged students, who call these spaces "*shari' al-gypsy*" or "*shari' al-nas*" (gypsy's and people's street, respectively). These spaces are usually overcrowded even on Saturdays and during class time. I was told more than once that, "There is no point in studying hard, nor in attending classes in which the professor is simply repeating what is to be found in the textbook. It is much more fun to go around, seeing people, friends, looking after girls and more importantly not being at home!"

The very fact of being in a group of friends, including both boys and girls, chatting, laughing and flirting, smoking and drinking, is quite peculiar to the best faculties. Girls in Jordan normally do not smoke in public, nor do they engage in prolonged conversations with boys, and laughing is not considered acceptable for a "true" Muslim girl, at least not in public and with boys around. Since gossip is highly damaging for the reputation of women, and especially of those who are less able to defend themselves or who cannot afford to have a bad reputation, most girls have to pay attention to their public behaviours.

Discussions among students on what is truly Islamic and what is not also take place among students at the best faculties, and more importantly they constitute the basis of the moral judgement that is imposed on others. Interestingly, almost all the students state that such judgement is hardly bearable, and yet they actively contribute to shaping it. Not only are actions judged but also the intentions, as in the case of a reportedly immodestly veiled girl or a newly religious boy who still drinks. The behaviour of girls in public is particularly scrutinised by other students (both male and female) who pass judgements on whether the girl is "easy"; those who travel more frequently and are able to speak other languages are often targets for hidden prejudices, such as having become "American", which usually denotes something imported, distorted, if not fake, and in any case alien. There are of course other forms of judgement, more in line with the societal distinctions that I will mention below, but religion definitely plays a crucial role in this process. In private conversations, many students admit that their behaviour is not in line with the tenets of Islam. This honest recognition, however, does not bring forth any particular change in the public setting of the campus, since the common assumption shared by almost all students is that the commandments of Islam and the everyday rules that inform students' practices are not open for discussion.

These socialisation patterns reflect a rift in Jordanian society, between the more affluent who are accustomed to travelling abroad and having contact with foreigners, and those who are of more humble origins, with less opportunity for getting to know a world different to their own. This rift has widened in recent years, partly as a result of the liberalisation policies implemented by the regime which are changing the structure of Jordanian society.

As Jordan is a small country, it is usual for a student to be identified with one of the main social groups – being from Amman or not, Jordanian or not, from a well-known family or not, and the like – even though this is seldom admitted outright and only prolonged mutual acquaintance allows this kind of information to emerge, especially if this identification has negative consequences. The division into these categories is quite important for the daily lives of the students, and the religious division, important as it is, is simply a part of this. Particularly for financial matters, such as obtaining a job after graduation, or social matters, such as marriage strategies, these categories are perhaps more relevant than the religious division. Yet religion plays a central role in determining self-representations and practices on a daily basis. Thus all religious representations are to be understood within this social context, partly as a consequence of the social and economic background that enables a certain student to behave in one way or another, rather than as a result of individual preference.

Conclusion

The public educational system in Jordan brings together students from very different social and economic backgrounds. By sharing the same campus, they have the opportunity to meet, or at least become aware of (or be exposed to), the existence of the "other". As noted, there are differences within the university and there are different possibilities of expressing them; these differences, and their social and political implications, are well understood by the majority of the students. The condition of privilege that some experience makes it hard to have real contact with students from other backgrounds or those from less prestigious faculties, or from other backgrounds. Speaking of a mutual exchange of experiences and points of view would therefore be misleading, since social borders are not easily bypassed in this context. At the same time, however, there is a spatial proximity that makes the university an interesting place for looking at how students build, represent and enact boundaries and differences among themselves. The flexibility of the ethnographic method used, that of a thorough participant observation, enables the research to account for the complexity of students' lives, allows time to gain a better understanding of the situations observed, such as self-representations and practices evolving over time and in specific situations, and allows differences and complexities to be accounted for with the aim of deepening the comprehension of what being a Muslim means in contemporary Jordan.

I agree with Samuli Schielke when he says that traditional forms of reasoning are increasingly mixed with newer problems and desires, such as consumerism, the highly idealised romance as opposed to religious prescriptions, and political (and economic) worries for the future.[6] This is particularly, but not exclusively, to be seen in the best faculties. I have tried to show the importance of social contexts and material conditions when regarding the different religious practices of university students in Jordan. The fact that the religious sense of belonging is not entirely reducible to material categories should of course go without saying. My aim, in addition to introducing the religious world of students, has been to demonstrate that contrasts and tensions are a common reality for students, regardless of their social backgrounds, and that the context of the university is relevant in showing the ways in which they present themselves, their ideas about what it means to be (and to be considered) a good Muslim, the social and political consequences of their religious acts and the implications of their beliefs.

Notes

1. See W. Armbrust, "The Riddle of Ramadan: Media, Consumer Culture, and the 'Christmasization' of a Muslim holiday", in Donna Bowen and Evelyn Early (eds), *Everyday Life in the Middle East*, Bloomington: Indiana University Press, 2002, pp. 335–48.
2. All names have been changed for reasons of privacy.
3. The fact that I was present might have changed the subject of conversation, either for the sake of my conversion or simply to show the "right" way of being Muslim to a foreigner. Not just in this regard, my research has been highly reflexive, since almost all the encounters with students implied a mutual exchange of experiences.
4. It should be kept in mind that Jordan is not a liberal country, and breaking the fast during Ramadan is forbidden under university regulations.
5. The Qur'anic prescription of "commanding what is good and forbidding what is wrong" (Qur'an 3.104, 110). See also Chapter 5 in this volume.
6. Samuli Schielke, "Being Good in Ramadan: Ambivalence, Fragmentation, and the Moral Self in the Lives of Young Egyptians", *Journal of the Royal Anthropological Institute*, vol. 15, no. 1, 2009, pp. 24–40.

Chapter 12

Referring to Islam in Mutual Teasing: Notes on an Encounter between Two Tanzanian Revivalists

Sigurd D'hondt

In this chapter, I examine how two Kiswahili-speaking adolescents negotiate a Muslim identity (or at least, one particular version of such an identity) within the hustle and bustle of a single tape-recorded episode of spontaneous everyday interaction. The setting is utterly mundane: a street corner in one of the many suburbs of Dar es Salaam, Tanzania's commercial capital. Around the time the episode was recorded, two of the three protagonists overtly sympathised with revivalist Islam. On repeated occasions, they explicitly (and eagerly) identified themselves as *mujahidina*. According to Nurudini, the participant who recorded the incident, it represents the Kiswahili equivalent of the English "fundamentalist" (though it is not included in any current Kiswahili dictionary). In this chapter, I shall use "revivalism" instead of the more common "fundamentalism", as the latter does not adequately capture the anti-traditionalist and individualised nature of this reform movement. In the fragments that I shall look into, Nurudini and his interlocutors exchange a series of playful challenges to this revivalist identity.

Since the 1980s, Tanzania has faced a rise in revivalist Islam. Prominent players in this movement are the "returning youth" who studied Islam abroad, often in Egypt, Sudan or Saudi Arabia, and who, upon return, started taking issue with the "impurities" they discovered in locally practised versions of Islam.[1] This revivalist movement shares many characteristics with Salafi movements found elsewhere across Muslim contexts, such as the vehement rejection of locally nurtured Sufi practices. It would nevertheless be a mistake, as Turner aptly points out, to analyse the rise of this movement as "yet another" instance of the ongoing conflict between global Salafism and local Sufism. For one thing, its success is intensely nourished by local political dynamics (for example, the recuperation of traditional Sufi religious authorities by the socialist government in the 1970s and 1980s). Revivalists also frequently articulate their critique of the status quo in terms of global issues, such as human rights and good governance.[2]

This chapter is also concerned with elucidating the local dynamics of identity formation, although it focuses on a very specific type of dynamic. It concentrates on the interactional encounters in which identities are forged, attributed and contested. Adopting the framework of ethnomethodological conversation analysis (EMCA), it presents an analysis of the methods and practices by which these encounters are constituted and by which ascriptions of identity are managed in their local contexts.[3] As an ethnographic method,[4] EMCA is exquisitely tailored for the proposed reappraisal of "Islam" as embedded in a complex of situated lived practices (rather than as an abstract, formal symbol or belief system) that is the central tenet of the various chapters in this section. In this instance, the method is helpful in drawing to attention something that is all too frequently overlooked in many of the contemporary discourses about Islam that circulate in the aftermath of the terrorist attacks of 11 September 2001: the agency of so-called "Muslim fundamentalists".

Don't You Pray?

The interaction we shall examine was recorded in Dar es Salaam in the spring of 1996, in the context of fieldwork on the structures of everyday interaction and the way Dar es Salaam residents collaboratively construct their lived realities through situated talk.[5] Importantly, the fieldwork was guided by Harvey Sacks's principle of "unmotivated looking": rather than positing specific research goals in advance, I assumed that any instance of naturally occurring interaction could potentially shed light on hitherto unforeseen aspects of how human beings organise their everyday practice.[6] To sample such naturally occurring interactions, I gave a small tape-recorder to Nurudini, a younger relative of an old friend of mine, with the request that he record spontaneous interactions in his daily environment. A few days later, he returned the tape-recorder along with a sixty-minute audio-cassette, the first side of which contained five short stretches of naturally occurring conversation in Kiswahili. The encounter reported here was one of them.[7]

Strolling around in the vicinity of his parents' home in a semi-residential suburb near the university, Nurudini accidentally bumped into Juma, one of his many acquaintances in the neighbourhood. Nurudini and Juma are both in their late teens. They have known one another since childhood, and they regularly attend prayer together in the local mosque. Both sympathise with revivalism. The third party to the encounter, Charlie, is an acquaintance of Juma. Juma supplements his meagre income as a truck driver with moonlighting as a self-employed "house agent", and Charlie had come after him to inform him of a vacant room in a tenement nearby. When Nurudini arrived, Charlie was busy supplying Juma with the details of the vacancy. Nurudini switched on the tape-recorder immediately after exchanging greetings with Juma and his companion.[8]

The encounter is extremely brief and lasts just over two minutes. The fragment is nevertheless analytically challenging because it contains two occasions where Nurudini explicitly calls into question Juma's Muslim identity: the first happens immediately after the tape-recorder is switched on, and the second occurs right before Nurudini walks away from the scene.

Let us begin by taking a look at the first of these two challenges. Directly after the exchange of greetings is completed (not captured on the tape), Nurudini asks Juma why he is no longer attending prayer:

```
001  Nur:    mbona sikuoni oni ↑masjidini.
             why don't I see you around in the mosque?
002  Jum:    °ah°    hunioni ↑WApi bwana.
             you don't see me where mister?
003          w[ewe unasalia wapi.]
             where do you pray?
004  Nur:    [aa:::::rh]   naswalia >hapa hapa<
                           I pray right here
005          lakini siku↑o::ni mimi
             but I don't see you around
006          rafiki    [yangu.]
             my friend
007  Jum:              [aa]    ↑we unaswalia NJE wewe.
                               you pray outside you
008  Nur:    ↑mi niswalie nje?      mimi NDANI bwana.=
             me praying outside?    I am inside mister
009  Jum:    =mimi nakuwaga ndani bwa[na.
             me I am always inside mister
010  Nur:                            [sa mbona
                                     [now why-
011          unatafuta ↑NINI hapa tena.
             what are you looking for this time?
```

Together, these few lines succinctly illustrate the strong inferential link between activity and identity: being seen (or in this case, verbally claiming) to participate in prayer is sufficient for generating a corresponding categorisation of the actor as [Muslim]. The episode also demonstrates the eminently moral character of this inferential link;[9] it illustrates that not participating in prayer (or arriving late, by the time the mosque is already packed with worshippers and there is no space left inside) is a noticeable phenomenon and may constitute grounds for questioning someone's moral integrity as a category member. Importantly, this inferential link is not a stable cognitive structure "inside the head" of the participants but is locally forged and continually updated in situated practice. In this particular case, its local character is evident, inter alia, in the fact that having to "pray outside" is taken to indicate a lack of religious zeal, a reflection of the local circumstance that Nurudini and Juma's neighbourhood mosque is too small to accommodate the growing number of worshippers.

In addition, and specifically relevant to our purposes, this inferential link also entails a particular "analysis" of the collectivity it alludes to. In challenging Juma's membership of the identity [Muslim] on the basis of his failure to attend prayer, Nurudini endorses a view of the collectivity [Muslim] as a "morally organised" unit, of which membership can be assumed by participating (and being seen to participate) in activities that are constitutive of that group. As Jayyusi points out, the fact that the collectivity is held together by its members' moral predisposition towards certain activities furthermore implies that these activities "need not be spatially bounded or localized [sic] in their operations ..."; rather, they "extend their operations and concerns spatially (and 'temporally' so that they 'reproduce' their character and work across time)".[10]

The fragment analysed here confronts us with the decontextualising effect of this spatio-temporal extension of activities and demonstrates its impact on the way identities associated with such a morally organised collectivity are attributed. For one thing, the way Nurudini challenges his interlocutor completely denies the reflexive embedding of the category [Muslim] in the practical context in which his interlocutor publicly "embraced" that category and treats it instead as "an object that is analytically independent of the actions by which it is produced."[11] Such "reifications" are characteristic of judiciary contexts, where legal experts produce abstract categorisations of offenders on the basis of yet other abstract categorisations, formal legal descriptions of unlawful acts that take no notice of the practical circumstances in which the offenders committed them. On the basis of such mechanisms, social structure is reified in (and through) situated courtroom practice.[12]

In the case at hand, a comparable process of reification is taking place as Nurudini publicly subjects Juma's membership of the category [Muslim] to critical scrutiny. Here as well, Juma is de-categorised as a member of the [Muslim] collectivity by means of a series of descriptions that completely ignore the practical circumstances that occasioned Juma's failure to follow the behavioural rules associated with the collectivity. Conduct that is the product of very specific contextual circumstances (what was Juma up to when he should have been at the mosque?) is thus subjected to evaluation on the basis of a regulatory framework of formal prescriptions that accounts for an abstract categorisation – [Muslim] – in terms of yet other abstract categorisations (assessments of conduct on the basis of these prescriptions). This is where reification sets in. Instead of treating the categorisation [Muslim] as the product of very specific biographical and contextual circumstances, Nurudini and Juma do exactly the reverse: they interpret their social environment in terms of secondary categorisations derived from the category [Muslim] and thereby "objectify" that category as an externally compelling force. Juma makes no effort to contextualise his alleged transgression; instead, he vigorously asserts his regular attendance.

These observations allow us to further disentangle the categorial implications of what is going on here between Nurudini and Juma The relevant choice for Nurudini and Juma, so it seems, is not one between [Muslim] and [non-Muslim] or between [Muslim] and [members of unspecified other denominations], but between candidate [Muslims] who fully accept and live up to the reifying logic governing the ascription of membership of this morally organised collectivity and those who fail to do so. The exchange of mutual accusations does not contest the internal "logic" of the category in question or the way it is made to relate to other denominational categories, but solely touches upon the empirical question whether the "facts" of the applicants' individual religious-biographical records are consistent with their membership claims.

The issue of Juma's alleged lack of religious zeal is thereupon abruptly abandoned. In line 11, Nurudini shifts into a lower gear and asks what Charlie and Juma are up to.

This does not last very long, however. Only two minutes later, in line 131–2 below, Nurudini decides to reiterate his challenge.

```
128  Cha:   ↑kama siyo bahati mbaya, basi kapangua (**).
            if it is not a miscarriage, then she got rid of it
129  Jum:   kama yupo sa↑lama, tuanze u:pya.
            if she is all right, let us start all over
130         (1.5)
131  Nur:   kwani wewe: una:::::
            but you, you d-
132         ↑vipi,    si una↑swali wewe?
            how?     don't you pray, you?
133  Jum:   eh?
134: Nur:   si una↑swali wewe.
            don't you pray, you?
135  Jum:   >sasa nataka kuoa<
            this time I want to get married
```

136	Nur:	>aa:. unataka kuoa.	s(h)awa sawa.
		you want to marry	all right then
137		a[salaam *alei*(gh)kum<]	
138	Jum:	[heh heh *heh*:]	
139		(.)	
140	Nur:	↑hih hi:h	
141		(1.5)	
142	Jum:	KA:ZI KUBWA BWANA.	
		a big job mister	
143	Nur:	SA:WA BWANA.	
		indeed mister	
144		((Nurudini continues his stroll))	

This second episode is different in many ways from the first one. First of all, a shift can observed from "locutional" to "embodied" categorisation work; unlike in the opening excerpt, the identities that are relevant to this part of the encounter are not "talked about" but are "enacted" in and through discursive form. This is the case, for example, in Juma's utterance in line 129: "if she is all right, let us start all over." How are we to interpret this utterance? One minute earlier, a young girl, Julie, had suddenly made her appearance in front of the corner where Juma and Charlie (and Nurudini, at the time) were loitering. After she left, Juma remarked that a while ago she gave the impression of being pregnant but that at present there was no indication that she had delivered a baby. For about a whole minute, Juma and Charlie wonder how Julie's pregnancy ended: did she terminate it or did she suffer from a miscarriage? In line 128, Charlie proposes to terminate the discussion by summarising (or "formulating")[13] it in a way that communicates clear indifference: as far as he is concerned, the question which of the two outcomes is correct is of little significance. In line 129, then, Juma produces the corresponding follow-up to this closing proposal (a confirmation) by ostensibly "upgrading" the insignificance Juma attributed to the topic: "If she is all right [that is, sexually available again], we can start all over!" Importantly, this "ostensible upgrade" involves the construction of a joint identity, a version of [masculinity] allegedly shared by Juma, Charlie and Nurudini alike, which is based on a shared sexual interest in Julie. In talking in such a derogatory way about Julie, Juma iconically "embodies" this identity: merely producing an utterance such as line 129 constitutes an icon of the specific form of [masculinity] this kind of utterance projects.

Admittedly, the contrast between locutional and embodied categorisation work is not as sharp as this exclusively binary account suggests. The categorisation in the opening segment may indeed be primarily locutional, but the challenge directed at Juma also contained an embodied knowledge claim on the part of Nurudini; because attendance during prayer is a knowledge domain that only fellow [Muslims] are assumed to be familiar with, it reflexively instantiates his membership in that category.

It is Juma's "let us start all over" in line 129 that sets the stage for Nurudini to reissue his initial challenge. In lines 131–2, Nurudini sets a trap for Juma; by "reminding" Juma that he attends prayer (something Juma himself forcefully insisted on in the opening segment), Nurudini presents the [masculinity] embodied by Juma in line 129 as fundamentally "at odds" with the [Muslim] identity which he claimed for himself in locutional terms in the opening episode. That Nurudini is making an assertion about something Juma is somehow supposed to know is evident from the negative predicative particle *si*, the effects of which are comparable to a negative tag in English, and the 1.5 seconds pause and the hedge-like delay preceding the utterance. These last two "postponements" present the reminder as a kind of "last resort"; Nurudini gave Juma ample opportunity to correct his fault, but Juma failed to do so.

Juma's response to Nurudini's trap, in line 135, is remarkable. He unequivocally refrains from amending his earlier claim that he attends prayer or from otherwise modifying his "stake" in the identity [Muslim]. Instead, he requalifies his sexual interest in Julie so that it is no longer illicit within the framework of pre- and pro-scriptions associated with the category [Muslim]: "This time I want to marry."

The floor now returns to Nurudini. In lines 136–7, he produces a rejoinder to Juma's sudden announcement that he is keen on marrying Julie. Nurudini's rejoinder consists of four separate components: (1) an indication that his interlocutor successfully "solved" the inconsistency ("aa:"); (2) a repetition of the proposed solution ("you want to marry"); (3) a positive evaluation ("all right then"); and finally (4) an "embodied" recognition of Juma's category membership (*asalaam aleikum*).

It is worthwhile digging a little deeper into exactly what Nurudini is expressing his positive appreciation of in this last utterance. A key issue here is the manifest insincerity of Juma's vow to marry in line 135, evident from the marked contrast between the solemn content of the utterance and its hasty, casual delivery. According to Clift, the "public" character of insincerities like the one in line 135 sets in motion a process of "ironicisation"; public insincerities index a shift in footing that suggests that the utterance in question is surrounded by an outside "frame", consisting of a set of shared norms with which to evaluate its manifestly insincere content.[14] Both Juma's utterance in line 135 and Nurudini's utterance in lines 136–7 qualify as ironical, but the reframings they suggest each follow a different trajectory. The insincerity of Juma's commitment in line 135 frames that utterance at two levels simultaneously. It indexes an outside frame from which to evaluate the "content" of the utterance proper (an outside frame that comprises a set of shared opinions about what a "proper" marriage should be like), while its manifest insincerity concomitantly frames the encounter in its entirety as a playful event, where the standard for evaluating what is said is not truthfulness but wit and cunning.

Nurudini's rejoinder to Juma's reframing proposal, in lines 136–7, projects a different but equally subtle layering of frames. In officially taking Juma's utterance in line 135 at face value and thus reciprocating its insincerity, Nurudini's rejoinder goes along with Juma's proposed reframing of the encounter as a playful event. However, because his manifestly insincere rejoinder also contains an embodied recognition of Juma's membership of the category [Muslim], Nurudini's response simultaneously indexes yet another outside frame, which surrounds not only his individual turn but the "playful event" in its entirety; the entire episode of banter, including the embodied categorisation work in line 129, is to be re-evaluated according to the framework of moral obligations associated with the category [Muslim]. That these two outside frames are indeed simultaneously at play can be inferred from the range of responses this sequence elicits: it is met with laughter (by Juma in line 138 and Nurudini in line 140) and also with a comment ("a big job, mister", line 142) in which Juma explicitly acknowledges the many difficulties a [Muslim] faces daily as he tries to live up to religious proscriptions (of which this encounter provides a vivid example).

This final episode presents a particularly ambiguous picture. The participants leave the reified nature of their social environment and the de-contextualising force of abstract categories like [Muslim] intact, but the exchange also demonstrates their ability to temporarily exempt their encounter from the exigencies of such reification.

Comments

One of the ethnographic merits of a detailed utterance-by-utterance analysis of such an everyday encounter between two revivalists is that it lays bare the agency that these alleged cultural others possess. Let me briefly explain what I mean here by "agency", as my reclamation of this notion in the context of a piece of EMCA research is likely to raise an eyebrow here and there.

Inspired by Goffman's dictum "not ... men and their moments ... rather moments and their men",[15] EMCA consistently rejects situation-transcendent, dichotomous conceptions of agency and structure. In their place, it highlights the formative role of the interactional environments (or "ecologies") that render behaviour meaningful; participants articulate themselves as "agents" through the particular position they assume vis-à-vis the locally salient contextual frameworks that project possible courses of action (and thereby make conduct intelligible).[16] Hence, in Sidnell's words, "there are no 'social actors' only brides and grooms, witnesses and lawyers, judges and juries, speakers and hearers".[17] The notions of agency and structure, in this view, completely collapse, as participants' capacity to demonstrate agency (irrespective whether they actually behave in the way that is expected of them) is grounded in the very structures that constrain them. In fact, the two notions are not even necessarily part of what participants themselves find relevant in making sense of one another, and hence their relevance is largely limited to "theoretical" debates between ethnomethodologists and outsiders.

This chapter touches upon a different phenomenon, however. In the encounter that we analysed, the classical dichotomous understanding of agency and structure is resuscitated in the flow of what is made publicly available in the talk.[18] Participants themselves appear to entertain these notions in making sense of each other's conduct (and in rendering their own conduct intelligible to their interlocutor). This is most obvious in the second excerpt. Importantly, the "internal logic" of the identity category [Muslim] here no longer functions as the ultimate yardstick for making sense of what is going on. Instead, Nurudini and Juma collaboratively negotiate a noticeable "distance" from the identity categories that supposedly inform their talk. The moment their encounter slips into banter, our two protagonists are no longer speaking "from within" the identity [Muslim], the category of which they coveted exclusive membership in the preceding parts of the quarrel. This momentary "non-identification" comes to an end when Nurudini and Juma exchange post hoc comments on their own fallibility (which corroborates the proposed analysis of this episode in terms of reframing and the performance of "outside-ness").

Agency can thus be understood as a form of "performed autonomy" vis-à-vis the constraints perceivably imposed by structure, which conflicts with classical functionalist explanations that assign these twin concepts an ontological status. It is remarkably consistent, however, with Lacanian notions of a "split subject", which locate subjectivity in the structural impossibility of full identification with the symbolic.[19] It is because of such a "split", the structural failure to fully coincide with the tradition one claims to embrace, that Islamic revivalism (so-called "fundamentalism") ultimately constitutes a modern subjectivity.[20] Not the "content" of the discourse but the "point of enunciation" from where it is produced is crucial in this respect. The EMCA analysis of the incident reported on here allowed us to identify this point of enunciation and to spell out how it is rooted in interactional practices, as a collaborative display of agency that resists reduction to the coveted identities that are at stake in the exchange in question.

Conclusion

In re-specifying these revivalists' agency in praxiological terms, as a form of performed autonomy vis-à-vis the constraints exerted by social structure, the utterance-by-utterance analysis of this incident discreetly directed us toward an unexpected form of shared modernity. It is precisely the identification of such elements of hitherto undetected commonality that an ethnographic account of revivalist Islam in its "ordinary", day-to-day manifestation has to offer: the hustle and bustle of the everyday, with all its momentary failures and passing inconsistencies, encapsulates a core of common ground that transcends established boundaries of otherness.

Notes

1. John Campbell, "Nationalism, Ethnicity and Religion: Fundamental Conflicts and the Politics of Identity in Tanzania", *Nations and Nationalisms*, vol. 5, no. 1, 2003, pp. 105–25; Simon Turner, "These Young Men Show No Respect for Local Customs: Globalisation and Islamic Revival in Zanzibar", *Journal of Religion in Africa*, vol. 39, no. 3, 2009, pp. 237–61. A wider-ranging perspective on the relationship between Islamic revivalism and Sufism in sub-Saharan Africa can be found in David Westerlund, and Eva Evers Rosander, *African Islam and Islam In Africa*, London: Hurst & Co., 1997.
2. Turner, "These Young Men".
3. For CA, consider: Paul ten Have, *Doing Conversation Analysis*, 2nd edn, London: Sage, 2007. For the affiliated tradition of membership categorisation analysis, see: Stephen Hester and Peter Eglin, *Culture in Action*, Washington: International Institute for Ethnomethodology and Conversation Analysis and University Press of America, DC, 1997.
4. Similar positions can be found in: Jack Sidnell, *Talk and Practical Epistemology*, Amsterdam/Philadelphia: Benjamins, 2005; Baudouin Dupret, Barbara Drieskens and Annelies Moors, *Narratives of Truth in Islamic Law*, London: Tauris, 2005.
5. Field research was carried out while I was a doctoral fellow at the Belgian National Science Fund. I am indebted to the Department of Modern Languages and Linguistics of the University of Dar es Salaam for their practical support and to the Tanzanian Commission for Science and Technology (COSTECH) for granting me permission for this research.
6. Harvey Sacks, "Notes on Methodology", in Paul Atkinson and John M. Heritage (eds), *Structures of Social Action: Studies in Conversation Analysis*, Cambridge: Cambridge University Press, 1984, pp. 21–7.
7. For an earlier analysis, see: Sigurd D'hondt, "Framing Gender: Multiple Gendered Identities in Dar-es-Salaam Adolescents' Talk", in Paul McIlvenny (ed.), *Talking Gender and Sexuality*, Amsterdam/Philadelphia: Benjamins, 2002, pp. 207–36.
8. In order not to disturb the natural course of interaction, Nurudini did not inform Charlie that he was tape-recording him and his companion. Permission to use the recorded data was solicited later, after Nurudini had returned the tape to me. In

order to guarantee anonymity, all proper names have been replaced with pseudonyms.
9. Lena Jayyusi, *Categorisation and the Moral Order*, London: Routledge and Kegan Paul, 1984.
10. Jayyusi, *Categorisation*, p. 50.
11. Douglas W. Maynard and Thomas P. Wilson, "On the Reification of Social Structure", in S. G. McNall and G. N. Howe (eds), *Current Perspectives in Social Theory*, Greenwich: JAI Press, 1980, p. 287.
12. Maynard and Wilson, "On the Reification", p. 310.
13. John Heritage and Rod Watson, "Formulations as Conversational Objects", in George Psathas (ed.), *Everyday Language*, New York: Irvington, 1979, pp. 123–62.
14. Rebecca Clift, "Irony in Conversation", *Language in Society*, vol. 28, 1999, pp. 523–53; Erving Goffman, *Frame Analysis*, Cambridge: Harper and Row, 1974.
15. Erving Goffman, *Interaction Ritual*, New York: Pantheon, 1967, p. 10.
16. Giolo Fele, "La rinuncia all'*agency*: forme di cooperazione e di interazione sociale tra gli operatori dell'emergenza", in Aurora Donzelli and Alessandra Fasulo (eds), *Agency e Linguaggio*, Rome: Meltemi, 2007, pp. 173–93.
17. Sidnell, *Talk and Practical Epistemology*, p. 10.
18. See also: Sigurd D'hondt, "Good Cops, Bad Cops: Intertextuality, Agency and Structure in Criminal Trial Discourse", *Research on Language and Social Interaction*, vol. 42, no. 3, 2009, pp. 249–75.
19. For useful overview of the notion of "split subject" and its relevance to social theory, consider: Saul Newman, "The Place of Power in Political Discourse", *International Political Science Review*, vol. 25, no. 2, 2004, pp. 139–57.
20. Consider, in this respect, the following quote from De Kesel on Osama Bin Laden: "Bin Laden is undeniably the prototype of the anti-modern fundamentalist. He is a devoted Muslim who despises every form of innovation and modernisation and who defends a hyper-traditionalist interpretation of Islam. *And yet he is not a traditional Muslim*. He professes a traditional kind of Islam, but he does not do so *from within* Islam. At the most fundamental level, he does not rely on his tradition, but on his own sovereign choice *for* that tradition. This distinction is critical, because the formal point from where such a decision is taken falls by definition beyond the scope of tradition itself. It presupposes a moment of doubt during which, if only for a short while, there is no longer any basis for the tradition ... In this sense, Bin Laden is modern, too. In what he says and does he is our absolute counterpart. But formally speaking, the point from which he enunciates his opinion on the world is identical to the one from which we relate to the world" (Marc De Kesel, "Bin Laden als cartesiaan: over de moderniteit van het fundamentalisme", *De Witte Raaf*, vol. 19, no. 108, 2004, pp. 11–13, my translation).

CHAPTER 13

Salafis as Shaykhs: Othering the Pious in Cairo

Aymon Kreil

In the shadow of the Islamic awakening at the end of the 1970s, partly as a result of the trauma of the 1967 war and the Sadat regime's deliberate use of religious references for the purpose of legitimising itself, individual signs of religiosity – for instance beards, galabiyyas,[1] the use of religious formulations in language, and the veiling of women – became familiar in the public sphere.[2] This phenomenon could also be seen in the media, as preachers and intellectuals claiming religious and moral wisdom were broadcast and became very popular among Egyptians. Through the internet and satellite channels, these figures have gained even more social visibility, with yet more trends competing publicly for religious hegemony.

One of the powerful trends of this religious renewal is the one described as Salafi. Most of the famous shaykhs appearing on TV today belong to it, and many followers of the Salafi trend can be seen in Cairo's streets, recognisable through specific types of clothing and beards. The word Salafi itself is imprecise, as it means literally "belonging to the Salafs", the pious companions of the Prophet Muhammad. Almost all Islamic reform movements since the nineteenth century have referred to a return to the principles of early Muslim preaching in Mecca and Medina as the true path to strengthening the umma, and consequently have considered themselves Salafis. Nevertheless, since the mid-twentieth century or before, what has become most widely known as the Salafi movement is a trend insisting on an unquestioning following to the letter of the Qur'an and the hadith, God's command, in all aspects of life, which involves a specific appearance: a beard without moustache, and often a short white galabiyya.

Salafi groups are strongly divided.[3] There are many points of contention about the correct interpretation of Islam and the best path to reform society, the main disagreement being between supporters of political violence and its opponents. Another important issue at stake for Salafis concerns the most appropriate behaviour to adopt with non-Salafi Muslims in the quest for religious purity. Yet the marginal position of Salafis in terms of the practices of most Muslims is perceived as God's will, as only few believers will deserve access to paradise in the end, and as a gap bridged through preaching to gain hegemony over minds. The specific role that Salafis assume as the only bearers of truth competes here with proselytising and the need to engage in society that work requires. How can a chosen minority encompass all of society, or even a large amount of people? This is maybe a further explanatory factor for the fragmentation of the Salafi trend, as distinctiveness requires an ever-growing need for dogmatic bordering against others.

This point leads us to the main issue of this chapter, the way non-Salafi Muslims perceive the Salafi trend and its followers. My contribution intends to illuminate how people who are not committed to the movement perceive Salafis.[4] One element of these perceptions is their general categorisation as "Sunnis" or as "Salafis", regardless of which group within that trend they belong to, on the basis of their appearance and because of their strict following of all the habits of the Prophet, called *Sunna al-Rasul*. Ethnographic data shows that many interviewees, despite considering Salafi opinions as reflecting the correct interpretation of Islam, do not feel compelled to conform to its commands. Because of this, the hegemonic tendencies of Salafi discourse do not determine social practice. In my opinion, one reason is the othering of the Salafis as particular Muslims compelled to exemplarity, a category that matches up with that of shaykhs as specifically religious men. Indeed, "shaykh" is, among other uses, a common way to address a Salafi during interactions.

Ethnographic accounts are only excerpts of research. A large part of the context remains unwritten in fieldwork notes. A researcher is not a tape machine; one has to order, structure and interpret information in order to make sense out of it, and to relate it, first to one's own notebooks, then to readers. This is an evolving process, as research inputs constantly reframe the topic of enquiry and consequently the reading of the surrounding environment. Finally, when publishing, one has again to make choices from the descriptions gathered from one's notebooks.

However, ethnographic research is the only way to obtain insights about everyday relations to Salafis, as these relations are embedded in common situations and not in writings.[5] Thus, they often remain unnoticed. Most research in the field of Islamic studies or political science focuses on the evolution of dogma and the discourse of religious players, especially of those belonging to political Islam. In Egypt, in the aftermath of the fall of former president Hosni Mubarak,

Salafi groups are gaining an important political aspect. For this reason at least, there is an urgent need to understand how Egyptians perceive them.

Relatives, Acquaintances and Salafi Groups

In this section, I will first present some excerpts that concern Salafis from my ethnographic data on a group of relatives and acquaintances.

Sayyid and Karim are brothers, the sons of Usama. They come from the wealthy branch of the family. Usama and his wife are both high-level functionaries, who managed to save money during time spent working in a Gulf country. They live in a wealthy neighbourhood. Sayyid married a French woman and Karim studied in Europe. Karim works as an engineer and Sayyid teaches Arabic to foreigners.

In the close family around Sayyid, with Karim, their unveiled sister, and Usama and his veiled wife, there is a clear distance to the Salafi movement. Sayyid defends quite a relativistic vision of Islam, where each trend can be considered as a *madhhab* (a school of interpretation) on its own, even Shi'ism, and where their followers are all equally entitled to express their views. Karim often boasts among friends about girls he met at parties and about alcohol, yet presents himself as Muslim and sometimes speaks about religion. He likes to depict himself as the enemy of "terrorists", the jihadi groups, and it is often difficult to distinguish them in his talk from more peaceful Salafis. It is the same for Usama. Nevertheless, distance does not mean open hostility.

Sayyid introduced me to Magdy, his cousin (*ibn 'amm*), living in a popular neighbourhood in the south of Cairo, and Ahmad and Yasir, close acquaintances from the same building as Magdy's family. At that time, Magdy was working as a craftsman, Ahmad was working for an IT company and Yasir was still studying. Ahmad and Yasir are the sons of Shaykh Muhammad, an influential Salafi preacher in the neighbourhood. However, they were unwilling to become shaykhs themselves. One of them, furthermore, was a dedicated hashish smoker. They all lived in the same building.

Magdy, Ahmad and Yasir have a very different relationship to the Salafi trend than Sayyid and Karim. Magdy, who does not show any visible sign of commitment to it, such as a beard or a galabiyya, and who loves American action films and love-chat on the internet, presents himself as sympathetic to Salafism. He always warmly greets the young, recognisable bearded Salafis we meet in the street. Ahmad and Yasir, Shaykh Muhammad's sons, though unwilling to follow their father's path, would never question the accuracy of his religious views. Shaykh Muhammad, especially in Magdy's eyes, is a bearer of perfect knowledge and able to solve any question according to the true principles of Islam. I was myself witness to the discursive apparatus Shaykh Muhammad mobilises on the basis of Qur'anic verses, the hadith and classical Arabic in order to convey the image of a complete science perfect in its axioms and conclusions.

Eventually, I met Sharif and Salih. Salih is also a cousin (*ibn 'amma*) of Sayyid, and Sharif is his closest friend. They live in a popular neighbourhood, but in the far north-east of the city, and have a very distant relationship with Magdy, Ahmad and Yasir. Indeed, the rest of the family seemed a bit bemused to see me visit Sharif and Salih. Sharif at that time was a student and Salih was unemployed.

Sharif and Salih are both former members of radical Salafi groups. Sharif has bitter memories of this period, accusing them of manipulation, intolerance and a disproportionate commitment to appearances. Salih, who seems quite unstable, alternates between a radical discourse involving extreme elements of jihadi thinking with an ideal of living based on flirting and a dream of a career in the arts.

With regard to this panel of individuals, the various points of view on Salafism should be noted. Family is not the determining factor, as the sons of Shaykh Muhammad do not want to follow his path. Nor is class the main relevant issue. Even if Sayyid and Karim's branch of the family, which is the richest one, shows more distance from Salafism, many rich Salafis can be found. On the other hand, among the inhabitants of the popular quarter we have seen here, the Salafi way seems only to appeal to Magdy. Shaykh Muhammad's influence on him is obvious, and Magdy admires him.

Nevertheless, all have in common, except perhaps Sayyid, that they have each made certain points of the Salafi discourse their own. They claim a strong contrast between their idea of a shaykh and the idea of a shaykh they attribute to Sufis, which is based on divine grace (*baraka*) and miracles (*karamat*). A shaykh must distinguish himself by his knowledge; he is mainly an ulama, or at least he has to convey the ulama's opinions to less knowledgeable people. They all criticise the concept of men of religion, evoking the theological principle that there is "no clergy in Islam" (*la kahnut fi l-islam*). However, even Magdy, Ahmad and Yasir, who consider Salafi preaching the true expression of Islam, do not apply its injunction of a life dedicated to religion. The picture of a Salafi tide advancing without hurdles is inaccurate to reflect the complex interplay of involvement and distance at stake.

The Shaykhs and the Others

I would like here to give examples of discussions of religion found in my notes on the group I have just talked about. This will give further insights on how religious positioning works.

Once, sitting with Sayyid, Ahmed, Yasir and Magdy at a coffee shop, I asked

Magdy what a shaykh is. "The shaykh brings the words of the ulama to the people", he said. I asked him how can one orient oneself among shaykhs of different trends? "You have to find the opinion that makes you feel comfortable". The term shaykh has two meanings in Magdy's eyes: "An old man" or "A young man who lets his beard grow and learns religious science". Magdy presents himself as convinced by Salafi thinking. I ask him about the excommunication (*takfir*) of unbearded men. "There is no such thing!" he answers.

Sayyid compares Salafis to people who try to sell you a mobile phone with Qur'anic verses. Magdy categorically refuses this analogy. In his eyes, they are referring to the Prophet himself, through knowledge of the hadith. The science gets deeper and deeper because they correct each other. A shaykh can change his opinion after coming across new information. Shaykhs transmit the considerations of the ulama: "This is *haram* for this and this reason in the opinion of one, and for this and this reason in the opinion of another … at the end, it's all the same!"

They discuss the shortening of clothes according to Salafi principles. Sayyid says it does not matter. They debate siwak, a twig used for cleaning teeth, which Magdy likes.[6] He cites a hadith and argues for its proven hygienic properties. Sayyid sees the hadith as contextual most of the time. In his eyes, siwak is useful, but there are other products as good as siwak, so why not use them? He also cites the *higgama*, the cupping glasses. In his opinion, it is Bedouin medicine. Sayyid relies only on the Qur'an and the hadiths which quote God's words. He makes fun of the "half-sleeved shaykh" (shaykh *ibn el-baluna*) who has an opinion about everything. He speaks about Shi'ism, for him a *madhhab* like any other, as well as the Ibadites in Oman. He gets a phone call and leaves us shortly to talk. His three cousins are wondering about his opinions and stubbornness. Magdy: "He would speak that way even in front of Shaykh Muhammad!" Sayyid comes back. Magdy accuses him of being a Muslim Brotherhood member. I ask about the relationship between Salafis and the Muslim Brotherhood. Magdy replies, "There is a war between them". Salafis don't get involved in politics: "They reform society".

Later during that week, I meet Shaykh Muhammad at his house. He is with a young man, Fu'ad. Shaykh Muhammad is around fifty years old and Fu'ad is twenty-five. The conversation is held in classical Arabic. Their talk is full of hadiths as arguments, of Qur'anic verses. Fu'ad speaks the most and Shaykh Muhammad listens to him, adding here and there a lighter comment or a story. According to them, shaykh can be used to mean: an old man (but this is less common than *hagg* or *'amm*), any person who lets his beard grow, or someone with religious knowledge. Shaykhs have differing opinions but there is only one dogma (*'aqida*) based on the same pillars (*arkan*). They quote an excerpt from a hadith:

> There are seventy-one Jewish groups, one of them will go to paradise and seventy will go to hell; Seventy-two Christian groups, one of them will go to paradise, seventy-one will go to hell; by God, my community is divided in seventy-three parts, one of them will go to paradise, seventy-two will go to hell.[7]

The path is to follow the example of the Prophet. You have to go back to the Qur'an, to the Sunna and the *igma'*.[8] You cannot invent your own opinion, you must refer to an existing one. On the other hand you do not have to follow a special *madhab*. You have to imitate the Salafs, not a *madhhab*. You have to imagine all the ulama are in the room for discussion. "This is for the old things, for new things it is different", concludes Fu'ad. I ask them about the *zebiba* verse and its interpretations.[9] While Fu'ad seems more willing to support the interpretation that considers *simahum* as a kind of facial harmony, Shaykh Muhammad considers *simahum* as the *zebiba*. In the end, Shaykh Muhammad states, "The verse expresses the greatness of prayer".

A few days later, I am sitting with Salih at a coffee shop. He seems profoundly disturbed. He speaks most of the time with a very weak voice, sometimes barely comprehensible, but when he speaks about religion, he raises his voice and is often nearly screaming. In his opinion Sufis constantly repeat the name of God, and that is senseless. If you want to pray, you have to address God with regard to his specific attributes. If you are looking for mercy for instance, you have to call him "the Merciful [al-Rahman]", and not endlessly repeat "Allah! Allah!" He also condemns the cult of tombs which Sufis practise. You have to show respect to shaykhs, but "there are limits". I ask him about diversity in Islam: "The credo is one!"

Salih also explains to me that you have degrees of associationism (*daragat al-shirk*), as you have degrees of impiety (*daragat al-kufr*). Sufis, for instance, who treat shaykhs like God, are associationists. A government that does not apply the shari'a is *kafir*. On the other hand, to make fun of a girl wearing a full veil is also associationism and *kufr*, because your joking and flirting interfere with religion, but to a lesser degree. I ask him about his opinion of 'Amru Khaled, the well-known TV preacher. He compares him to people who belong to the Muslim Brotherhood:

> They are thinking about their interests ... It's the most important thing for them ... For instance, someone wearing sneakers and thinking only about sport, it's better if he prays ... or an actress, far away from mores, from her traditions and uses, she can wear the veil ... it's politics!

They are bound to their time. He cites some more uncompromising shaykhs, like Muhammad Hassan, a Salafi TV preacher.

A shoe-shiner takes his shoes. Salih seems worried that he cannot see him returning. Eventually he does bring them back. Salih pays him, then looks at his feet with obvious satisfaction. It is good to have shiny shoes in case you meet a girl, he explains.

In these instances of religious argument, there are common points. In the first discussion, especially according to Magdy, shaykhs are seen mainly as transmitters of religious science. God's word is one, and they are seen as able to decrypt it and convey it to the people. Shaykh Muhammad embodies this knowledge. Sayyid, who defends a more relativistic point of view, is seen as making false compromises. In this regard, he appears to Magdy to be close to the Muslim Brotherhood, who are always suspected of neglecting religion in favour of political aims. While talking with Shaykh Muhammad, I saw his knowledge at work. When a point of disagreement appeared between him and Fu'ad, as it did regarding the prayer mark, they managed to save the situation in front of me through a general statement on the greatness of prayer. Finally, the discussion with Salih shows how far an ambivalent commitment to Salafism can go, to borrow Samuli Schielke's words.[10] In his case, it is bound to a profound instability. In his anathema of Sufis and compromising shaykhs seeking influence and money, he introduces an interesting grading of faults and an implicit hierarchy of behaviour. Thus, his own desire to flirt with girls can be religiously framed.

Othering the Pious in Cairo

The notion of the shaykh is an interesting pointer for exploring the way religious commitment is apprehended by a majority of Cairenes.[11] Patrick Gaffney defines the word as defining "a relative degree of social distance".[12] This appears in the discussions I have cited, through the figure of Shaykh Muhammad or in the hierarchy of behaviours evoked by Salih. Further, I would argue that there is a general trend to consider Salafis as a new kind of shaykh. In this regard, calling anyone wearing a beard a shaykh can implicitly mean that exemplarity actually only applies to his behaviour, as the data from my fieldwork suggests.

The use of titles in Egypt is extremely generous, since any student can be called a doctor or even a professor, any employee an engineer, and so on. Here, flattery and irony are inseparable and the title of shaykh is no exception. It could apply to any individual displaying religious knowledge but is also used to designate a bearded man. Indeed, this was experienced by an acquaintance of mine, an Italian anarchist growing his beard as a tribute to Wladimir Bakounine. The use of the colloquial verb *istishiyakha* is therefore revealing. It means "becoming a shaykh" or "playing the shaykh"; it could mean to mend one's ways, or be used to sarcastically refer to someone pretending they have religious authority without any serious knowledge; or to someone having become Salafi. This last meaning prevails among my youngest interviewees. The sarcastic nuance must be emphasised to be reasserted. Talking about someone giving religious lessons without knowledge, for instance, a girl told me "*da bye'mil mistashiekh*", which could be translated as "that one there is pretending to be one becoming the shaykh!"

A vast sarcastic and even disparaging repertoire denouncing hypocrite shaykhs is also constantly employed in Egypt. Indeed, the behavioural exemplarity claimed by some devout believers could at any time be turned against them. In contrast, most people see themselves as one of the "normal people", following less rigorous religious prescriptions. Here one can see the outline of the referents of normality, providing orientation for common religious practices. For instance, a man who was usually called a shaykh because of his regular and assiduous prayers refused the title when smoking hashish with friends: the break between normality – implying fallibility – and exemplarity clearly appears here. In an environment where different referents such as love, religion and professional success compete, and Salafi involvement appears in constant danger of fading, strong differences can arise in a network of relatives and acquaintances, even between a Salafi shaykh and his sons.

As I said before, there is tension among Salafis between the claim for distinctive doctrinal purity and the will to convert all Muslims to the Salafi creed. My observations suggest a mirroring of this tension among non-Salafi Muslims. Salafis are seen as a new group of shaykhs, so they do not belong to common people. It is a way of othering them. Salafis, as shaykhs, are others in terms of knowledge, dedication and exemplarity. As with all representations arrived at through othering, this permits the rise of stereotypes and the enclosing of Salafis in the bounds of a restricted identity. Eventually, this leads us to the important issue of religious authority. How far does it reach? Claiming the truth of Salafi interpretations does not mean abiding by its principles. For many Cairenes, these are true opinions about Islam, not a way of life they claim.

Notes

1. *Galabiyya*: the long Arab tunic.
2. Fadwa El Guindi, "Veiling Infitah with Muslim Ethic: Egypt's Contemporary Islamic Movement", *Social Problems*, vol. 28, no. 4, April 1981, pp. 445–85.
3. Roel Meijer (ed.), *Global Salafism: Islam's New Religious Movement*, New York: Columbia University Press, 2009.
4. For those with a similar interest in the perception of Salafi trends in Egypt, see: Patrick Haenni, "Ils n'en ont pas fini avec l'Orient: de quelques islamisations non islamistes", *Revue du Monde musulmans et de la Méditerranée*, no. 85/86, 1999, pp. 121–47.
5. Some films released in the 1990s that aimed to fight the Islamists raise the topic; however, this is a subject of a separate article.
6. A twig used mainly by Salafis to clean their teeth.

7. This famous hadith reflects the tensions I evoked among Salafis, between exclusiveness and the will to convert all Muslims. If the saved ones have to be a minority, the rallying of a majority to one's opinions would mean that they are wrong. This version can be found in Shaykh Nasir al-Din al-Albâny's collection, *al-Silsila al-Sahiha*, vol. 3, hadith no. 1492.
8. The consensus of the ulama.
9. The *zebiba* is the mark on the foreheads of many men caused by the prostrations of prayer. In verse 29 of *Sura al-Fath*, the word *simahum* is interpreted either as designating the *zebiba* as an attribute of true believers or a general harmony of features, according to my Egyptian interviewees.
10. Samuli Schielke, "Ambivalent Commitments: Troubles of Morality, Religiosity and Aspiration among Young Egyptians", *Journal of Religion in Africa*, vol. 39, 2009, pp. 158–85.
11. Aymon Kreil, "Se faire cheikh au Caire: exemplarité et intériorité religieuse", *Archives de Sciences sociales du Religieux*, no. 149, January 2010, pp. 255–72.
12. Patrick Gaffney, *The Prophet's Pulpit: Islamic Preaching in Contemporary Egypt*, Berkeley; Los Angeles; London: University of California Press, 1994, p. 31.

Chapter 14

Ethics of Care, Politics of Solidarity: Islamic Charitable Organisations in Turkey

Hilal Alkan-Zeybek

Within the social sciences, giving to the poor is analysed primarily through its impact on receivers. Research questions in this area are usually limited to a few variants: how effective is a certain kind of giving for the alleviation of poverty?[1] How does it construct the poor?[2] Or how does it affect the class structure in society?[3] Yet, any kind of giving requires the involvement of at least two actors and, as a process, it has effects on both sides. Those who, in a specific moment, occupy the position of the giver are also shaped and transformed by the act and the context that surrounds it.

With this understanding, a general category of religious giving – in this case Islamic giving – requires further elaboration and a detailed analysis that illustrates the differences between forms of giving, levels of engagement and their political and social potential. In this article I will follow the analytical differentiation between charity and solidarity. According to Bora, these two ways of fighting poverty share the common characteristic of being dependent on individuals' benevolence and will to share their wealth with those in need.[4] Yet they are different in their implications and potentialities. While charity is the act of giving without establishing any personal relationships, the recognition that any hint of intimacy may turn the encounter into one of obligation; solidarity aims to do exactly what charity tries to avoid, which is to establish personal contact.

In the following sections this difference will be explored by providing an ethnographic account of what happens at the moment of beneficence; that is, at the moment of the encounter between benefactors and beneficiaries. It is the use of the ethnographic method, with a focus on the moment of the encounter, that allows moving away from canonical explanations of importance given to charity in Islam towards an understanding of the piety practised in different kinds of giving. Most saliently, the ethnographic account illustrates that religious giving is not only about alleviating poverty but also about transformation on the side of the giver.

This article is based on ethnographic research that I conducted between August 2008 and July 2009 in Kayseri, a central Anatolian city in Turkey. With its population of almost one million, Kayseri is a relatively wealthy city, where wealth, religiosity and benefaction are interwoven with each other as structural elements of the self-representation of local identity. In a recent scholarly report, the economic boost of the town is explained in Weberian terms of Protestant ethics.[5] In the report, the entrepreneurs of the town are identified as Islamic Calvinists with asceticism and a unique ability to generate profit.

However, in this illustration, beneficence appears to be another business of Muslim "businessmen". Fine distinctions between those who donate money and those who organise the distribution of those material resources, and therefore have close encounters with beneficiaries in an everyday manner, become irrelevant. It is in this context that I will introduce the ethics and politics of benefaction and emphasise its layered and often conflicting nature, which only becomes visible through a fine ethnography.

Among Charity Workers

In June 2009, I spent a day with Nihal and Fatma, two middle-aged female volunteers, travelling all around Kayseri in Nihal's car. We were on a mission to pay house visits to supplicants of the institution that these two women had helped to found and had since been working at as volunteers. This organisation helped poor couples who wanted to marry but could not afford it financially. With the help of sponsors, the organisation would provide some basic household items, furniture, a wedding gown and a suit for the groom. They would also cover legal marriage expenses. Employees of the organisation used a checklist to make preliminary assessments of supplicants, with the aim of verifying their poverty and/or orphanhood. Then these two women would pay house visits to cross-check the stories.

Our trip on that particular day started with getting lost on the outskirts of the city and taking more than an hour to find the first address, which had been provided with inadequate detail. When we arrived, both Nihal and Fatma were tired and irritated to such a degree that they reminded each other to be patient and congenial. The house of the supplicant was situated in a garden, typical of the summerhouses of the wealthy inhabitants of Kayseri, but it was visibly old and weary. It was a lovely day, so although the lady of the house invited us in, Fatma and Nihal preferred to sit on the benches in the garden. When we were settled, the lady rushed back inside to make us tea, despite Fatma and Nihal's objections. On her return, she told us that she was trying to arrange her son's wedding. She was facing difficulties because all the family's wealth had been lost as a result of her ex-husband's lifestyle.

She was particularly concerned about keeping her application to the organisation hidden, because she wanted to keep up appearances with her in-laws. Fatma was particularly taken by the story and openly empathised with her wish. After checking with Nihal (without saying a word, but by exchanging a knowing glance and nod) Fatma then approved the application and explained the necessary steps they would have to take afterwards. We sat there for almost an hour, sipped two glasses of tea, and while we were leaving Fatma and Nihal hugged the woman and affectionately kissed her youngest child, a ten-year-old boy.

On our second stop on the other side of the city, we were welcomed in a shanty house, lacking the most basic household items. Here, the lady of the house offered us peanuts and tea and explained that she was trying to organise her daughter's wedding. Again, we spent nearly an hour chatting about the situation of the bride-to-be. Fatma and Nihal offered her advice on how to get more than the routine package, consisting of a bedroom set, an oven and a sofa set. We left the house after hugging and kissing everybody, including the neighbours who happened to drop by while we were there. When we got to the car, Fatma told Nihal to put a note on the family's file indicating that they should be given extra food boxes.

There were ten addresses on our list that day and it was already past noon. Nihal and Fatma therefore discussed refusing any food or drinks, and cutting the visits as short as possible. They wished to stick to their primary aim, which was investigation. Yet, because they were both unhappy about the connotations of refusing somebody's hospitality, we ended up eating a plateful of cherries at our next stop. They had to spare the next day (which was a Sunday) to complete the visits, since we could only cover half of the addresses that day.

According to Sennett, in the established Western traditions of social work, it is common practice to keep at a distance from the beneficiaries (or clients as it is preferred); to maintain a calm and reserved attitude; and to avoid physical contact.[6] In that context, the attitudes of these two women may seem extraordinary, as they were not reserved, they seemed to lack clear-cut personal boundaries, and they frequently established physical contact during their encounters with the beneficiaries. They were also comfortable receiving gifts from beneficiaries in the form of food and drink. Yet these differences cannot be simply summed up as cultural dissimilarities since they imply significant distinctions with ethical and political implications *within* the charitable field of Kayseri.

Bodily attitudes towards beneficiaries vary greatly between those who work in charitable organisations and those who donate money to charitable projects.

Who you eat with or touch as a "benevolent person" is not a random question, as dispositions about bodily boundaries are defined in gender-specific racial and class terms in Kayseri. The boundaries are especially pronounced between Turks, Kurds and Roma; and between the upper-middle classes and those who live in poverty. In this respect, bodily dispositions are at the heart of an important distinction between two different sorts of benevolence, *vakıfçı* (those who work for charities) and *hayırsever* (philanthropists). Let us explore this distinction, for it provides an array of meanings and practices in Kayseri.

BETWEEN PHILANTHROPISTS AND CHARITY WORKERS

In Kayseri, public figures are proud of the fact that their town does not need public funds to build schools or mosques, as their business community provides more than enough. The philanthropists of the city display this pride by giving their names to such facilities. But the climate of public beneficence does not only generate bricks-and-mortar civic gifts, but also supports a diverse array of charitable organisations. These non-governmental organisations (NGOs), although their legal statuses differ greatly, call themselves *vakıfs*, with reference to the Islamic civil welfare institution more frequently known by its Arabic transliteration, *waqf*. They specialise in different tasks such as providing food, clothing, furniture and bursaries to the poor of the city. They also run bathhouses, educational facilities and shelters for the mentally ill and cancer patients. Yet, these institutions are not only dependent on the support of the business community. The charitable scene of Kayseri shows an intermeshing of public and private funds, NGO and municipal involvement and the efforts of individuals who are not necessarily related to any of these parties.

Among those who work in this field in Kayseri, a significant distinction is made between vakıfçı, the men and women of vakıf; and hayırsever, the benefactors/philanthropists. Although these two categories are often used descriptively, they are also notably value-laden. Vakıfçı refers to those who devote their labour, time and energy to charitable work like Fatma and Nihal, whether in private or institutional settings. They are the volunteers, employees, managers and active board members of the charitable organisations. They may also be the men and women who do not have any institutional engagement but are still known for "devoting their lives" to beneficence. Vakıfçı are in close contact with the people they help. Hayırsever, on the other hand, literally means those who love philanthropy, connoting a lesser degree of hands-on involvement and, instead, moral and financial support from outside. Hayırsevers are usually *not* involved in the daily operations of the institutions but support them with donations, preferring, especially, large-scale projects such as building schools or mosques. Yet of course most of the vakıfçı financially support their institutions and engage in private benefaction by giving money away too. So it is not possible to apprehend this distinction by focusing on the form and quality of what is given.

What distinguishes vakıfçı from hayırsever is the former's proximity to the beneficiaries. The philanthropists rarely meet the people for whom they are donating, unless they are invited by the organisations to witness the use of their donations. Yet these occasions are less about establishing an engagement than observing the use of money. In contrast, being a vakıfçı involves extensive encounters with the people in need, as well as occasionally establishing long-term, sustained relations. The difference between these two emic categories matches the distinction made by Bora between charity and solidarity, and it has significant implications that will be discussed in the final section of this chapter.

The distinction between vakıfçı and hayırsever has important gender and class dimensions. In corollary with the uneven distribution of property ownership among men and women in Kayseri (as in Turkey generally), hayırsever of the city are almost exclusively men. Although it is quite common to come across schools or soup kitchens named after women, this is because of an established tradition where husbands or sons sponsor civic gifts to commemorate the women of their families or carry their name. Yet among vakıfçı, men and women are equally active, either as volunteers or as paid employees.

Again as a direct derivative of wealth, hayırsever exclusively belong to the upper classes, while among vakıfçı there are industrialists who work actively in the organisations they have founded, as well as workers surviving on low salaries.

As I have mentioned, vakıfçı have first-hand, face-to-face encounters with the beneficiaries and supplicants of their organisations and they are responsible for the immediate care-giving and care-taking activities that their organisations offer. Their daily contact with beneficiaries and supplicants lead vakıfçı to revise their attitudes and be forced into situations they would otherwise have avoided. The singularity of the encounter and the intimate content of the care relationship impel vakıfçı into directions they appreciate but find hard to bear. It forces them, first of all, to alter their embodied dispositions against the poor and poverty. At the same time it leads them to engage in reciprocal gift relations that, to a certain extent, level the hierarchical positions of givers and receivers.

My observations in Kayseri have demonstrated that for the middle and upper-class women of the town, poverty necessarily implies dirtiness and poor health. Also, imbued with racial prejudices against the Roma and the Kurds of the town, these women find it difficult to transcend the class and racial boundaries that separate them from the poor on the grounds of hygiene and cleanliness. Entering the houses of poor people, eating their food or kissing their children poses quite a challenge for these women. But again the experiences of Nihal and Fatma, with their daily encounters, illustrate how racialised and discriminatory dispositions are alterable. Indeed, they need to be altered if one wants to be a vakıfçı.

Nihal and Fatma, two seasoned vakıfçıs with more than ten years of experience working in the field, have specific ways to relate with beneficiaries of their institutions. This is the outcome of an ethical transformation they have lived through during this period of time and which is widely shared by other vakıfçıs. When I asked Aliye, a female volunteer of another organisation providing for the poor, how volunteering affected her life, she said: "I have gone beyond myself. I used to refrain from eating strangers' food but I began eating it. I used to refrain from sitting down in a poor house but I started to do that. I witnessed great changes in myself, and I am very happy about it."

Aliye is a wealthy woman aged over sixty. She covers her hair with chic silk scarves and always wears elegant clothes. Her gold-rimmed glasses and rings with precious stones disclose her upper-class position. She is responsible for running the public bath of a charitable organisation in Kayseri, where she interacts with the poorest women and children of the inner city. Catering to those who do not have access to running water, she is at ease with women who roam around the bath naked, making casual and friendly conversation or smoking in the foyer without the slightest embarrassment about their nakedness. And here, Aliye sits and chats with them, checks their papers and has the Turkish bath experience on a fortnightly basis, including being washed by one of the employees of the bath. Bathers at the public bath usually bring some food with them and share it with bath house employees, including Aliye. Aliye accepts and reciprocates with her own food offerings. Aliye eats her lunch with a score of naked and half-naked women and their children, as well as with two employees who were once beneficiaries of the organisation, but who were offered employment at the bath house a couple of years ago. From feeling uncomfortable about even entering slums at one point, she now has the most intimate contact with their inhabitants, although not without conflict and restlessness.

In the following section I will focus on care as a dimension of solidarity and as a corporeal phenomenon that opens up a space for transformation in the case of charity workers.

Embodied Ethics

The ethical transformation Aliye and other vakıfçıs lived through does not necessarily imply a radical change from conceiving of the poor as dirty. Although it definitely leads to a habitual presumption that they are not dirty, this change of behaviours does not begin or end with such a change of assumptions. It is rather a piecemeal transformation that involves action more than reflexive questioning of beliefs and conceptions. The crux of the ethical transformation is that it is acted out before becoming one.

In her ethnographic monograph about the female participants of the Mosque Movement in Egypt, Saba Mahmood discusses the premises of positive ethics in understanding ethical and pious agency.[7] According to Mahmood, in post-Enlightenment thinking, ethics are often conceived as an abstract system of principles, values and regulations.[8] In this Kantian tradition, ethical reasoning is more emphasised than ethical practices. Practices are either seen as habits that do not qualify as virtue or as actualisations of some abstract values and principles. In this understanding, ethics always starts with critical reasoning, hence within the person, which then creates a change in behaviour. Therefore the direction of the ethical transformation is from inside to outside. Yet in positive ethics – Aristotelian ethics – moral actions are not seen as contingent but as constitutive elements of the content of the ethical norm.[9] Therefore the variety of relationships that can be established between various elements of the self (including the body, affects and reason) and the accepted norm becomes a matter of analysis.[10] This variety allows the transformation to take the opposite direction: values and attitudes that change with an alteration of actions and behaviours. Rituals, prayers, fasts and meditation may all be counted as classic examples of technologies of transformation starting from the outside. Following this vein, I approach the formation of an ethical being through the never-ending processes of becoming a vakıfçı as a matter of adapting actions, donning new stances and meticulously working on behaviour.

In our case, there is, of course, a norm, which is hardly surprising: a vakıfçı should be indiscriminately compassionate to all creatures of God. This norm is repeated piously among vakıfçıs as it represents the will of God for being a good Muslim. Yet, if one wants to enquire about the mechanisms through which religious ethics are embodied, it is neither fruitful nor explanatory enough to simply ask about the norms or question if they are being observed. For the vakıfçıs of Kayseri the ethical odyssey of becoming better Muslims involves, maybe more than anything, letting their bodies learn how to enact compassion and how to transgress the boundaries their dispositions pose. This corporeal process requires them to act compassionately in order to be compassionate, not vice versa. It also requires physical contact with the poor, before (or even without) questioning the assumptions about the dirtiness of poverty. Therefore what we see here is an aspect of religious ethics that is not focused on distinguishing what is dirty from what is clean, but an aspect that challenges established racial and societal prejudices about cleanliness.

This corporeal ethical process does not follow a path of linear progress and is never complete. A person acting in one way in a certain context does not necessarily guarantee similar behaviour in a different context. Between each reiteration there is always an opening that allows different interpretations, challenges, renunciations and retreats.[11] Still, by repetition, slowly, intermittently and equivocally one's body changes its posture, its limits, and its tendencies to fear, recoil, show disgust and wince. This is the habituation of virtue, which Kant disregards as a part of moral establishment,[12] yet this is what can be observed in the bodily attitudes of Fatma, Nihal and Aliye in most of their interactions with the beneficiaries of their organisations. Hence their religious ethics find expression in practices that are germane to their vakıfçı activities.

The religious ethics of vakıfçı is primarily an ethics of care that is shaped by daily acts of attending to the other party's needs. These needs are often very material, like those of housing and nutrition, but they are also psychological and spiritual like the need for recognition. Both these needs and their provision have very visceral and corporeal dimensions for the care to be fully practised. An emphasis on this bodily and practical aspect of care is widely found among scholars of care, whether they are philosophers, political scientists or psychologists.

In an attempt to consider the ethics of care through the lens of phenomenology, Maurice Hamington approaches it as an ultimately embodied phenomenon and argues that bodies are not only objects or instruments of care, but also the very possibility of care.[13] This possibility is related to the unarticulated nature and primacy of the body's knowledge and its communication of this knowledge through behaviours. Because of this inherent bodily aspect, Hamington argues that "as a corporeal potential, care can be cultivated or diminished through practices and habits".[14] In a similar fashion but coming from a different background, political scientist Selma Sevenhuijsen argues:

> the core idea of the ethic of care in my view is that care is a practice, and that it is crucial for developing a moral attitude – and thus also a moral vocabulary – of care by engaging in the practice of care. By doing so care can in fact grow into a disposition, a part of our everyday thinking and doing.[15]

The crux of the difference between vakıfçı and hayırsever lies in the practice of care. If, among many other things, charity/benevolence is an act of caring about others, being a vakıfçı is actively caring for them. In that sense, the distance that keeps hayırsevers separate from the people they care about also makes them more prone to established bodily limits and societal prejudices. On the contrary, with the active practice of caring, vakıfçıs are more open to impact and ethical change that is shaped by the corporeal aspects of care itself.

Therefore, as much as charity or being a hayırsever is a hygienic and contingent way of (non)engagement, solidarity or being a vakıfçı makes one susceptible to the other's material and inner world. This contact brings forth an ethical transformation at an individual level that is encouraged and supported by religious premises. Yet, more importantly, at the social and political level it brings forth a transgression of social barriers and a potential for understanding and caring about the suffering of those who are socially distant. Moreover, paying attention to practices of piety at the moment of encounter between givers and receivers teaches us about the potential for a religiously-informed, ethical transformation that cannot be immediately assumed by looking at what is commonly said and written about charity in Islam.

Notes

1. Amartya Sen, "Poverty: An Ordinal Approach to Measurement", *Econometrica*, vol. 44, 1976, pp. 219–31.
2. George Simmel, "The Poor", *Social Problems*, vol. 13, 1965, pp. 118–40; and Lydia Morris, *Dangerous Classes: The Underclass and Social Citizenship*, London, New York: Routledge 2001.
3. Ayşe Buğra, "Poverty and Citizenship: An Overview of the Social-policy Environment in Republican Turkey", *International Journal of Middle East Studies*, vol. 39, 2007, pp. 33–52.
4. Tanıl Bora, "Sadaka, sosyal yardım, dayanışma, örgütlenme", *Birikim*, vol. 241, 2009, pp. 19–23.
5. European Stability Initiative, *Islamic Calvinists: Change and Conservatism in Central Anatolia*, Istanbul: ESI, 2005.
6. Richard Sennett, *Respect in a World of Inequality*, New York: W. W. Norton & Co., 2003.
7. Saba Mahmood, *Politics of Piety: The Islamic Revival and Feminist Subject*, Princeton, NJ: Princeton University Press, 2005.
8. Ibid., p. 119.
9. Ibid., p. 120.
10. Ibid., p. 120.
11. Judith Butler, *Gender Trouble: Feminism and the Subversion of Identity*, New York: Routledge , 1999.
12. Mahmood, *Politics of Piety*, p. 26.
13. Maurice Hamington, *Embodied Care: Jane Addams, Maurice Merleau-Ponty, and Feminist Ethics*, Urbana: University of Illinois Press, 2004.
14. Ibid., p. 5.
15. Selma Sevenhuijsen, "Trace: A Method for Normative Policy Analysis from the Ethic of Care", paper presented to *the Centre for Women's and Gender Research*, University of Bergen, Norway, 2003.

CHAPTER 15

Making Shariʻa Alive:
Court Practice under an Ethnographic Lens

SUSANNE DAHLGREN

In this chapter, I present a court case litigated in one of the family sections of the Aden Magistrates' Court, situated in the southern part of the Republic of Yemen. I will argue that while in current Yemeni legal debates opponents have labelled the 1974 Family Law as "deviating from the shariʻa", legal practice needs to be taken into consideration to see how shariʻa was actually practised during the course of that law (1974–92). My aim is also to demonstrate that by applying the ethnographic method in a study of court practice, something new can be discovered in the legal history of a particular country.

In Adeni divorce litigation, several normative sources for legitimate rights are present. These include the statutory family code (during the years 1974–92, Law no. 1 of 1974 in relation to the family), abstract understandings of the shariʻa and norms that spring from the ʻurf (customary law). Although in Aden, ʻurf does not constitute a sophisticated "tribal law" as in other parts of Yemen, it nonetheless remains a vivid structure of understanding as to what is right and wrong and by which moral expectations individuals are bound in various positions. In a divorce court, these three sources of rights come into play between the judge, the litigants, and their barristers and witnesses.

In the Family Court, men and women come to litigate cases of divorce (khulʻ and faskh, and under the 1974 law also the talaq),[1] child custody, maintenance and inheritance disputes. I will show how legal practice is "made" Islamic, that is, how small events in court contribute to people's understanding of how Islam is practised as a legal approach.

Divorce in Court: An Ethnographic Account

The Family Section of the Aden Magistrates' Court is a small courtroom closed to the public. Outside the courtroom, people sit and squat along the long corridors as they wait for their turn to be called in. An usher, an elderly woman called Hajja (a woman who has conducted the pilgrimage to Mecca) and dressed in the traditional black chador drawn over her hair, controls who can come in and out of the court. When a new case begins, the judge asks the usher to call out the names of the litigants. It is late morning and this is the first case of the day. There are not many hours left in the working day, as everything winds down in the court building after the midday prayer call. Those present are usually the judge, the scribe, the court secretary and archivist, the tea maker, the litigants, the possible witnesses the court will hear and the barristers, the legally trained jurists who help to prepare the cases and speak on behalf of the litigants.

The case I will discuss was tried in 1989 when the old 1974 Family Law was in force. This law, which made it possible for women to bring a family dispute to court, was throughout the 1970s and 1980s increasingly employed by women to gain their rights.[2] The marriage counselling system, or obligatory arbitration (*tahkim*) that the law introduced, made a contribution to curbing men's "easy divorces", which talaq at that time was understood to be (Family Law 1974 §25b). Out-of-court talaq became illegal with the 1974 law, and it became mandatory to bring all divorces to court, even those that were not disputed.[3] In addition, every couple was obliged to consult a representative of the neighbourhood Popular Defence (People's) Committee or the district clubhouse of the General Union of Yemeni Women. Often couples were sent to both on several occasions. People's Committees were neighbourhood organisations based on the Cuban model[4] and assigned to issues relating to public order, minor offences and social problems. They were usually chaired by a man. Women's clubs in districts had a female social secretary in charge of counselling. It was thus likely that the couple met a male arbitrator in the People's Committee and a female one in the Women's club. This arrangement was an attempt to avoid gender bias. The judge's decision was based on each party's testimony of the "facts" that led to the marital breakdown. These included character witnesses, recommendations by the official arbitrators, and any other evidence.

Under study here is a divorce case where a couple jointly decided to seek divorce. It follows the procedure of court talaq, separation upon mutual consent without fault. According to the 1974 law, the wife is entitled to maintenance (*nafaqa*) during her *'iddat* (the waiting period of three menstrual cycles before she can remarry). The husband acts as the plaintiff.

In my field notes I recorded the following account of the court case:

We have gathered in the smallest courtroom of Sira Court to witness the litigation of a divorce case. The judge is a woman in her mid-thirties, a graduate of the Aden University Faculty of Law. She wears her ordinary work attire, a Western-style cotton dress, and allows her hair to be uncovered. She sits at her desk, an ordinary worn-out office table arranged at the end of the room. Placed against the desk, in front of her, is another table that has long benches on both sides, the place for the scribe, barristers, litigants and witnesses. Her male secretary sits on one side of her desk and handles the clerical work. The secretary is about the same age as the judge, and he wears the typical government employee attire, straight slacks and an ironed white shirt.

A young female law student serves as the scribe assigned to write the record of the sessions and to interview the people who give a statement in the court if the judge prefers not to do it herself. She is a fourth-year law student and is undertaking her on-the-job training, part of her final year of studies. Uncommonly for this period (1989), she is a *muhajjaba*, that is, she is a woman who wears a black coat (*balto*) and a scarf that covers her hair (*hijab*). She has occupied the closest seat on the bench to the judge. On each side of the table sit the litigants, a couple in their mid-thirties. The man works as a guard in a government office. His modest and weary attire, a *futa* (loin cloth) and untidy colourful shirt, speak of his modest social position. The thin man looks tired and depressed. He sits in a flattened position on the bench opposite the scribe, embodying his disillusioned state of mind.

The woman is a factory worker. She works at a conveyor belt and wears the usual attire of a woman from a modest social background: a colourful *dar'a*, the traditional transparent Adeni voilé dress and a black overcoat *chador*. Occasionally she pulls the chador over her head and holds it tight with her teeth. She covers her hair with a loose headscarf (*mandil*). The testimony she is about to deliver gives the impression that she is satisfied with the situation. She sits in an upright position and follows the court proceedings carefully.

The physical attire of each person present symbolically links to the social hierarchy that will structure the court session today. The judge leads the proceedings in a respected position, a position that not only her formal education but also her personal 'charisma' (*karama*) have bestowed on her. The session proceeds under her disciplinary grip and the litigants open their mouths only when she grants permission.

I sit at the end of the bench in my usual attire in Aden: Western-style clothes that respect the modesty code, and I try to be as unobtrusive as possible. The court translator sits next to me, a man in his fifties who acquired his skills in translating from Arabic to English during the British era when the judge was British. The court translator is not a modest man and does not bother wearing the work attire of the white-collar employees, but settles for his leisure-time attire, the futa and an untidy white shirt. Occasionally I have to ask him to lower his voice, as he tends to carry out his interpretation so loudly that I can no longer follow the proceedings. This man works on a freelance basis and I have asked him to accompany me in order not to miss the slightest detail of the session. Earlier, I had met with the director of the Magistrates' Court, the head *qadi* (judge) who works for the Ministry of Justice, to grant me permission to attend. I had also asked the judge of this court for permission to observe the case, and once the litigants arrived, I explained my study to them and enquired whether they objected to my presence, which they did not.

After all the commotion of barristers and litigants of other cases coming and going and everybody trying to finish things before the session starts, the door is finally closed and the initial hearing can begin.

The court scribe announces the names of the litigants and enquires about the facts. While interviewing the litigants, she writes down the information on a form where the details of each case are recorded.

> *Court scribe:* The marriage is registered in the district of Crater. Have you had sexual intercourse?
> *Man and woman:* Yes.
> *Scribe:* Do you have any children?
> *Woman:* No.
> *Scribe:* Are you presently pregnant (to the woman)?
> *Woman:* No.
> *Scribe (to the woman):* Do you agree on the divorce?
> *Woman:* Yes.
> *Scribe:* Are you convinced of the divorce without any compulsion?
> *Woman:* Yes.
> *Scribe:* Is there any chance to reconcile?
> *Man:* We have agreed on the divorce.
> *Scribe to the woman:* Do you want anything from your husband?
> *Woman:* No.
> *Man:* Only the divorce.
> *Judge to the man:* Do you want the *mahr* (dower) paid back to you?
> *Man:* No.

The scribe now proceeds to ask for the woman's identity card to write down her personal data. At this point, it is the woman's turn to speak under oath. She stands up and raises her right hand to swear the oath: "I will speak the truth and nothing but the truth. Allah is my witness." As she has her menstrual period, she cannot place her hand on the Qur'an while taking the oath.

The scribe goes through the same questions with the woman who now speaks under oath. She repeats the question as to whether the woman is willing to divorce and ascertains that she has not been subjected to any duress.

Scribe: Do you renounce all your rights?
Woman: Yes.
Scribe: Do you demand anything from your husband?
Woman: Only my wardrobe (*kiswa*). I will pay half of its value to him, 3,175 shillings (158.750 Yemeni dinars).[5]

The purchase is agreed upon. The court then proceeds to discuss the maintenance issue (nafaqa). The man has agreed to pay 10 Yemeni dinars each month, about a fifth of his monthly salary during her 'iddat as alimony. The judge asks if this can be taken directly from his salary. The man insists that he pays on a monthly basis through the Popular Defence Committee to receive written proof of the payment. The final deliberations of the judge are that the court will first seek reconciliation and if that fails, the court will allow the divorce in due course.

In the next court session, a couple of weeks later, the judgement is read. Present are the same people as in the first session.

Judge: In the name of the people, the Court gives the following decision. (to the man): Is this the first divorce?

The man takes the oath. He stands up, places his right hand on the Qur'an and looks into the eyes of his wife, as he is instructed to do, and announces solemnly: "I will divorce thou". The scribe counts the wife's 'iddat as three months, and the judge announces that after the lapse of 'iddat, she will be free to marry another man. The husband is ordered to pay the alimony to her as maintained in the first session.

The court session proceeded smoothly, as there was no tension between either the divorcing couple or between the judge and the litigants or their barristers. The case was based on agreement between the husband and wife, and for the judge, on a legitimate reason for divorce: the couple could not have children. As the appeal for divorce came from the husband and it was supported by the wife, the court did not have to discuss the medical question, as would have been the case if there was discord.

Analysis

Let us turn to the ethnographic facts presented above to see how the court session can be read as a practice of shari'a. To highlight the structural elements that are present but not immediately visible, I will apply the *practice perspective* as outlined by the American anthropologist William Hanks. According to Hanks, practice has both schematic and emergent aspects. Schematic aspects are features that are repeatable and relatively stable that actors have access to as they enter into engagement. Emergent aspects are those that emerge over the course of action, as part of the action. Unlike the schematic aspects, the emergent aspects are not given to agents prior to engagement. In other words, the emergent aspects are neither prefabricated nor stable but in process.[6] To apply this conceptualisation to the litigation process, we can treat legal structure and the normative systems applied as schematic aspects while emergent aspects are manifested in the argumentation and actions in court. This type of analysis allows consideration of legal practice both in space and time as unfolding the process of making.[7]

The session begins with an enquiry as to whether the marriage has been consummated, which follows the classical Islamic jurisprudence (*fiqh*) on determining the status of marriage. The couple are asked about children, that is, if the divorce will involve custody considerations. The scribe also determines whether the woman is currently pregnant, a matter that has consequences for the length of time she has to wait until she can remarry ('iddat).

By asking the woman if she agrees to the divorce, the court is able to determine the type of separation that is in question as well as the nature of the demands both are allowed to make. The matter of compulsion in divorce is then addressed, in order to ascertain whether the divorce is based on mutual consent (*mubara'a*) under Islamic law. Then the husband is asked if he wants to receive compensation for the divorce, that is, for the wife to return the dower he paid at the time of their marriage and stated in their marriage contract. The husband declines. Thus, this is not a case of khul', meaning divorce on the initiative of the wife in exchange for economic compensation for the husband. As the couple did not exhibit discord, the court could proceed with treating the husband's appeal as court talaq.

The 1974 law promulgates divorce under the heading "Judicial Separation" (Part II, §§ 25–30). Paragraph 25(b) states:

> No divorce shall be effective or notarised except with the leave of a competent divisional court, and such a court shall not grant such leave unless the matter was first referred to the People's Committee and after failure of all attempts to reconcile the married couple and is satisfied that the divorce is justified by reasons which render it impossible for the married life and the happy union to continue.

The conditions for divorce continue as follows: "Every divorce shall be reversible except the one competing with the third divorce" (§ 27). Court talaq differs from court termination of marriage in that the latter requires legitimate reasons (§ 29).

A man is free to repudiate his wife according to the Shafi'i school[8] by uttering talaq in any combination of written or oral expression. He is entitled to take her back during her 'iddat, irrespective of the wife's willingness to return.[9] In contrast, the 1974 law outlaws repudiation without the wife's consent and also sets her consent as a condition for her return to her husband.

In the case described above, the judge was not willing to grant divorce in the first session. When the wife took the oath, she could not touch the Qur'an, as she was having her menstrual period. According to Shafi'i fiqh, divorce that takes place during the wife's menstruation is void. Even though this is not indicated in the 1974 law, the judge decided that the court could not grant a divorce. This procedure makes the divorce a *sunna* divorce as outlined in a local commentary on the fiqh.[10] Another factor that is pertinent to the law also delays the announcement: the People's Committee has to reconcile between the spouses before the divorce becomes effective.

Other schematic aspects unfolding in the process include the oaths the litigants were asked to take. As the woman has her menstrual period, she is excused from touching the Qur'an. Her oath, however, is still considered to be legitimate. In fiqh, bleeding transforms a woman into an impure state. The court required testimonies given under oath, which is not standard practice in this area. As Maktari explains in reference to agricultural courts in the neighbouring province of Lahij, disputants are normally not asked to give testimony under oath. An oath is needed only to affirm the truthfulness of a testimony if not presented by two witnesses, or when one of the witnesses is discredited. This is because according to Islamic law, complete *bayyina* (evidence) consists of two witnesses.[11] Oath-taking in Adeni courts follows the Anglo-Muhammadan law that was practised here in the colonial era until 1967. In English courts, the oath is taken by placing one's hand on the Bible. This has been transformed into an Islamic practice by replacing the Bible with the Qur'an.

Still, oath-taking has become a central method in Islamic jurisprudence for verifying legal claims. It is not proof as such, but an indication of proof for the qadi.[12] Nevertheless, an oath taken in the court discussed here does not have the same function, although it is applied to all testimonies. The way the oath is practised here echoes the Anglo-Muhammadan legacy, a legal culture that embeds several sources of law including classical fiqh. It represents many of those instances where classical fiqh is blurred with other, later sources of law, resulting in new understandings of shari'a.

Promoting reconciliation between a couple in marital discord echoes the common belief in Aden that God abhors divorce.[13] The way divorce is executed in the second session follows conventional shari'a practice. The husband is asked to announce "I divorce thou". To make the announcement in a respectable way, the husband is instructed to look into his wife's eyes and to pronounce the formula. Even though classical Shafi'i jurisprudence does not require witnesses when the divorce is announced, it is recommended that witnesses of *'adala* (morally sustained) quality are present in case the divorce is later disputed.

Under the 1974 law, talaq was brought to court to ensure that the legal consequences of divorce, such as custody and maintenance, were acted upon. During the colonial period in which Anglo-Muhammadan law was practised, maintenance issues were treated under a separate appeal in another court. The British often complained that the litigants, in particular women, applied different strategies in these two courts in order to maximise their benefits. According to the 1974 law, the steps taken to perform court talaq could be considered a guarantee for avoiding "bad" divorces such as *talaq al-bid'a*.

Conclusions

In this chapter, I have tried to demonstrate through my ethnographic observations how a judge in a divorce court attempts to adjudicate Islamic law, sometimes with the help of statutory law and on other occasions by relying on classical Islamic jurisprudence or local customs understood to be in accordance with shari'a. When getting to know the judge, I got the impression that she was highly concerned that justice be served in her court. In other cases that I followed in her court, I observed how she made every attempt to serve justice to the weaker party, which was not always a woman. As a female judge, she was aware of the prejudice that the "Women's law"[14] favours female litigants. In the court case discussed here, the issue was not to guarantee a weaker party's rights but to ensure that talaq was processed in a sound manner. In other words, in her emergent aspects of practice, not required by the 1974 law, the judge participated in *making* shari'a into practice.

Notes

1. *Khul'* is divorce instigated by the wife in exchange for compensation to the husband; *faskh* is the annulment of marriage or divorce by the court on prescribed grounds initiated by the husband or wife; and *talaq* is the husband's repudiation of the wife, normally out of court.
2. During the British colonial era (1839–1967), divorce was litigated in the Supreme Court under a British judge, following the model from British India called Anglo-Muhammadan law. See Susanne Dahlgren, *Contesting Realities. The Public Sphere and Morality in Southern Yemen*, Syracuse, New York: Syracuse University Press, 2010. In the 1950s, divorce cases initiated by women were rare, while out-of-court *talaq* was very common (Ronald Knox-Mawer, "Islamic Domestic Law in Aden", *International and Comparative Law Quarterly*, 1956, pp. 511–18). In 1957–8, the *madhun* (marriage registrar) recorded seven to eight divorces for every ten marriages

contracted (Aden Colony, *Reports for the Years 1957 and 1958*, London: Her Majesty's Stationery Office, 1961, pp. 92–3).
3. Family Law, *Law no. 1 of 1974*, Official English translation, Information Department of the Ministry of Information, Aden, Yemen: 14 October Corporation, 1976, § 25a.
4. The Committees for the Defence of the Revolution is the largest mass organisation in Cuba, charged with solving social problems in neighbourhoods.
5. This sum amounts to about three times her monthly salary.
6. William F. Hanks, *Language and Communicative Practices*, Boulder, CO: Westview Press, 1996, p. 233.
7. Sherry Ortner has suggested that in the social sciences, "making" can refer to a dynamic way of seeing things emerge in attestation, resistance, negotiation and enactment: see Sherry B. Ortner, *Making Gender: The Politics and Erotics of Culture*, Boston, MA: Beacon Press, 1996.
8. The four Sunni law schools differ little in determining how talaq should be uttered. The majority of Adenis follow the Shafi'i school.
9. Ahmad ibn Naqib al-Misri, *Reliance of the Traveller. A Classical Manual of Islamic Sacred Law*, Beltsville, Maryland: Amana Publications, 2008, pp. 559–60, 564–5.
10. Islamic jurisprudence distinguishes between the different categories of divorce: *sunna* (commended); unlawful innovation (*bid'a*); and that which is neither (al-Misri, *Reliance of the Traveller*, p. 558). The nineteenth-century Adeni jurist al-Mekkawi calls "the best form of divorce" the one that is made in between two menstrual periods and observes the iddat (Shaikh Abdul Kadir bin Muhammed al-Mekkawi, *A Treatise on the Muhammedan Law*, Cairo, Egypt: Moustapha El Baby El Halaby & Sons, 1959 [1886], pp. 291–2).
11. Abdulla M. A. Maktari, *Water Rights and Irrigation Practices in Lahj: A Study of the Application of Customary and Shari'ah Law in South-West Arabia*, Cambridge: Cambridge University Press, 1971, p. 99.
12. Knut Vikör, *Between God and the Sultan. A History of Islamic Law*, Oxford: Oxford University Press, 2005, p. 178, n. 24.
13. al-Mekkawi, *A Treatise on the Muhammedan Law*, pp. 289–90. The idea is based on the hadith "No permissible thing is more detested by Allah than divorce" (al-Misri, *Reliance of the Traveller*, p. 556 and Vikör, *Between God and the Sultan*, p. 309).
14. The 1974 law was popularly called the Women's law, as people believed that with this law, women gained their rights for the first time in history: see Susanne Dahlgren, "Women's *adah* vs 'Women's Law': The Contesting Issue of *mahr* in Aden, Yemen", in Baudouin Dupret and François Burgat (eds), *Le shaykh et le procureur: systèmes coutumiers et pratiques juridiques au Yémen et en Égypte. Égypte/Monde arabe*, no. 1, 3rd series, Le Caire: CEDEJ, 2005, pp. 125–44.

CHAPTER 16

Referring to Islam as a Practice: Audiences, Relevancies and Language Games within the Egyptian Parliament

Enrique Klaus and Baudouin Dupret

In this chapter, we address the question of referring to Islam as a social practice, not in abstract terms, from an overhanging viewpoint, but as it is embedded in members' routine activities. Hence, the relevance of ethnography in our undertaking, for referring-to-Islam is a situated accomplishment that must be described in context and in action. What it contextually means and "does" to refer to Islam can only be elucidated through a close description of people's orientation to, and reification of, categories as they emerge from their actual encounter with social matters.

The context we are dealing with is the Egyptian parliament in the course of a session that was part of the broader polemic resulting from the publication of declarations allegedly made by the Minister of Culture Faruq Husni, in which he considered the Islamic headscarf as a mark of backwardness. This session constitutes a "perspicuous setting"[1] for the study of referring-to-Islam as a situated practice, since there were numerous references to Islam as the session unfolded. Our data consist of the official verbatim transcription produced by the parliament's secretary, and submitted to the deputies for approbation for all practical and bureaucratic parliamentary purposes.[2] The secretariat's concern for accuracy is obvious in these documents, through following endogenously developed rules, but also in respect of a procedure which accounted for a genuine editorial work (the formulation used to refer to the participants, the description of specific actions, or the elision of injurious words). As such, the official minutes prove sufficiently detailed (registers of language, errors of syntax, repetitions, interruptions, applause, and so on) to attest to their faithfulness to the original interactions during the parliamentary session.

In previous works, we have reconstituted the "dialogical network" around which the polemic is articulated, and studied the mechanisms specific to the birth, the growth and the death of this scandal. Focusing on the parliamentary session, we have detailed the procedures which constrain talk at the people's assembly (*majlis al-shaʿb*) – mainly the speech allocation system – in order to document its very institutional character.[3] Here, we intend to study the discursive resources at the participants' disposal to play with such institutional constraints. Through the detailed description of a limited number of speech-turns, three different resources of discursive alignment are considered. With reference to Islam in scope, we will observe how members of parliament (henceforth MPs) (1) resort to particular sets of relevancies, (2) address physical and virtual audiences alike, and (3) explore specific language games, in order to have their fellow MPs side with them.

A parliamentary session is a peculiar moment in public debates. It is grounded in an institutional context which is oriented towards specific practical ends (for example, votes for the law; questions to the government; budget approbation), and which is organised around a set of procedural rules (the by-laws). The debate unfolds in a sequential way, through a succession of contiguous and interactive interventions. At least five different kinds of intervention are distinguishable: (1) the assembly speaker's turns, which are mainly procedural (agenda, speech allocation, repairs to breaches made to the allocation system); (2) legitimate speech turns by MPs (that is, those regularly allocated by the speaker); (3) discursive, sonorous or gesture interruptions to the latter, which are always illegitimate (except for the speaker) and might be ignored by the legitimate orator; (4) interruptions taken into account by him; and (5) salvos of applause that might punctuate or interrupt some speech turns.

In the course of a parliamentary debate, MPs routinely address various audiences and mobilise different sets of relevancies, that is, repertoires on which a discursive alignment is operated and whose observance is claimed, including the principles that rely on the order of truth that they establish.[4] The fact that the session is inaugurated in the name of God immediately accounts for the legitimacy of resorting to a set of relevancies considered Islamic. In parallel, the fact that it is also opened in the name of the people warrants the validity of the democratic and constitutional relevancies, that is, the mechanism of parliamentary representation formally warranted by the Constitution and the basic principles of the rule of law. However, relevancies are never permanently given for granted and always remain emergent. The mere invocation of the legitimacy of a set of relevancies does not suffice to ensure its actualisation.

In the debate on the minister's statements, other categorical relevancies also found their way in, be it Egyptian identity or Arab nationalism. Therefore, sets of relevancies are multiple, intertwined and open for modulation, and only a detailed description of their contextual unfolding allows one to measure their importance and observe their mechanism:

Excerpt 1: Parliamentary Session, 20 November 2006

Mr the Honourable Deputy 'A. 'Abd al-Ghani

138 Mister speaker, this is a subject of the highest importance and we all have to take care
139 of it. Yes, we are an Islamic State. Yes, our Constitution stipulates that the shari'a is the
140 main source of our legislation. Yes, we are all Muslims. Yes, we are all fond of the Islamic
141 religion, the Islamic predication (*da'wá*) and the principles of Islam.

Resorting to a set of relevancies sets forward the terms in which the debate will properly unfold, thus leading to the impossibility of taking part in the debate without relying on the resources that such a register offers. In other words, the terms of the debate are established and, somehow, it becomes impossible to escape them. Excerpt 1 is one of the many occasions in which a close link between Islamic and constitutional relevancies is projected. The statement "Egypt is an Islamic State" (line 139) not only refers to a religious belonging, but also to a constitutional provision (Article 2), which the orator exploits to underscore the inscription of law in the Islamic frame. The projection of both relevancies to the foreground leans on various rhetorical devices, such as scansion (lines 139–40: "Yes, we …") and listing (lines 140–1: "the Islamic religion, the Islamic predication and the principles of Islam").

Obviously, both constitutional (relating to the principle of legality) and democratic (relating to the principle of majority) relevancies constitute grade-one registers at the people's assembly:

Excerpt 2: Parliamentary Session, 20 November 2006

Mr the Honourable Deputy M. Dawûd

599 Mister speaker, the truth is that the human being which is inside of us is really pleased by
600 what is going on at the Egyptian people's assembly, today, on behalf of both the majority
601 and the opposition, regarding a specific minister, with all my respect for the person of
602 the minister. But, Mister speaker - and this is a very important thing - it is the people's
603 assembly that the people have chosen and it is the Minister of Culture who comes to
604 us from the days of the 'Atif Sidqi cabinet. Each prime minister who took office found
605 himself with an imposed minister, Faruq Husni, the one who can scorn today the will of
606 the people of Egypt, which is the land of al-Azhar, the source of Islam, and the beacon
607 of Islam. Today, we stand up to protest against the blow struck on the veil in France and
608 in any other country. Today, what will we do, Mister speaker, as people of Egypt? And
609 who will answer the deputies of the Egyptian people's assembly, from both the majority
610 and the opposition? Because there's a blow struck on the foundations of religion, Mister
611 speaker. This is what Almighty God said, not Ahmad Nazif. No, Mister speaker, we
612 cannot leave the subject and treat it with indifference; otherwise, Islam will be a subject
613 of mockery for the government of the national party. At the same time, I am grateful to
614 my colleagues, the deputies from the national party, the deputies from the opposition
615 and the independents, because there is a common position against a minister who has
    struck a blow against the true religion …

This excerpt is one of the most explicitly political speech-turns during this session. It is noteworthy that this orator is a member of an ultra-minority opposition party in the Egyptian parliament (the neo-Wafd). His argument is grounded in a contrast between the MPs, who stand as representatives of the nation as they are elected by the people (lines 602–3), and Faruq Husni, an irremovable member of the cabinet whose presence has been imposed on successive governments for the past twenty years, without regard for the popular will (lines 603–5). Out of this, the orator builds up a second contrast between the cabinet as a whole, which might rise to mock Islam (lines 612–3), and the deputies – whatever their political leanings – who hinder attacks on "the true religion" (lines 614–15). In other words, the argument is founded on the idea that, as an emanation of the popular will, the people's assembly cannot be but faithful to a "true" conception of religion, and that its very democratic legitimacy constitutes it de facto as the ultimate guardian of its respect. In contrast, the successive cabinets, on whom the minister has been imposed, are deprived of popular representation and, consequently, ministers may well hold religion up for derision. In sum, democratic relevance draws a discriminatory line between representation and authoritarian rule, and its association with the register of Islamic relevance allows the orator to put into equation democracy and genuine "Islamic-ness".

In this excerpt, several audiences are called upon as recipients of the speech-turn: the speaker, different groups of deputies, the majority party, the Egyptian people, a former and present prime ministers, Almighty God and foreign states. The projection of these recipients authorises the convocation of what can be called in semiotic terms "actants", whether virtual or "material", who embody the relevancies. In a game interweaving audiences and registers of relevance, deputies categorise the public they represent and address them to mark the camps that are present to create antagonisms and alliances and to provoke alignments. This rhetorical strategy is founded on the idea that speech possesses performative virtues.

The speaker and the deputies from the opposition and the majority constitute audiences who are physically present alongside the orator. At the opening of this speech-turn (line 599), the speech is formally addressed to the speaker in a routine fashion, thus constituting him as a procedural audience (see also Excerpt 1, line 138). Yet, as he is one of the party's pundits, his many convocations within this intervention (lines 602, 608, 610–11) show that the speaker's alignment with the orator's position is not irrelevant to the latter. By addressing MPs directly as one of them, and by underscoring their convergent viewpoints, the orator projects the existence of a kind of negative solidarity on the primacy of Islam and its intangibility without consensus on the content of this principle.[5] Playing with the multiple audiences, he is able to transcend the classical parliamentary oppositions and to produce a "we", from which no other participant can retract. This "we" is first constituted by the MPs (line 599) and comes up to encompass the whole of the Egyptian people (lines 603, 606–8), before being circumscribed, once again, to the MPs (line 611). Another illustration of the game of audiences interwoven with registers of relevance is noteworthy in the reference to "France and any other foreign country" (line 607), which pops up as a kind of contrast. The foreign audience, to whom Egypt has addressed its opposition on different occasions, enables the orator to establish a dichotomy between the Egyptian and Muslim "we" and the foreign and non-Muslim "they", thus paving the way for the rejection of the minister in the latter category.[6] The Islamic and national relevancies mobilise – for the practical and immediate purposes of the unfolding parliamentary debate, and through membership categorisations – the use of contrasted audiences previously established in the debate.

Excerpt 3: Parliamentary Session, 20 November 2006

Mr Speaker
815 The subject is closed, but the chairman of the commission for religious and social affairs
816 and *awqaf* asks for the floor. After you.

Mr the Honourable Deputy A. Hashim
817 In the name of God, the Clement, the Merciful. Thank you, Mister speaker. While we are
818 discussing the subject, we have to put in balance that such a phenomenon has previously
819 been discussed, when the book *Banquet for seaweed* was released,[7] and we are discussing it
820 now with the affair of the veil. It is an affair that has already been treated, about which
821 there is no controversy. And it is not possible to infringe on it because it is clearly [stipu-
822 lated] in the Book of God: 'They [fem.] shall not show their attire but what appears of it'.[8]
817 What is revealed in the Book of God and what is revealed in a text from the Qur'an,
818 nobody needs to talk about it, neither make concessions on it, whatever the circumstances.
819 (applause) ...
878 (applause) Our religion is eternal ... Our religion is eternal ... Our religion is the religion
879 of the [true] values, our Prophet is the Imam of the Sent Ones, our religion is an eternal
880 religion. Our Islamic community has been described in the Book of the Lord as 'the best
881 community [ever] conceived of for men', without complaisance towards it, but from the
882 fact that it encapsulates the rest of the faith on the surface of earth. He said: "You form
883 the best community conceived of for men, you order what is acceptable and you forbid
884 what is blameable. You believe in God."[9] By the One who holds my soul in His hand, and
885 by the One who is second to none, if we applied the teachings of the Prophet – upon him
886 be the prayer of God and salvation – we would be, as the Qur'an establishes, "the best of
887 the communities". So, let us edict a law that criminalises and forbids all those who try to
888 offend Islam or any other religion. Because we are the community to whom it was asked
889 to believe in the whole of the [revealed] Books and in all of the prophets. Have I testified?
890 May God be witness![10] Have I testified? May God be witness! May the peace of God and
891 His mercy be upon you. (applause)

Excerpt 3 contains the opening and the closing of Hashim's speech-turn, in which the main point he is trying to make is calling for a law criminalising what he depicts as offenses to Islam and other religions (lines 887–8). While law proposals lie at the very heart of parliamentary work, the orator is pursuing this goal in a rather unconventional way, by making use of a specific language game which departs from more traditional interventions in Parliament (for example, Excerpt 2). By virtue of this language game, his speech turn is virtually turned into a sermon (*khutba*) and, correspondingly, the MP is transfigured into a preacher. As for relevancies, the indexation of a language game is never achieved once and for all: language games are always pervasively emergent and need to be actualised through devices irreducible to the language game at work.

Right after the closing of the debate, Hashim is remarkably given the floor in his capacity as chairman of the commission in charge of religious affairs (lines 815–16). His ex officio intervention may explain the fact that his speech-turn is one of the lengthiest in the whole debate, in an obvious departure from the practical parliamentary grammar. Like other MPs (eleven out of twenty-five), he acknowledges his taking of the floor by means of a set expression called *al-basmalah* (line 817), thus forecasting the Islamic relevance, before procedurally addressing the speaker. Then, he contrasts the anteriority of the topic MPs were discussing (lines 817–20) with the fact that such a topic is not open for discussion (line 820–1). In the words of Heritage and Greatbatch, the comparison with a former affair coupled with the assertion concerning the very possibility of talking about the debated issue creates a puzzle that calls for resolution.[11] Part of the solution is given in the form of a verse from the Qur'an (lines 821–2), which is meant to apply to the subject under discussion. This is a typical move as far as sermons are concerned, where quotations from the Qur'an are embedded in the course of an argument. Yet, this is not enough to disambiguate the previously set puzzle. The punch line is delivered in a statement holding God's word as intangible (lines 822–4), thus producing a first round of applause.

Overall, seven salvos of applause scatter this speech-turn, that is, a bit more than a third of the total number of bursts of applause during the whole debate. Such a reflexive attitude on behalf of Hashim's fellow MPs reminds one of similar expressions of pragmatic alignment in the course of a sermon. It is as if the direct physical audience constituted by the MPs replaced interjections commonly heard at the mosque (for example, "Allah!" or "amin!") with applause, which is more appropriate in the institutional context of parliament.

Reaching the sixth salvo of applause (line 878), and comforted by so many pragmatic alignments, the orator makes use of another typical device of the sermon, namely, scansion, employed here for the predication of Islamic religion and community (lines 878–82). This predicative move is sustained by a second quotation from the Qur'an, in which the Islamic community is depicted as "the best community [ever] conceived of for men".[12] Then, the orator thrusts forward, by swearing twice to God (lines 884–5), that it would be so, only if the Prophet's teachings were applied, thus constituting both God and Prophet Muhammad as transcendental audiences. The logical linkage (line 887) of this argument with the main point defended here (that is, promulgating a law that would criminalise offenses to Islam) completes the intertwining of the parliamentary task of law proposal with the accomplishment of God's word in a kind of formulation[13] that announces the closing of this sermon-like allocution.

The speech-turn is closed with a device that elicits a final salvo of applause: a three-part list. Consistent with the sermon language game, the latter is composed of two set-phrases referring to Islam. One is the traditional greeting in Islamic society, which also punctuates prayers, and which here closes both the list and the speech-turn. The other is asserted twice and corresponds precisely to the words used by the Prophet at the very end of his last sermon. This explicit reference to "the farewell sermon" (*khutbat al-wada‘*) retrospectively allows the speech-turn to be heard as instructed by the language game specific to the sermon.

Throughout this chapter, we have considered the social activity of referring to Islam as a practical accomplishment. We have described three different devices through which participants of a debate in parliament referred to Islam, namely: orientation towards specific relevancies, calling upon certain audiences, and exploring particular language games.

Mobilising relevancies brings to the foreground the circles of an unfolding debate. This is accomplished in a rather coercive fashion, insofar as it becomes difficult for prospective participants to retract from the "imposed" relevancies. Relevancies can overlap, as we have seen in the parliamentary session under study, where the Islamic, institutional and constitutional relevancies were closely intertwined. Parties in a debate can employ relevancies by themselves (see Excerpt 1), or they can rely on different kinds of audiences to "embody" them (see Excerpt 2). Audiences are multiple, by definition, and they can be either physical or virtual. They play an important role in the many orientations that a debate can take as it unfolds, as they allow the underscoring of partition lines between the different camps that are present, thus sealing antagonisms and alliances. If relevancies and audiences can interweave, they can also be embedded to sustain a specific language game, which is always contingent upon the specificities of the interactions in which it is used. The use of specific language games almost subliminally marks an orientation towards a specific relevance. As we have seen in Excerpt 3, the orator adopts some conventional forms of speech, typical of sermon preaching, thus marking his orientation towards the religious/Islamic relevance.

Our close descriptions of these devices as they actually appeared in the course of a parliamentary session prove that referring to Islam is not a monolithic and transcendental undertaking, merely amounting to the orientation towards a "set" corpus of authoritative sources (the Qur'an, the Sunna and fiqh). It is, rather, a practical achievement that has to be described in the actual context of its instantiation. Hence, only ethnography can provide us with the necessary tools to come to the conclusion that the social activity of referring to Islam cannot be anything but the contextual product of situated interactions informed by a cluster of various practices.

Notes

1. Harold Garfinkel and D. Laurence Wieder, "Two Incommensurable, Asymmetrical Alternate Technologies of Social Analysis", in Graham Watson and Robert Seiler (eds), *Text in Context: Contributions to Ethnomethodology*, London: Sage Publications, 1992: , pp. 184.
2. The session is archived online (*www.parliament.gov.eg*).
3. See Enrique Klaus, Baudouin Dupret and Jean-Noël Ferrié, "Derrière le voile: analyse d'un réseau dialogique égyptien", *Droits & Sociétés*, vol. 68, 2008; Baudouin Dupret, Enrique Klaus, and Jean-Noël Ferrié, "Scandal and Dialogical Network: What Does Morality Do to Politics? About the Islamic Headscarf within the Egyptian Parliament", in Richard Fitzgerald and William Housley (eds), *Media, Policy, and Interaction*, Aldershot: Ashgate, 2009; and Baudouin Dupret, Enrique Klaus, and Jean-Noël Ferrié, "Parlement et contraintes discursives. Analyse d'un site dialogique", *Réseaux*, no. 148–9, 2008.
4. Jean-Noël Ferrié, Baudouin Dupret and Vincent Legrand, "Retour sur la politique délibérative en action: une position praxéologique", *Revue française de science politique*, vol. 58, no. 5, October 2008, p. 798.
5. Jean-Noël Ferrié, *Le Régime de civilité en Égypte. Public et Réislamisation*, Paris: C.N.R.S. Éditions, 2004.
6. See Ivan Leudar, Victoria Marsland and Jiří Nekvapil, "On Membership Categorisation: 'Us', 'Them' and 'Doing Violence' in Political Discourse", *Discourse & Society*, vol. 15, no. 2–3, 2004.
7. A novel by Syrian writer Haidar Haidar, which was first published in Beirut in 1983 and which was reprinted in Cairo in 2000, stirred up virulent demonstrations by Islamist militants who held it as injurious for Islam.
8. Qur'an 24.31.
9. Qur'an 3.110.
10. Literally: "*alla qad Ballaghtu, allahumma fa-ashhad*"
11. John Heritage and David Greatbatch, "Generating Applause: A Study of Rhetoric and Response at Political Party Conferences", *American Journal of Sociology*, vol. 92, no. 1, 1986.
12. Later in his speech, the orator also uses a hadith.
13. John Heritage and Rod Watson, "Formulations as Conversational Objects", in George Psathas (ed.), *Everyday Language*, New York: Irvington Publishers, 1979, pp. 123–62.

CHAPTER 17

Contesting Public Images of 'Abd al-Halim Mahmud (1910–78): Who is an Authentic Scholar?

HATSUKI AISHIMA

In recent decades, professional boundaries between Islamic studies and sociocultural anthropology have blurred, as anthropologists have started to produce insightful work on scholarly cultures of Islam, illuminating the diverse manners in which canonical texts are acquired, produced and performed in a given sociohistorical context.[1] Such ethnographies from Muslim societies have shed light on the profane life of sacred texts, analysing the everyday contexts in which ordinary Muslims skilfully employ the words from the Qur'an and hadiths (accounts of Prophet Muhammad) quoted by religious authorities for their purposes.[2] At the same time, field research has become a common approach in Islamic studies when exploring the topics where written accounts are scarce.[3]

My study furthers such enquiries into Islamic knowledge and scholarship through the prism of a former Shaykh al-Azhar, 'Abd al-Halim Mahmud (1910–78) who continues to receive exceptionally high media attention, as compared to his contemporaries.[4] I approach Islamic intellectual fields as markets for producing specific cultural commodities, which result from dynamic interactions between authors and their intended audiences. This article is largely based on the ethnographic data I gathered from my two-year period of fieldwork in Egypt (April 2006–October 2008) where I organised "tutorials" with educated Egyptians who were willing to assist me with reading the books by 'Abd al-Halim Mahmud. These tutorials provided the perfect arena to discuss my interest in exploring the notion of an "authentic scholar" (*'alim salih* or *sahih*) of Islamic sciences or "Islamic thinker" (*mufakkir islami*) from the perspective of Egyptian Muslims of educated middle-class backgrounds. I took note of the interpretations my informants gave of 'Abd al-Halim's writings, and of the discussions we had on the notion of being a modern scholar and, in general, on the status of the

Islamic knowledge derived from our readings. I was interested in exploring the ways in which educated Egyptians define the profile of a public personality such as a *muthaqqaf* (cultured person, intellectual), *mufakkir* (thinker, intellectual) or an *'alim* (scholar).

Three decades after his death, radio recordings of 'Abd al-Halim Mahmud's lectures and reprints of his publications continue to attract new generations of urban professionals who aspire to maintain a cultured life after completing school education. His attempt to market literatures of Sufism as essential knowledge of Islamic culture gained a favourable following among non-specialist audiences. Yet his colleagues from scholarly communities – Egyptian Orientalists (professors and graduate students specialising in Islamic philosophy or Sufism as a scientific field of the humanities and social sciences, rather than embodied knowledge for enhancing one's religious beliefs and practices) – tend to be rather critical of his success in the mass media. In their view, although 'Abd al-Halim Mahmud's credentials as an authentic scholar of Islamic sciences are questionable, as demonstrated in the lack of erudition in his writing style, he managed to cleverly manipulate his symbolic capital – his doctoral degree in Islamic mysticism from the Sorbonne and the *'alimiya* degree from al-Azhar – to gain public fame. It is worth noting that the writing style of 'Abd al-Halim Mahmud which raised eyebrows among Egyptian scholars, appeared to non-specialist audiences as definitely "scholarly". In other words, what is contested are *registers of judgement*, rather than the actual knowledge contained in 'Abd al-Halim's writing.

Hence, instead of presupposing who 'Abd al-Halim Mahmud *was* simply from his biography, this chapter illustrates the complexity of defining his public intellectual profile through the discussions I had with my Egyptian interlocutors on what they would expect from an "authentic scholar" of Islamic sciences. While the core of my informants consists of educated audiences outside the scholarly community, I also discussed 'Abd al-Halim's work with Egyptian Orientalists. This was to compare and contrast public notions of what it means to be a scholar with those of the scholarly community, in order to better understand the manner in which authentic scholarly credentials are fought over and established in discursive ways. By applying an ethnographic approach to analysing textual materials, my study demonstrates the diverse ways in which Egyptian Muslims *consume* knowledge of their faith produced by public intellectuals, in order to navigate within the ever-contested currents of Islamic resurgence in contemporary Egyptian society.

An Authentic Scholar in the Eyes of the Educated

Most educated Egyptians outside scholarly circles with whom I spoke agreed that 'Abd al-Halim Mahmud was a kind of *'alim*, since he was a professor at al-Azhar University. However, they differed greatly on whether he was also a mufakkir islami or an 'alim salih, depending on how they identified themselves, and their quest for true knowledge, with regard to their faith. For more religiously committed persons an 'alim ought to be a mufakkir, hence 'Abd al-Halim Mahmud was both; but for those who ascribe to the Western ideal notion of an "intellectual" as an independent thinker, the mufakkir's place is somewhere above an 'alim.

One evening, I listened to a debate between Yusuf, a young representative of an internet provider with a BA in commerce, and some of his brothers-in-law who are Salafi-leaning Azharite preachers. According to Yusuf, a mufakkir cannot be an 'alim because the former is credited with thinking freely, whereas the latter's mind is entrapped in institutional knowledge. 'Abd al-Halim Mahmud appears as a government-oriented scholar to Yusuf because he remembers reading 'Abd al-Halim's writing as a part of the national religious education curriculum. Thus Mustafa Mahmud (1921–2009)[5] or Jamal al-Ghitani (born 1945),[6] two famous writers and public figures who studied Islam on their own, are prime examples of mufakkir islami, while 'Abd al-Halim Mahmud, who was a product of the Azhar establishment, could not be more than an 'alim. On the contrary, according to Yusuf's in-laws, a mufakkir islami has to be a professional scholar trained in Islamic sciences. For them, although Mustafa Mahmud could be an 'alim of medical science, he could not be a mufakkir islami because his understanding of Islamic sources was necessarily limited. In the end, the preachers advised me to study Ibn Taymiyya (1258–1326) as a model of a mufakkir islami, because as a Sufi, 'Abd al-Halim Mahmud would only provide a distorted image of Islam to a non-Muslim student like me.

One can add more nuances to this discussion of 'alim and mufakkir. With regard to education and culture, my Arabic teacher Ihsan, who is a young *muhajjaba* (veiled woman) with a BA in English literature, pointed out that a mufakkir does not need to have completed school education, indicating 'Abbas Mahmud al-'Aqqad (1889–1964)[7] as an example of a self-educated writer. She stressed that al-'Aqqad had not even finished elementary school, but that he had trained his mind rigorously through extensive reading in private and produced a number of insightful books. While an 'alim needs intensive training in one specific discipline in order to produce his scholarly work, a self-taught mufakkir is perceived as being able to produce knowledge via individual readings of the sources. Some end-products of a self-taught mufakkir can therefore be as valuable as those produced by a trained 'alim. However, the work of 'Abd al-Halim Mahmud, who is both an 'alim and a mufakkir in her eyes, would be more "reassuring" in terms of its truth value because his ideas are supported by authentic sources such as the Qur'an and hadith. Referring to 'Abd al-Halim Mahmud's autobiography,[8] Ihsan said that he qualifies as a mufakkir islami because he starts with his own ideas (his own motivation to write about his life and God's grace), and then develops his thoughts by relating them to the Qur'an and hadith.

In contrast to the favourable views non-specialist audiences had of my research project, members of the scholarly community were sceptical of the value of studying the life and thought of 'Abd al-Halim Mahmud. For instance, 'Adil, a graduate student of Dar al-'Ulum (the College of Islamic Sciences at Cairo University) who aspires to be a scholar of Islamic philosophy, was initially supportive of my project. However, as we started to go through a book by 'Abd al-Halim, he gave me concrete examples of why this writing – the text was published in a simple paperback without proper footnotes or a reference list – would not qualify as serious scholarship. In a similar context, when I told Nur, a doctoral student at al-Azhar University and an enthusiastic member of a Shadhili Sufi order, about my project, she mentioned that with all respect for *Duktur* 'Abd al-Halim, she would not consider his work as a subject for scholarly research as it was intended for popular audiences. For instance, his book on Ahmad Badawi (1199–1276) is the type of paperback that educated Egyptians might pick up at the railway-station kiosk to read on their way to Tanta in the Nile Delta when attending his *mawlid* (annual birthday festival).[9]

Many scholars were doubtful about 'Abd al-Halim's credentials as an authentic scholar not because of the knowledge contained in his books, but because of the rhetorical style of his writing. 'Abd al-Halim's writing occasionally irritated Doctor Farag, my tutor at al-Azhar University who was a former student of 'Abd al-Halim, because, according to him, 'Abd al-Halim Mahmud *neglected* the rhetorical rules of classical Arabic. For instance, the professor repeatedly stressed that, "If one were to write in a scholarly manner, s/he ought to end the first paragraph of the preface with *amma ba'du*, and start the following sentence with *fa*".[10] On the contrary, 'Abd al-Halim Mahmud ended the paragraph with *wa ba'du* and started the next one with *fa*.[11] Likewise, when we encountered a phrase "*'ala marri al-zaman*" ("the course of time"), Dr Farag asserted that when writing about philosophical or theological subjects, a professional scholar should use a term *al-zamaan* (the time) in contrast to *al-makaan* (the place) to discuss the temporal and spatial order of the universe. Although "wa ba'du ... fa" or "zaman" were not grammatically incorrect, but were rather synonymous expressions, this was unheard of for a man who went through the scholarly training of al-Azhar; they were the style conventionally used by "common people" rather than scholars. Dr Farag once said to me that "Dr 'Abd al-Halim was a learned man, but because he was in France for too long, he had forgotten these basic rules of Arabic". Consequently, he recommended that I look into *The Philosophy of the Kalam* by Harry A. Wolfson,[12] which was his favourite book ever since he discovered it in the SOAS library, so that I would not waste more time on the writings of this pseudo-scholar.

The criticisms of 'Adil, Nur and Dr Farag initially sounded to me like a trivial matter which did not explain much about the nature of 'Abd al-Halim's writing. However, similar conversations took place when I interviewed other Egyptian Orientalists to further my understanding of the evaluation of 'Abd al-Halim Mahmud's work. As in the case with 'Adil and Dr Farag, they would sound delighted to meet a foreign researcher who was interested in the intellectual culture of their country. Yet, many of them attempted to steer my interest towards other intellectual figures, as they were perplexed by my approach to 'Abd al-Halim's writing as a serious scholarly subject. Such conversations reconfirmed my hypothesis that 'Abd al-Halim Mahmud intended his works to be read by non-specialist audiences, rather than only by his colleagues at al-Azhar.

Nobody's Shaykh but Everybody's 'Abd al-Halim Mahmud

'Abd al-Halim Mahmud was (and posthumously, remains) a public intellectual who reproduced scholarly knowledge of Sufism through publications and radio broadcasts that were accessible to the broader public. Compared with the numerous people I encountered in Egypt who claimed to *know* about 'Abd al-Halim Mahmud, it was, however, very rare to find individuals who had had personal interactions with him or even read his books. He seems to be nobody's shaykh but everybody's Shaykh 'Abd al-Halim at the same time. His name is inscribed on the entrance to the College of Fundamentals of the Religion (*kulliyat al-usul al-din*), al-Azhar University, yet there is no sign of "a school of 'Abd al-Halim" developing within the College. In reply to my question with regard to the place of 'Abd al-Halim Mahmud in contemporary Egyptian society, a blind Azharite 'alim[13] who studied with him said: "Dr 'Abd al-Halim was 'a social phenomenon', on a par with Muhammad al-Ghazali [1917–98][14] and Muhammad Mutawalli al-Sha'rawi [1911–96]".[15] These three personalities have in common that they were leading public figures of Islam whose fame was generated and sustained by their constant presence in the mass media – quite apart from any concrete specialist knowledge or experience of them that a given individual might have had. This former student gave me one or two titles of books that 'Abd al-Halim Mahmud had used in his lectures, but had nothing more to tell me about his late professor than that he was a revered 'alim. In this way, as in the case with any other kinds of public knowledge, although memories of 'Abd al-Halim seem to be well rooted in wide sections of the Egyptian public, it is difficult to locate those roots with precision. One thing that my meetings with his former students made clear was that 'Abd al-Halim Mahmud was a celebrity to whom members of the general public were eager to claim connections. Most of them did not have more information about their late professor than what I could acquire from magazine articles, yet they often asserted that they recognised in him the original station of their personal *silsila* (chain, intellectual and spiritual genealogy).

The fragmented nature of memories about 'Abd al-Halim Mahmud can be explained by what sociologist Saeko Ishita characterises as "the nature of a mass media community".[16] Mass media produces abstract audiences, well before the receiver of the information comes into existence. When speaking of somebody's fame, we employ this concept as if it is knowledge shared by "everybody". However, in reality, we have never personally encountered specific instances of "everybody", and so this sense of community in the judgement of fame is a product of images we experience through mass media. While the knowledge of "fame" accumulated through media experiences tends to be vague and fragmented, the possession of this knowledge licenses us to become a part of the community of judgement.

Although very few academic studies have been undertaken on 'Abd al-Halim Mahmud either inside or outside Egypt, there is no doubt that he is one of the more "famous" public religious personalities among educated Muslims and the wider public of Egypt. For instance, 'Abd al-Halim Mahmud has an entry in *Encyclopaedia of 1,000 Egyptian Personalities* which lists iconic figures of the twentieth century. His portrait is in the company of forty-six faces on the front cover of the encyclopaedia, including Sa'd Zaghlul, Taha Hussein, 'Abbas Mahmud al-'Aqqad, Shaykh al-Sha'rawi, and others who "left tangible imprints on the key matters of modern Egyptian society".[17] Such techniques of visually representing an object without verbal explanation (for example, using an uncaptioned photograph of the Eiffel Tower in a travel guide) indicate the highest degree of fame in modern society where mass media has become omnipresent. This technique communicates to the viewer that what s/he is looking at is "something famous" which is widely known among many people.[18] However, as Ishita argues, "fame" is a double-edged sword.[19] While "fame" represents a symbol of success in contemporary society, it also entails a notion of falsity, as the phrase "famous person" may evoke the perception that s/he is a mere name, and the praises attributed to her/him do not match the actual ability of the person. This is especially notable for public intellectuals like 'Abd al-Halim Mahmud and others, as the measure of their "fame" is indicated largely by the frequency of their appearances in the mass media. 'Abd al-Halim Mahmud's presence in the mass media made his work *authentic* in the eyes of the general public. He became a national hero whose legacy was considered worth celebrating by the production of a biopic television series in 2008. However, in contrast to the general public, his efforts to educate people by popularising the scholarly knowledge of Sufism through mass media had the opposite effect on the ways in which the "specialists" – Egyptian Orientalists – evaluate 'Abd al-Halim's scholarship and his status as an authentic scholar. The recognition of 'Abd al-Halim as "a great *'alim*" equivalent to "the Ghazali of the twentieth century"[20] is limited to non-specialist audiences and is less widespread within the scholarly community. Many high-ranking scholars of subjects related to Islamic studies that I met in Cairo, expressed their reservations about the value of studying the work of 'Abd al-Halim Mahmud as a subject of a doctoral thesis on the intellectual and scholarly culture of their country.

Conclusion

The goal of this chapter has been to analyse the public image of 'Abd al-Halim Mahmud among educated Egyptian Muslims from middle-class backgrounds in order to demonstrate the contested nature of the notion of "authentic scholar". The ethnographic approach has revealed diverse ways in which educated Egyptians assess 'Abd al-Halim's intellectual profile in relation to what they know about this public personality and the way they think about the intellectuals of their society. While there seems to be a consensus in terms of the definitions of various expressions related to the subject of knowledge, the credibility of 'Abd al-Halim Mahmud's scholarship and his status as an authentic scholar or Islamic thinker differs greatly between scholarly and non-scholarly audiences. This divide is rooted not only in the ways and degrees to which individuals identify themselves with the Islamic faith, but also in the ways they assess the value of knowledge produced and disseminated through the mass media. Although Egyptian Orientalists are deeply resentful of 'Abd al-Halim Mahmud's success in public Islam, his publications and radio recordings facilitate the maintenance of his status as "the Ghazali of the twentieth century" in the Egyptian public sphere.

Notes

1. See Dale F. Eickelman, *Knowledge and Power in Morocco: The Education of a Twentieth Century Notable*, Princeton: Princeton University Press, 1985; Brinkley Messick, *The Calligraphic State: Textual Domination and History in a Muslim Society*, Berkeley: University of California Press, 1996 [1993].
2. See John Bowen, "Salat of Indonesia: The Social Meaning of an Islamic Ritual", *Man*, New Series, vol. 24, no. 4, January 1989, pp. 600–19; Charles Hirschkind, *The Ethical Soundscape: Cassette Sermons and Islamic Counterpublics*, New York: Columbia University Press, 2006.
3. See Valerie J. Hoffman, *Sufism, Mystics, and Saints in Modern Egypt*, Columbia: University of Carolina Press, 1995; Malika Zeghal, *Gardiens de l'islam: les oulémas*

d'Al Azhar dans l'Égypte contemporaine, Paris: Presses de Sciences Po, 1996.
4. A French trained scholar of Sufism and a Sufi celebrity from the Sadat era (1970–81). For 'Abd al-Halim Mahmud's biography, see Hatsuki Aishima, "A Sufi-'alim Intellectual in Contemporary Egypt: 'Al-Ghazali of 14th Century A. H.' Shaykh 'Abd al-Halim Mahmud", in Eric Geoffroy (ed.), Une voie soufie dans le monde: la Shadhiliyya, Paris: Editions Maison-Neuve Larouse, 2005, pp. 319–32.
5. A former Marxist writer trained in medical science. Mustafa Mahmud became a renowned public intellectual from the late 1960s onwards through his Qur'anic exegesis and autobiographical writings on how he came to accept the Islamic faith. His wonders-of-nature style television documentary programme, Al-'Ilm wa al-Iman (Science and Faith), was immensely successful in the 1980s. See Armando Salvatore, "Decentering Social Services and Recentering Normative Authority: Mustafa Mahmud's Social and Public Islam", in Eberhard Kienle (ed.), Politics from Above, Politics from Below: The Middle East in the Age of Economic Reform, London: Saqi, 2003, pp. 214–28.
6. Editor-in-chief of Akhbar al-Adab (Literature News) and a prolific writer. His latest novel Kitab al-Tajalliyat (The Book of Illumination) is an autobiography narrated through his spiritual interactions with legendary Sufis.
7. A self-taught writer, poet and literary critic, who dedicated his life to spreading liberal and anti-authoritarian views in Egypt. He is known for a fourteen-volume series 'Abqariya (Geniuses), featuring major figures in Islamic history, including the Prophet Muhammad. See Hideaki Sugita, "Aqqad", in Kazuo Otsuka, Yasushi Kosugi, Hisao Komatsu, Yasushi Tonaga, Masashi Haneda and Masayuki Yamauchi (eds), Iwanami Dictionary of Islam, Tokyo: Iwanami Shoten, 2002, p. 107.
8. 'Abd al-Halim Mahmud, Al-Hamdu lillah Hadhihi Hayati (Praise God, This is My Life), Cairo: Dar al-Ma'arif, 2001 [1976].
9. Ahmad Badawi is one of the most venerated Sufi saints in Egypt. The annual festival to celebrate his birthday exceeds all others in its size and fame. The event lasts for a week and is estimated to attract a total of 500,000 pilgrims. See Samuli Schielke, "Snacks and Saints: Mawlid Festivals and the Politics of Festivity, Piety and Modernity in Contemporary Egypt", PhD dissertation, University of Amsterdam, Amsterdam, 2006, p. 216.
10. According to The Hans Wehr Dictionary of Modern Written Arabic, "amma ba'du ... fa" is "a formular phrase linking introduction and actual subject of a book or letter" which could be translated as "Now to our topic". See J. Milton Cowan, "Amma", in The Hans Wehr Dictionary of Modern Written Arabic, 4th edn, Ithaca: Spoken Languages Service, INC, 1994, p. 32. There are some books by 'Abd al-Halim which started with "amma ba'du ... fa" rather than its less formal equivalent "wa ba'du ... fa" (for example, 'Abd al-Halim Mahmud, Tafkir al-Falsafi fi al-Islam (Philosophical Thought in Islam), Beirut: Dar al-Kitab al-Lubnani, 1989 [1955]). However, the majority of his publications do not open with either of these formular phrases.
11. See Abd al-Halim Mahmud, Qadiyat al-Tasawwuf: Al-Munqidh min al-Dalal (The Issue of Sufism: The Deliverance from Error), Cairo: Dar al-Ma'arif, 2003 [1967], pp. 7, 17.
12. Harry Austryn Wolfson, The Philosophy of the Kalam, Cambridge, MA: Harvard University Press, 1976.

13. Taha Habayshi, personal interview, 13 March 2007. At the time of the interview, he was Head of the Department of Philosophy and Doctrine at the College of Fundamentals of the Religion at al-Azhar University.
14. An Azharite scholar who was once a prominent member of the Muslim Brotherhood. Even after his expulsion in 1953, al-Ghazali continued to occupy significant space in the publications of the Brotherhood. He dedicated himself to educating the public by occupying a number of important positions related to da'wa (public "outreach") at the Ministry of Pious Endowments in Egypt. See Rachel. M. Scott, "The Role of the 'Ulama' in an Islamic Order: The Early Islamic Thought of Muhammad al-Ghazali (1916–96)", *The Maghreb Review*, vol. 32, nos. 2–3, 2007, pp. 149–74.
15. Al-Sha'rawi is regarded as the best Egyptian orator of the twentieth century. Many Egyptians became fascinated with his televised lectures on *tafsir* (exegesis) of the Qur'an, which were broadcast from mosques showing him sitting on the floor with the audience, explaining the Qur'an verse by verse, using animated gestures and Egyptian colloquial Arabic. For his biography see Hava Lazarus-Yafeh, "Muhammad Mutawalli al-Sha'rawi: A Portrait of a Contemporary *'alim* in Egypt", in Gabriel R. Warburg and Uri M. Kupferschmidt (eds), *Islam, Nationalism, and Radicalism in Egypt and Sudan*, New York: Praeger, 1983, pp. 281–97.
16. Saeko Ishita, *Yumeisei toiu Bunkasouchi* (The Cultural Apparatus called Fame), Tokyo: Keisoshobou, 1998, pp. 33–8. The nature of the media community described by Ishita is similar to Benedict Anderson's *Imagined Communities*, in the sense that this is a community consisting of people who will never actually meet each other, yet nevertheless feel themselves to be connected: Benedict Anderson, *Imagined Communities: Reflections of the Origin and Spread of Nationalism*, London: Verso, 2003 [1983].
17. Lam'i al-Mut'i, *Mausu'a 1000 Shakhsiyat Misriya* (Encyclopaedia of 1000 Egyptian personalities), Cairo: Maktabat al-Dar al-'Arabiya al-Kitab, 2006, back cover.
18. Ishita, *Yumeisei*, p. 25. For the historical process through which the Egyptian public became accustomed to visual media, especially illustrated popular magazines, see Walter Armbrust, "Ramadan, Marketing, and Heritage: Visualisation and Commodification", paper presented at the *Fifth Mediterranean Research Meeting. Workshop 6: Euro-Mediterranean Expressive Culture(s) between Markets and Cultural Policies*, Florence, 24–8 March, 2004.
19. Ishita, *Yumeisei*, pp. 3–4.
20. The original Ghazali is the medieval philosopher Abu Hamid al-Ghazali (1058–1111) who is distinguished for theoretically bridging the gap between knowledge of *fiqh* (Islamic jurisprudence) and *tasawwuf* (Sufism).

Part Three

The Ethnography of History

Chapter 18

Possessed of Documents: Hybrid Laws and Translated Texts in the Hadhrami Diaspora

Michael Gilsenan

The Judge and the Muftis

In a complex Muslim inheritance case in the Singapore High Court in 2004, contesting siblings disputed the validity of a particular gift of property by their late father that favoured one group over the other.[1] The defence attempted to have a fatwa by the Mufti of Egypt introduced into evidence. The plaintiffs objected. Sustaining the objection, the judge ruled that the "purported opinion (just about a page and a half in length)" was inadmissible because its "maker" was not present to give oral testimony and be cross-examined. Moreover, he remarked that the fatwa was "more in the form of a pronouncement than an opinion".

The main ground for the fatwa's inadmissibility was thus the mufti's unavailability as a witness. In addition, the document's *form* clearly did not meet the court's expectations of what an "opinion" should be. At "a page and a half", the relevant issues could not be addressed, which I understood to be the problem. Finally, the document was what I would call legally "impure". A kind of hybrid, more "pronouncement" than "opinion", the fatwa could not be convincingly translated by the defence into the "secular" forms of the legal system's documentary practices and procedures.

The Mufti of Singapore was present for cross-examination, however. For different reasons that are not the focus of the present chapter, the judge accepted neither his fatwa on the case nor his reading of the relevant sources of Islamic law. One key element in the ruling emerged when defence counsel said that the mufti could only testify to Muslim law "and he would be 'ill-equipped'" to answer questions on the implications of section sixty of the Administration of

Muslim Law Act (rev. edn 1999) which were essential to a key point in the case. It was, said the judge, "most unfortunate" as it meant that his fatwa was "bound to be deficient". Lack of expert knowledge of the *statute* regulating how Muslim law is to be "administered" was as significant as knowledge of Islamic legal interpretations, if not indeed more so.

The judge's observations, which have their own history in inheritance cases going back to the 1860s, are framed in terms of a fundamental category *difference*: Muslim law, unlike "Western or other secular law", is "not man-made", it is divinely inspired. For Western legal discourse, this marks its pre-modern nature and justifies its subordination to what is imagined as the entirely distinct secular order, while allotting it a circumscribed sphere within that same order.

The fate of the mufti's fatwa has a bearing on three deeply inter-related dimensions of my research on the Hadhrami Arab diaspora in South-east Asia.[2] The first concerns the practical, structural and epistemological dilemma that has faced all such litigants in all such suits since the beginning of the colonial period in the early nineteenth century: how to convert, translate and deploy forms of authority, interpretation, legal documentation and argument from the Muslim discursive tradition, whose set of legal practices are meant to govern inheritance, into the Western tradition in the context of a Western hierarchy of laws. The second involves the study of the legal intermingling and criss-crossing of discursive boundaries in Muslim inheritance cases before non-Muslim courts in Singapore. Given changing diasporic contexts and forms of property, cases and inheritance disputes more generally have often entailed institutional, discursive and documentary criss-crossings of state and jurisdictional boundaries, as well as travel by individuals involved to different sites where interested parties reside. The third is the ethnographic and historical analysis of the processes through which inheritance disputes become "cases". Such cases help us to understand the significance of the generation, circulation and use of many different kinds of documents, their pathways and mappings, and how those inscribed in them in whatever way understand such processes.

My particular focus is on the ways in which in the Hadhrami diaspora, different forms of capital – economic, social and cultural – have been transmitted over time and across British and Dutch colonial, political and jurisdictional spaces between the Hadhramaut (their place of origin in what is currently south-east Yemen), Singapore, Johore, Sumatra, Java, Timor, Pontianak, Sulawesi and many other places. The main site of my research is Singapore, an investment hub in the diaspora in which many documents in Arabic, English and Malay concerning migrant/settler land, properties and other forms of income have been produced and from where they have circulated for more than a century.

Transfers of wealth and properties in the form of land and houses, real estate, as well as inheritance claims to trust and endowment capital or incomes, generate complex, hybrid documentary regimes of law and kinship. In the diaspora, such transfers have entailed new interests, calculations and strategies for transmitting goods in swiftly changing circumstances. Knowledge of changing patterns of law and property necessary to make decisions might be uncertain, ambiguous and difficult to obtain. Mediation, translation and complex inter-textualities have been fundamentally *constitutive* of all these processes. The transmission of goods could no longer be a matter of the *habitus* concerning patrimonies and the biological and social continuities of genealogy, lineage and family.

It is important to understand that while "Muhammadan law" was subordinated to British colonial law, this development nonetheless opened avenues to Hadhramis (and others in different colonial settings such as India) for new legal tactics and procedures, new ways of challenging a testator's (the person making the will if a will had been made) wishes or the conditions of a trust on new grounds. New possibilities arose for making and disputing claims and reinterpreting Muslim wills or gifts, according to British criteria of "charity" or "administration" for example.

Moreover, where Hadhramis made trusts and settlements under British legal acts that tied up capital and property for many decades (often up to eighty years or more), these could be challenged by later generations seeking to change the terms or render certain key provisions legally void. In 2009, for example, the High Court ruled on a case concerning the trusteeship of the estate of someone who had died in 1883.[3] The apparently simple question of who had the rights to collect and remit to the legal heirs in Hadhramaut the rent of a house that was bought in 1935 in Dunlop Street, Singapore, exploded in the late 1990s into a case that involved allegations of fraud, multiple journeys between Singapore and Hadhramaut, complex procedures of witness and kin identification after so long a period, and newspaper articles about a property scandal.

In the 1950s, 1960s or 1970, it was not at all uncommon for settlements and wills from the 1920s that had long been treated as unproblematic and dealt with in all sorts of ways that were assumed to be more or less acceptable, to be legally revivified in suits. These suits sought to change stipulations for beneficiaries or to have long-standing dispositions on charitable dedications declared legally void and the monies directed to particular living persons. Years after a testator's death, ramifying groups of heirs and would-be heirs may seek and discover documentary pathways to reverse once-ruling interpretations. New histories of what should have been are created, new interests are discovered, and new possibilities and life-chances are imagined. New court cases bundle up the manoeuvres, calculations and claims of those engaged in property disputes in terms of legal genealogies. Legal documents thus offer ways to study the wealth and property histories of individuals and their kin as the latter have become "legalised" in terms of inheritance.

Some Hadhramis have gone "jurisdiction shopping" across temporal and religious, as well as political, boundaries. They had an *interest* in different colonial, secular documentary regimes. Indeed, I think that British legal discourse became dynamically absorbed into the casuistical and practical repertory of contesting wills and inheritance divisions by Muslims quite prepared to try to use secular judges' authoritative interpretations of Muslim law where they thought it might be in their interest. Calculations of interest necessarily became more complex.

It is important to note that although inheritance is usually described as pertaining to "personal law" in British colonial legal discourse, and therefore under the supervision of Islamic judges or other authorities, in fact, the Singapore courts allowed the government-appointed qadis no authority over immoveable property or real estate, the Hadhramis' main investments. Wills involving such property had to be given probate in colonial state courts, that is, they had to be "proved" and accepted as valid in terms of their form and the rights of the dead to make the dispositions they stipulated.

The Family Solicitor, Translator and Friend

Muslims with property had no alternative but to become legally bilingual, learning about "Muslim law in translation" in English *and* as translated into court practice. For this they needed colonial legal specialists. They often formed very long-lasting relationships of trust with solicitors in Singapore. These solicitors became repositories of confidences, as well as key producers, preservers and deployers of British legal documents and emerging "modern" systems of documentation, including filing and accounting. Throughout the first part of the twentieth century especially, as documentary regimes grew more complex, *trust* in a firm of British solicitors therefore became as important a principle as that of trust in individuals. Frequently, it too was personalised, one particular partner becoming a "friend" over many years, invitations to garden parties, marriages and other occasions marking this blurring of professional/personal status and enmeshing it in a social network that was punctiliously maintained.

Relationships with solicitors' offices involved the generation and exchange of reciprocal knowledge of many kinds. Hadhrami clients, particularly those with large businesses in Singapore real estate, also acted as agents, trustees or executors for many others in the diaspora, tasks that entitled them to fees of 3–5 per cent but that had to be carried out through proper legal and accounting documentary processes. Hadhrami clients learned "legal writing" and "legal talk" in consultations and on social occasions. Some were skilled readers of legal documents in addition to being skilled in the precious knowledge of how to utilise those documents through specific channels and in particular arenas so as to bring about a desired conclusion, an essential part of "reading".

Hadhrami businesses involved in administering inheritances for distant heirs, tracking the location and legal status of persons in relation to property rights in Singapore, finding out who had been born and who had died, organising rent collection and sending remittances overseas, administering properties and many other matters, established office practices following the model of their solicitor "friends". They moved quickly from script to typewriter in official correspondence when writing in English, managing communications in three languages (Arabic, Malay and English) and so forth. They filed wills after obtaining probate, property records, papers for legal suits and other documents as solicitors did, in strict chronological sequence, noting dates, referring to the previous correspondence in succeeding letters, using English modes of address and locutions appropriate to "legal" letters, and so on.

Hadhramis educated their legal partners in Islamic law, inheritance rules and practices and genealogical links. One senior businessman told me that he used to joke with the Chinese junior member of the firm he always consulted that the junior knew the complex genealogies better than the businessman did. "He would go straight to the file", my informant said, he would know the kin connections relevant to the suit and tease his client with long strings of Hadhrami names – A bin B bin C bin D bin E – an idiom of descent that the junior found comical and "foreign", a strand in their pattern of interaction making difference a source of shared amusement. "He knew them better than I did", said my informant. The British partner would also joke about "you Arabs and your fractions" as the two of them tried to work out the exact shares of members of the third generation of trust beneficiaries. The two forms of knowledge were integrated, of course, as were the practical realms in which they were co-constitutive.

Hadhrami businessmen in turn developed their own *savoir* and *connaissances*,[4] a more sociological knowledge of "how to do things" ("Don't go to the British partner, go to the Indian chief clerk" as one informant said, illustrating the kind of thing you had to know in the old days, ways of "chatting", the right places to meet when the "races" were separated in different settings), of how solicitors' firms and the courts worked in practice rather than in terms of formal rules, of the ways in which government officials up to the most senior levels might be approached. This knowledge was vital to their social capital in the diaspora at large. They could be trusted, not only because of their relationships and "friendship" with the solicitors and clerks, but also because they regularly talked to certain Chinese businessmen in the property market, to Indian money specialists, bank compradors and other Singapore virtuosi in a burgeoning port society: the dynamic linkages that drove commerce and property.

The Textual Community?

New networks and skeins of knowledge developed, necessarily added onto, rather than replacing, the older patterns of knowledge. For until the later mid-twentieth century, Hadhramis of major families still needed the "pen of the family" back in Tarim in Hadhramaut. "There is a room there that is full of documents", a key informant told me. The diaspora communities had their written records *as well as* the man of impeccable reputation who travelled constantly and was trusted with complex transactions, sums of money, messages and the transferral of crucial information more or less entirely on the basis of his *word* and face-to-face exchanges. These men acted as key agents in the circulation of knowledge and the managing of affairs across the Indian Ocean. Personal presence was the foundation of the element that was crucial to diaspora networks: trust. In this way, presence, word and documents flowed together.

In short, my argument is that we need to consider the Hadhrami diaspora as a "textual community" in key aspects of social reproduction, its kindred links and rights established through the documentary processes of a developing legal culture creating propertied selves. I would also argue that they were increasingly constitutive of self-conscious "belonging" to the diaspora in terms of documentation of specific legal genealogical positions, rights and claims in Singapore and elsewhere. Documents in this kind of regime came to play a part as active in the motivation, the moving and conveying of goods across social, generational and geographical space as the people whose perceived interests they served.

Documentations and Disputes

To illustrate some of the issues I have discussed above, I now turn to three examples of ways in which very common legal documents required by English law that granted persons specific powers with regard to decision-making and the control of properties became pivotal in often long-running disputes between Hadhrami family claimants across the diaspora. The first concerns what is called the *power of attorney*; the second deals with the *duties of executors of wills and estates*; the third centres on the *duties and obligations of trustees*. In each example, later generations appealed to the 'letter of the law' in launching law suits against persons appointed by such documents, alleging various failures to abide by their fiduciary duties as therein defined.

I begin with the power of attorney. In the context of Hadhrami Indian Ocean migrations and returns, people needed to grant full legal powers in British legal form to someone to act on behalf of an individual or group with regard to their holdings in multiple places in the diaspora. As property regimes were under British law and became increasingly bureaucratically elaborate, written authorisations for such agreements, properly registered and authenticated, were required. Words alone were not sufficient. Trust was crucial but it also had to be documented and a specific set of functions had to be clearly delineated. People granted such powers of attorney (and the same would be true of the executors of wills) were usually close male kin in the Hadhramaut or elsewhere. They were trusted senior Arab residents of Singapore deemed to have the right connections and know-how, men such as those I referred to above. They were the publicly known "men of property" with the considerable and particular status honour, lifestyle and resources that this classification entailed in the colonial period.

In 1924, for example, twenty-seven "landowners" of sections of the Alkaff lineage or with affinal or other ties to them collectively gave power of attorney to Sayyid Abd ar-Rahman bin Shaykh Alkaff, the leading member of the family firm managing their considerable interests in Singapore. These powers applied to the Straits Settlements, the Federated and Unfederated Malay States, the Netherlands Indies, the Kingdom of Siam "or anywhere else" and covered a huge range of activities. Indeed, thirty clauses dealt with everything from purchasing and leasing, mining rights, insurance, timber cutting and plantation development, the payment of debts and enforcement of payments, lending mortgage monies, evictions, insurances, borrowing money, buying and selling or dealing in stocks, shares, bonds, debentures and securities of any kind, chartering ships and generally using all powers regarding properties and much else. The landowners also appointed Sayyid Abd ar-Rahman to "enforce or oppose all actions or proceedings in any court or tribunal" up to "the king's most excellent majesty in council" (that is, the Privy Council, the highest judicial instance in the British Empire). A routine power of attorney of the period thus offers a glimpse of the range of an elite individual's economic activities across many jurisdictions just after the First World War. Decisions on those activities were nonetheless in varying degrees *collective* and involved active correspondence and travel between Hadhramaut and Singapore. This was only the second generation after the founder of the Alkaff fortunes, Sayyid Shaikh, and Sayyid Abd ar-Rahman's siblings (from three different mothers) maintained, at least until after the Second World War, a largely effective group solidarity.

The document ends with the phrase "Witnessed and set hands and seals 26th Jan. 1924" using the Gregorian and not the Muslim calendar. It is under the seal of the "Na'ib Ash-shari'ah" (official of the Islamic court) in Tarim in Hadhramaut and the qadi's seal under each name indicates that the person signed "in his presence". The men all signed with varying degrees of calligraphic elegance and the women put their crosses; the document was put under the seal of the shari'a court in the Hadhrami town of Tarim.[5] The document then had to be translated into English by an official translator in Singapore and was admitted as a proper legal document by registration in Singapore on 18 February 1924.[6]

The appointment of executors charged with carrying out the terms of a will or the administration of an estate located in different places involved similar processes. In their case, what was at issue was the powers and duties of their position as executors in terms of the proper distribution of estates according to Islamic law and the decisions of the deceased. In the early decades, from the 1910s to the early 1940s, I have found many of the same names from power of attorney documents recurring as executors of wills. And executors increasingly found themselves bound by English-language translations and documents concerning colonial judges' conceptions of Muslim law and the same judges' rulings on what the *intention* of the deceased Muslim "actually was", as the judges construed it and whatever the views of the executors might be. I have found the same clusterings of names as executors and witnesses to their appointment occurring time after time in the earlier decades.

Both powers of attorney and the appointment of executors might lead to later conflicts as the authority of the older generations was subverted by economic crises, especially in the context of post-Second World War political and imperial upheavals in Hadhramaut as well as South-east Asia. Take the role of executor, for example. I have found many reports and cases from the early decades of settlement in Singapore where estates had not been finally distributed to heirs for years, sometimes over several generations. An executor had died and no longer lived in the colony, or was "travelling", or had returned to the Hadhramaut without appointing a successor and had paid no attention (deliberately or otherwise; this is difficult to know) to the matter. Nothing had been done, funds had not been remitted back to Hadhramaut, X had simply pocketed the rent, Y had completely ignored the rights of the widow and an elder brother had excluded his siblings from any control over an estate. This "traditional" assumption of hierarchy and family powers might be challenged in court by the new husband of the widow of the elder brother's deceased youngest brother. The elder brother might be the senior male of a powerful family cluster, accustomed to exercising powers of decision, disposition and distribution of resources without any accounting to formal legal process or to what the documents and his position enjoined. Patterns of authority and *trust* in shifting groupings of kind that were often defined in terms of those entitled to shares of estates or trusts through inheritance were questioned. New forms of interest and avenues of action based on opportunities opened up by colonial laws emerged, and were taken advantage of. *Trust* might be translated into officious examination of the legal performance of *trustees*.

Ways of taking those executors to court or overruling the wishes of the testator by asking the colonial court to appoint new administrators, a very common procedure in the many suits over estates, slowly came to be explored for all sorts of reasons indicated above. A plaintiff could thus claim that concerning the duties of an executor, the law be applied to the "letter of *British* law" to a person who had operated following a general, customary Hadhrami understanding of "how these things are done". The same was true for challenging individuals with power of attorney, power that had to be renewed or passed on once people died, moved residence, gained new properties or lost old ones. We find some of these challenges in the court reports of cases mostly from the 1870s and 1880s onwards as the laws concerning property and the increasingly bureaucratised colonial (and judicial) regimes developed. It is also the period during which the largest migration of people from the Hadhramaut to South-east Asia occurred.

For individuals of Arab descent, who so often had income and properties derived from real estate holdings, these changing relationships added additional complexity to legal disputes and social ties for two main reasons. First, for many years real estate was not a domain in which qadis or muftis had any legal authority so everything had to be dealt with under British law. Second, many Arab (and Chinese and Indian) property owners adopted the tactic of establishing settlements and trusts under British law. There were various reasons for this, not least that the British would not allow family endowments that continued "in perpetuity" as in the case of the Muslim *waqf*-s. Instead, they restricted them by a series of rules with the implication that the trust would have to be dissolved and its capital distributed, usually after a period of around seventy-five to ninety years.

The unintended consequences of this were a pattern of deferred conflicts between different generations and kinds of beneficiaries that tended to erupt in the trust's later years as its anticipated possible end date drew near. These conflicts were over entitlements, shares and, not infrequently, accusations of maladministration sometimes dating back over decades. Conflicts generate talk, a lot of talk. As I discovered in Singapore, they also generate documents of all kinds, sometimes over long periods: letters between multiple senders and places, communications between solicitors, trustee reports, accounts of various kinds, genealogies to demonstrate and prove kinship connections entitling a person to certain classes of benefits, property and court documents, summons, and much else besides.

Documents: Fantasy and Fetish

Documents easily become fetishes and vehicles for fantasy, not least because they point so directly towards realities, material and non-corporeal. They offer signs of the imaginary, signs that can be dangerous when read, both to the anthropologist and to other interested parties. And we are interested parties, for our sense of our social and cultural capital is at play. Mondher Kilani has described the seduction of the discovery that communities in the Gafsa oasis in

Tunisia constantly referred to documents when they talked about the oasis and lineage history.⁷ Finding his own *savoir* as an anthropologist so complicitously shared, he hastened to demonstrate his expertise as a way of forming relations with his interlocutors. He determined that he would systematically seek to relate what they said to documents, while confronting the documents with each other in order to "decode" the oasis. Hot in pursuit and with their eager encouragement, he plunged into research into all kinds of documents. At the same time, sure that his informants possessed only partial and scattered views of the precious "texts", he saw himself as filling in the many gaps in their knowledge and creating a new whole.⁸ Yet, when exhausted by his *"quasi-policiere"* investigations, he finally found the person who was supposed to possess a certain document, it was never available; it was lost, or difficult to get hold of, but it was certainly there and the owner was absolutely ready to find it as soon as possible, it was just that …⁹ It was only after some time that Kilani began to understand that it was the *absence* of the documents to which everyone appealed and the fact that no one doubted their existence that enabled everyone to rhetorically deploy "documents" in their arguments about lineage and oasis history.

I hope I have said enough to suggest that for those in Hadhramaut, Singapore and elsewhere who share something of the confusing and partial knowledge of the legalised conflicts of inheritance, the lived histories, the "family talk", the narratives of law suits and the accounts of hopes realised and dashed, powerful fantasies of what "documents" may contain and could, somehow, do or re-do are easily stimulated. People have historically become all too aware of the vagaries and, in some ways arbitrary, outcomes of the transmission of goods on which to some degree, great or small, their life chances and histories depended or might depend. The mixing and blurring of Muslim and colonial law, understandings, opinions, procedures, practices and translations creates fertile ground for reinterpretation, for imagining pasts and futures in which the possession of property is central.

Perhaps a person possesses a particular document, a share certificate from 1910 for example, or a map of supposed land holdings that might be reclaimed in Hadhramaut, or a fatwa from long ago. If only they could find someone who would know how to unlock the power of the document to prove a claim, to make it a powerful instrument in asserting their right to what they have always known to be rightfully theirs! Or perhaps they have a story of the will that vanished from the box in which they know for certain their father had placed it. Documents such as wills and property deeds are precious assets to be shown, read or revealed only under highly specific circumstances to specifically entitled people. They are intensely private documents until such time as they can be turned into public instruments for the transmission of goods from the dead to the living. Otherwise they are kept in lawyers' offices, hidden at home, locked in boxes, filing cabinets, drawers, chests, cabinets, safes or placed "where they are not supposed to be" to foil the eager searcher. Those hiding places may be forgotten, destroyed or broken into. In this sense, they are similar to the maps of buried treasure that drive the plots of adventure stories.

Hiding places are uncertain and legal time is supremely unpredictable. Years and decades pass, cases are resolved and yet continue, the fixed is not fixed. Rulings are reversed; principles of interpretation are changed; fatwas have and do not have authority. The sense of time in relation to law and inheritance is conveyed as much in the conditional and the subjunctive moods as in tenses: "If I am able to obtain my inheritance/properties/incomes"; "Were we to receive/ had we received/might we yet receive our inheritance/shares/rights"; "Had we had the documents" and so on. The subjunctive structures the narratives of memory, present experience and expectations of life chances in the future.

Personhood may thus seem to be a function of "the documents" and the changes in the propertied selves that they are potentially conceived to contain or have once contained. This personhood may of course be experienced as never having achieved the full realisation it might have attained or might yet attain in a constantly deferred achievement of possession and ownership.

The word "trust" referring to a legal trust becomes a trigger for joking about its legendary power to divide kin and destroy the wealth it was meant to preserve. Indeed, people point to this or that person's or group's investment in fighting a case for many years at enormous cost in terms of time, social relations, emotions, energy and material wealth that far exceed the monetary worth of the property. This reversal of everyday assessments of *value*, of the usual calculations and rationalities, is clear to at least some of the actors. It is nonetheless subordinated to their investment of self in the struggles over property that is "rightfully theirs".

Many are not troubled by such indeterminacies. Their inheritances, trust shares or settlement benefits have been distributed and paid up, whatever the court suits over the years may have been. Their affairs are, or seem to be, fully resolved. Others have never lived through legal challenges at all; they are no doubt the majority. Yet for others, possible pasts, transformed presents and uncertain futures are temporally constituted in part by the fantasy constructions of which the dangerous materiality of documents is the keystone.

Notes

1. *Mohamed Ismail Ibrahim & Anor v. Mohammad Taha Ibrahim*, High Court, Republic of Singapore, 22 September 2004, *www.cljlaw.com/public/cotw-050527.htm*. (last accessed 9 January 2010).
2. See Michael Gilsenan, "Topics and Queries for a History of Arab Families and Inheritance in Southeast Asia: Some Preliminary Thoughts", in Eric Tagliacozzo (ed.), *Southeast Asia and the Middle East: Islam, Movement, and the* Longue Durée,

Stanford: Stanford University Press, 2009, pp. 199–234; and "Translating Colonial Fortunes: Dilemmas of Inheritance in Muslim and English Laws across a Nineteenth-century Diaspora", *Comparative Studies in South Asia, Africa and the Middle East*, vol. 31, no. 2, 2011, pp. 355–71.
3. *Syed Abbas bin Mohamed Alsagoff and Another v. Islamic Religious Council of Singapore (Majlis Ugama Islam Singapura)*, SGHC 281.
4. It is difficult to translate these terms as they do not have separate verbs in English. However, *savoir* suggests a sense of knowing a thing(s), a knowledge about something or, as in *savoir faire*, a general sense of knowing how to act in a wide range of situations, being socially adept and adroit. *Connaissances*, in plural form, is wide ranging and relates to persons and activities, practices, rules and behaviours, trades and crafts (as in knowing one's metier).
5. Personal seals in the English translations of such documents from the Arabic are represented conventionally by ink or pencil circles filled in with red crayon. The signer not unusually writes his signature around the "seal".
6. Doc. 040000958, Collection of Koh Seow Chuan, National Library of Singapore. I am most grateful to the Library for permission to see certain documents in their collection.
7. Mondher Kilani, *La construction de la mémoire*, Geneva: Labor et Fides, 1992.
8. Ibid., pp. 22–6.
9. Ibid., pp. 40–1.

About the Contributors

Hatsuki Aishima currently holds a research fellowship at the National Museum of Ethnology (Minpaku) in Osaka, Japan. She received a DPhil in Oriental Studies from St Antony's College, Oxford in 2010. Her research interests include Islam and art and body culture in contemporary Egypt.

Hilal Alkan-Zeybek received her MA in Sociology at Boğaziçi University, Istanbul. She is currently finishing her PhD at the Political and International Studies Department at the Open University, UK. Her research interests include charitable giving, the Islamic institution of waqf, feminist studies and environmental work.

Cédric Baylocq is a post-doctoral fellow at the Centre Jacques Berque, Rabat, Morocco. He holds a PhD in Anthropology from the University Segalen Bordeaux II (2012). His dissertation dealt with religious authority and Islamic norms in France through an ethnographic approach. He co-authored *Profession imam* (Albin Michel, 2009).

Yazid Ben Hounet is a researcher at the CNRS, Laboratoire d'Anthropologie Sociale, Collège de France, Paris. He obtained his PhD in 2006 at the École des Hautes Études en Sciences Sociales (EHESS), Paris. He is the author of *L'Algérie des tribus* (L'Harmattan, 2009) and *Parenté et anthropologie sociale* (Ginkgo, 2009). He has taught at Paris VIII University, Lausanne University and Neuchâtel University.

Katia Boissevain is a researcher in Social Anthropology at CNRS-Idemec. She studied at the University of Paris X Nanterre and SOAS in London. She has worked on female sainthood in Islam, the organisation of the Hajj in Tunisia, the touristic use of religious heritage in the Maghreb and Christian converts in the region.

Daniele Cantini is a post-doctoral fellow at the University of Halle/Wittenberg, Germany. He teaches courses on Political Anthropology of the Middle East at the University of Modena/Reggio Emilia, Italy. His research interests are contemporary Egypt and Jordan, questions of youth, education, migration, citizenship, religion and secularism.

Susanne Dahlgren is an Academy of Finland research fellow at the Helsinki Collegium for Advanced Studies. She studied Anthropology at the University of Edinburgh, LSE and the University of Helsinki. She has published extensively on Islam, morality, sexuality and urban space and is the author of *Contesting Realities. The Public Sphere and Morality in Southern Yemen* (Syracuse University Press, 2010).

Sigurd D'hondt obtained a PhD in Linguistics from the University of Antwerp in 2001 and currently teaches Socio-linguistics and Linguistic Anthropology at the Department of African Languages and Cultures at Ghent University. His research interests include the analysis of face-to-face interaction, Kiswahili and East-African popular culture and interaction in judicial settings.

Akila Drici-Bechikh obtained an MA at the École des Hautes Études en Sciences Sociales (EHESS), Paris in 2009. She is currently a PhD candidate at the Department of Sociology at the University Segalen Bordeaux II. Her research focuses on French Salafi women.

Baudouin Dupret is Research Director at the French National Centre for Scientific Research (CNRS). He is also the Director of Centre Jacques-Berque, the French research institute in Rabat, Morocco. He has published extensively in the field of the anthropology of law and norms in the context of Arab societies.

Gisele Fonseca Chagas received her PhD (2011) and MA (2006) in Anthropology at Federal Fluminense University (UFF), Brazil. She is currently a researcher at the Centre for Middle East Studies at UFF. Her research interests are the construction of religious authority in Islam and its gender dynamics. She has undertaken fieldwork in Brazil and Syria.

Michael Gilsenan is David B. Kriser Professor in the Humanities, Professor of Middle Eastern and Islamic Studies and Anthropology, and Director of the Kevorkian Center for Near Eastern Studies at New York University. He is an emeritus fellow of Magdalen College, Oxford. His main publications include *Saint and Sufi in Modern Egypt* (Oxford University Press, 1973), *Recognizing Islam* (Pantheon Books, 1983) and *Lords of the Lebanese Marches* (University of California Press, 1996).

About the Contributors

Enrique Klaus obtained a PhD in Political Science from the Institute of Political Studies (IEP) in Grenoble, France. He currently teaches contemporary History of the Middle East and North Africa region and Media Studies at the International University of Rabat (UIR) in Morocco. He is also a researcher at the Centre Jacques-Berque (CJB) in Rabat.

Aymon Kreil is undertaking PhD research on love and sexuality in Cairo at the University of Neuchâtel, Switzerland, and EHESS Paris, France.

Katharina Lange is a researcher in Anthropology at the Zentrum Moderner Orient (ZMO), Berlin. She has undertaken fieldwork in Syria, Jordan and Egypt and has published on the indigenisation of Arabic anthropology, experiences and memories of the world wars in *al-Mashriq al-Arabi* (Arab East), and is currently working on oral and written historical narratives in northern Syria.

Thomas Pierret is a Lecturer in Contemporary Islam at the University of Edinburgh. A former post-doctoral fellow at Princeton University, he completed his PhD on the modern ulama in Syria at Sciences Po Paris and the University of Louvain.

Paulo G. Pinto received a PhD in Anthropology from Boston University. He is a Professor of Anthropology and Director of the Centre for Middle East Studies at the Universidade Federal Fluminense, Brazil. He has published on Sufism in contemporary Syria, Shi'i pilgrimages in Syria and Muslim communities in Brazil.

Kathryn Spellman-Poots received a PhD in Sociology from Birkbeck College, University of London. She is Associate Professor at the Aga Khan University, Institute for the Study of Muslim Civilisations in London. She has published in the areas of gender and Islam in the Middle East and North Africa, the Iranian Diaspora and Shi'i Muslims in Europe.

Emma Varley is Assistant Professor in the Department of Anthropology at the Lahore University of Management Sciences, Pakistan. Her current research examines the influence of Islamic reform movements and sectarian conflict over women's reproductive and maternal health in northern Pakistan.

Ward Vloeberghs is currently affiliated with the École de Gouvernance et d'Economie de Rabat, Morocco, where he is Deputy Director of the Centre for Research on Africa and the Mediterranean (CERAM). He holds a PhD in Political Science from the Université Catholique de Louvain, Belgium (2010).

Index

'Abd al-Halim Mahmud, 170, 171–6
    fame, 174–6
    scholarship, 172–4
Abd ar-Rahman bin Shaykh Alkaff,
    Sayyid, 187
Abu-Lughod, Lila, 38
Aden divorce court, 153–60
    dress, 154, 155
    judge, 155, 156, 160
    Popular Defence (People's)
        Committees, 154
    translator, 187–8
    women, 154, 155–6, 157, 158, 159
agency, 131–2
Ahl al-Bayt Society, 44
alcohol, 74
Algeria, south: ma'ruf ritual, 50–60
'alim, 172
Amman University (Jordan), 116–23
    clothing, 119, 120
    Ramadan, 116–19
    Shari'a law, 119
    social class, 121–2
    women, 119–20, 121
amulets 13, 14, 17, 18
anthropology, 3
Antoun, Richard, 3–4

al-'Aqqad, 'Abbas Mahmud, 172
Arab ethnicity: and Muslim identity, 77
Arabic language, 42, 73, 74, 77
Ashura, 40–9
Ashura procession (London), 42–6
associationism, 140
audiences
    Egyptian Parliament, 163, 165–6, 167,
        168
    mass media, 175

Badawi, Ahmad, 173
Bakhtin, Mikhael, 99
Battle of Karbala (680), 40–1, 44, 45,
    47
beads, 86, 88
Beirut
    Muhammad al-Amin mosque, 81, 91n1
    Rafiq al-Hariri tomb, 80–91
Bin Laden, Osama, 134n20
black magic, 12–13, 14
blood donation, 46–8
bloodletting *see* latmiya
body language, 53, 59, 149
body piercing *see* darb al-shish
Bora, Tanil, 144
Brazil *see* Rio de Janeiro

care, ethics of, 151
carnivals, 99
cemeteries, 33
chadors, 155
charity work, 144
charity workers, Turkish
    body language, 146–9
    clothing, 149
    ethics, 149–52
    food, 149
Chiffoleau, Sylvia, 27
child cruelty, 41
chillah, 17
China, 75
Chirac, President Jacques, 87
Clift, Rebecca, 130
clothing
    Ashura procession, London, 42
    charity workers, Turkey, 149
    Hajj pilgrims, 25, 26
    hijabs, 112, 155, 162
    imams, 74
    law courts, Aden, 155, 156
    Mawlid celebrations, Syria, 95
    mourners, 37
    Salafi Muslims, 111, 135, 139
    students, 119, 120
    see also veils
conversation analysis (CA) *see* ethnomethodological conversation analysis (EMCA)
courts, 41, 155–60
cults *see* Hariri, Rafiq

darb al-shish (Syria), 62–9
    cultural idiom, 67
    definition, 63
    initiation, 68
    performance, 63, 64–5
    religious context, 62–6
    tariqa Rifaʻiyya, 62–3
Dawûd, M. (Egyptian MP), 164, 165
dervishes, 97
dhikr, 35, 64, 68, 97–8

diviners, 13, 14, 15–18, 19
divorce, 13, 153–60
documents, 189–91
Doua, Imam Mahmoud, 109, 112–13
Durkheim, Émile, 3

education
    imams (Rio de Janeiro), 72
    Jordan, 115–16
    Syria, 35, 37
Egypt
    Mosque Movement, 150
    Parliament: audiences, 163, 165–6, 167, 168; language games, 167, 168; Qurʼan, 167–8; relevancies, 163–4, 165, 166, 167, 168
    religious referencing, 135
    saints' festivals, 99
    Salafi Muslims, 135–42
Eickelman, Dale, 3–4, 82
elders, 52, 53, 58
Encyclopaedia of 1,000 Egyptian Personalities, 175
ethics, 150
    Turkish charity workers, 149–52
ethnography, 1–8, 136
ethnomethodological conversation analysis (EMCA), 125, 131, 132

Fadlallah, Ayatollah Muhammad Hussein, 47
fairies, 13
fame, 175
fasting, 43, 117, 118–19
fatwas, 181
flagellation *see* latmiya
flags, 84, 86
flowers, 84, 86, 87
food
    ʻazza, Syria, 34
    charity workers, Turkey, 149
    Hajj preparations, Tunisia, 25
    maʻruf ritual, South Algeria, 57
    Mawlid celebrations, Syria, 95

mourning receptions, Syria, 34
Sunni Muslims, Rio de Janeiro, 77
France
   Association des Musulmans de la Gironde (AMG), 109
   Salafi Muslims, 106–14
   Union des Organisations Islamiques de France (UOIF), 114n5

Gaffney, Patrick, 141
Geertz, Clifford, 3
gender relations, 4, 38, 72
genealogies, Hadhrami, 185
al-Ghazali, Muhammad, 174
al-Ghitani, Jamal, 172
Gilgit-Baltistan
   amulets, 13, 14, 17, 18
   chillah, 17
   jinn, 13, 16, 17
   Shi'i Muslims, 13
   sorcery, 11, 12–13, 19
   Sunni Muslims, 11, 12, 13
   veils, 14
Goffman, Erving, 131
Goluboff, Sascha L., 38
Greatbatch, David, 167
grief, expressions of
   Ashura tradition, 41, 44
   Hajj refusals, 23
   northern Syria, 33, 35, 36, 38–9

Hadhrami diaspora, 182–3, 184–5
   and British law, 186–9
   genealogies of, 185
   and inheritance, 191
   and Islamic law, 183, 184
Hajj (Tunisia), 21–8
   age factors, 23
   as a family event, 25, 28
   food, 25
   guides, 23
   pilgrims, 22–5
   preparations, 22, 23, 25–6
   quota system, 22–3

"service providers", 26
state involvement, 26, 28
travel packages, 26
Hamington, Maurice, 151
Hanks, William, 157–8
Hariri, Fahd, 91
Hariri, Rafiq (*Rafiq al-Hariri*)
   cult of, 86–90
   tomb, 80–91; dignitaries' visits, 87–8; flags, 84, 86; flowers, 84, 86, 87; pilgrimage, 87; plaque, 87; site, 81–6
Hashim, A. (Egyptian MP), 166
Heritage, John, 167
Hezbollah, 49n2
hijabs, 112, 155, 162
hospitality, 33–4, 57, 146
Husni, Faruq (Egyptian MP), 162, 164, 165
Hussein, Imam, 40–1, 43, 44, 45

Ibn Hazm, 107
identities, 127–31, 132
   masculine, 129, 130
   Muslim, 77, 126, 130
Ikhwanis, 110, 111, 113
imams
   France, 109
   London, 75
   Rio de Janeiro, 72, 73–5, 78
   Tunisia, 28
inheritance
   Hadhrami diaspora, 191
   Singapore, 181–2, 183–4, 188–9
Iranian Islamic Universal Association, 42
Ishita, Saeko, 175
Islam
   peripheralisation, 3–4
   practice, 2, 3, 4; Egyptian parliament, 162–9; ma'ruf ritual (South Algeria), 50–60; revivalist, 124–33
   Salafi definition, 72
   Wahhabi interpretations, 90
   see also Muslims
Islamic Unity Society (IUS), 47

INDEX

Ithna'Ashariyya (Twelvers), 49n1

Jayyusi, Lena, 127
jinn, 13, 16, 17, 65, 66
Jordan education, 115–17: Amman University, 116–23
judges, 155, 156, 160
Jumblatt, Walid, 87–8

Ka'aba, 25
Kant, Immanuel, 151
Karim (Salafi Muslim), 137
Kayseri (Turkey), 145–9
Khomeini, Ayatollah: *Spiritual and Political Testament*, 110, 111
Kilani, Mondher, 189–90
Koran *see* Qur'an

language
    Ashura (London), 43, 44, 45–6
    Egyptian Parliament, 167, 168
    Hajj pilgrims, 27
    religious knowledge transmission (Rio de Janeiro), 72
latmiya (self-flagellation), 41–2, 44, 45, 46, 47
law, British, 186–9
law, Islamic
    Administration of Muslim Law Act (1999), 181–2
    divine nature of, 182
    Hadhrami diaspora, 183, 184
    see also Shari'a law; "Women's law"
Lebanon
    14 March movement, 84, 87
    Hezbollah, 49n2
    Oger Liban (contracting company), 84, 92n6
    Rafiq al-Hariri tomb, Beirut, 80–91
London
    Ashura procession, 42–6
    Holland Park Majma', 42
    Imam Hussein Blood Donation Campaign, 46–8

imams, 75
majales, 45–6

magicians, 12
Mahmood, Saba, 150
Mahmud, 'Abd al-Halim *see* 'Abd al-Halim Mahmud
Mahmud, Mustafa, 172
majales, 45–6
Maktari, Abdulla M. A., 159
Mamère, Noël, 109
martyrs *see* Hariri, Rafiq; Hussein, Imam
ma'ruf ritual (South Algeria)
    communitas, 54–8
    cultural significations, 59
    elders, 52, 53, 58
    liminas, 51–3
    talabs (religious students), 59
mass media, 175
Mawlid celebrations (Syria), 93–100
    dress, 95
    food, 95
    mosques, 94–7
    munshidun (religious singers), 95, 97
    musical instruments, 95
    prayer, 99
    Shari'a law, 95
    shaykhs, 96
    taqbil al-athar ("kissing the relic"), 98
    ulama, 93, 94–5, 95–6
    women, 95
mevlud recitals, 4
miraculous deeds, 63
Miran, Marie, 113
modernisation theories, 3, 4
Modressi, Sayed Mahdi, 46
Mosque Movement (Egypt), 150
mosques
    Hajj preparation (Tunisia), 26
    Mawlid celebrations (Syria), 94–7
    mourning practices (Syria), 33
    Muhammad al-Amin mosque (Beirut), 81

prayer (Tanzania), 127
Salafi-oriented (France), 109
mourning practices
  Beirut, 88
  northern Syria, 32–9; food, 34; gendered, 32, 35–7, 38; expressions of grief, 33, 35, 36; mosques, 33; shaykhs, 32, 34, 36; tents, 35; veils, 35
mrabtin, 60n8
mufakkirs, 172
muftis, 181–2
muhajjabas, 155
Muhammad, Shaykh, 137–8, 139–40, 141
Muharram commemorations, 42, 44, 46
mulid celebration, 32, 35
munshidun (religious singers), 95, 97
musical instruments, 39, 95
Muslim Brotherhood, 108, 109, 113, 139, 140, 141
Muslims
  Chinese, 75
  ethnicity, 77
  identities, 126, 130
  prayer, 99, 126–7
  religious practices, 2, 3, 4
  young: Ashura practices, 40, 41, 42, 44, 45, 46, 48–9; Islamic Unity Society, 47; and Ramadan, 116–19; and revivalist Islam, 124–33; and Salafism, 113, 137–8
  see also Hadhrami diaspora; Islam; Salafi Muslims; Shi'i Muslims; Sufis; Sunni Muslims

nakedness, 26, 37
Nakshawani, Sayed Ammar, 46
Nasrallah, Sayyid Hasan, 88
nomads, 50

occult practices, 11–19
  amulets, 13, 14, 17
  black magic, 12–13, 14
  jinn, 13, 16, 17
  magicians, 12
  sorcery, 12–13, 19
Oubrou, Imam Tareq, 109, 110, 112, 113

Pakistan *see* Gilgit-Baltistan
Parkin, David, 53, 58
philanthropists, 147–8, 151
pilgrimages *see* Beirut: *Rafiq al-Hariri* tomb; Hajj; 'Umra
poverty
  Turkey, 144, 145, 147, 148, 150–1
  water, 44
prayer
  Mawlid celebrations (Syria), 99
  Salafi Muslims, 140, 141
  Tanzania, 126–7, 130

Qazwini, Sayed Hussein, 46
Qur'an
  Adeni courts, 156, 157, 159
  Egyptian parliament, 166, 167–8
  healing benefits, 12
  invocations, 55–6, 57
  ma'ruf ritual, 50, 59
  mulid, 32, 35
  Rafiq al-Hariri tomb, Beirut, 88
  right and wrong, 120
  shaykhs' interpretations, 139–40
  sura of The Cow, 54–5

Ramadan, 116–19
reification, 127–8, 131
religious celebrations *see* Mawlid; mulid; Ramadan
religious experience *see* darb al-shish
religious knowledge
  darb al-shish (northern Syria), 68, 69
  Sunni Muslims (Rio de Janeiro), 72, 73–7, 78
  see also Qur'an
religious students, 59
al-Rifa'i, Shaykh 'Abd al-Karim, 99–100

Index

ritual
    Ashura, 40–9
    body language, 53
    darb al-shish, 62–9
    Hajj, 21–30
    magic, 11–19
    martyr worship, 80–91
    ma'ruf (South Algeria), 50–60
    Mawlid, 93–100
    mevlud (Turkey), 4
    mourning practices, 31–9

Salafi Muslims, 106–14
    beliefs, 135, 136, 138, 142
    dress, 111, 135, 139
    identity, 105, 135
    and Muslim Brotherhood, 106–8, 139
    and non-Salafi Muslims, 110–13
    shaykhs, 138, 139
    social class, 138
    women, 106–8
Salafiyya, 72
Salih (Salafi Muslim), 138, 140–1
Samir (Salafi Muslim), 110–11
Sayyid (Salafi Muslim), 137, 139, 141
Schielke, Samuli, 99, 122
seals, personal, 187
Sennett, Richard, 146
Sevenhuijsen, Selma, 151
Shafi'i Islam, 159, 160
al-Sha'rawi, Muhammad Mutawalli, 174
Shari'a law
    Amman University, Jordan, 119
    divorce, 153, 157–60
    oath-taking, 159
    religious singers, 95
Sharif (Salafi Muslim), 138
shaykhs
    darb al-shish (northern Syria), 63, 65, 67
    definition, 139–40, 141–2
    Mawlid celebrations (Syria), 96, 99–100

mourning receptions (northern Syria), 32, 34, 36
Salafi, 135, 136, 138, 139, 141, 142
Shi'i Muslims
    Beirut, 89
    Britain, 40, 41–9
    female mourners, 38
    Gilgit-Baltistan, 13
    Ithna'Ashariyya (Twelvers), 49n1
    marja' (supreme leaders), 41
shrines, 82
Sidnell, Jack, 131–2
Singapore: inheritance, 181–2, 183–4, 188–9
singers *see munshidun*
social class
    Aden divorce court, 155
    Amman University, Jordan, 121–2
    Salafi Muslims, Cairo, 138
    Turkish charity workers, 147, 148–9
social work, 146; *see also* charity work
solicitors, 184–5
sorcery, 11, 12–13, 19
spatiality, formulaic, 53
split subject, 132
Sufis
    brotherhoods, 7n4
    darb al-shish, 62–9
    divorce, 159
    and Salafi Muslims compared, 138, 140
Sunni Muslims
    Beirut, 88–9, 90
    beliefs, 110
    divorce, 161n8
    Gilgit-Baltistan, 11, 12, 13
    Rio de Janeiro, 71–8; birthday celebrations, 73–4; converts, 72, 73–4, 76–7, 78; gender divide, 72; Muslim Beneficent Society of Rio de Janeiro (MBSRJ), 71–2, 75, 76, 77, 78; religious elite, 72–3; sermons, 73, 74–6, 77
    Syria, 31–2, 98

Syria
- darb al-shish, 62–9
- Mawlid celebrations, 93–8
- mourning practices, 31, 32–9; gendered, 32, 35–7

Tabligh movement, 110
Tanzania, 124–33
- identities, 126
- masculinity, 129
- prayer, 126–7, 130

Tapper, Richard and Nancy, 4
teasing, 126–31
tents
- ma'ruf ritual (South Algeria), 51
- mourning receptions (northern Syria), 35
- *Rafiq al-Hariri* tomb (Beirut), 81, 91

Tunisia
- documents, 189–90
- Hajj, 21–8
- imams, 28
- Montazah Gammarth travel company (later SSNR), 26, 29n7
- mosques, 26

Turkey
- bathing, 149
- beneficence, 143
- charity work, 145–52
- *mevlud* recitals, 4
- non-governmental organisations, 147, 148, 150, 151
- philanthropists, 147–8, 151
- poverty, 144, 145, 147, 148
- social class, 147, 148–9

Turner, Simon, 124
Twelvers *see* Ithna'Ashariyya

ulama: Mawlid celebrations (Syria), 93, 94–5, 95–6, 97, 98, 100
Umar, Imam, 109–10
'Umra (the lesser pilgrimage), 22, 24, 27

veils, 14, 24, 35, 109, 135, 140

Wahhabis, 90
water poverty, 44
Wolfson, Harry A.: *The Philosophy of the Kalam*, 174
women
- Amman University (Jordan), 119–20, 121
- Ashura tradition, 41, 42, 44
- charity work, 145–52
- divorce, 154, 155–6, 157, 158–9, 160
- and Hajj, 23, 24–5, 26
- hijabs, 112, 155, 162
- Imam Hussein Blood Donation Campaign, 46–7
- as judges, 155
- as law students, 155
- Mawlid celebrations, 95
- mourning practices, 32–3, 35–7, 38
- Muslim Beneficent Society (Rio de Janeiro), 72, 73
- observance/ritual practice, 11, 13
- occult practices, 11–19
- religious knowledge, 73, 76
- Salafi, 106–8
- veils, 14, 24, 35, 109, 135, 140

"Women's law", 160

Zaidi, Syed Mustafe, 41
Zaynab (sister of Imam Hussein), 44

EU representative:
Easy Access System Europe
Mustamäe tee 50, 10621 Tallinn, Estonia
Gpsr.requests@easproject.com

www.ingramcontent.com/pod-product-compliance
Lightning Source LLC
Chambersburg PA
CBHW061829300426
44115CB00013B/2309